THE QUEST FOR
HUMAN
BEAUTY

THE QUEST FOR
HUMAN
BEAUTY

An Illustrated History

Julian Robinson

W. W. Norton & Company
New York • London

Printed in Hong Kong

First Edition

The text of this book was set in Sabon with the display set in Trajan
Book design by Germaine Clair

Library of Congress Cataloging-in-Publication Data
Robinson, Julian.
The quest for human beauty: an illustrated history Julian Robinson
p.   cm.
Includes index.
1. Beauty, personal. — History
2. Fashion — History   3. Social Science
I. Title.
RA778.R529   1998
646.7—dc21
97-19491
CIP

ISBN 0-393-04004-6

W. W. Norton & Company, Inc., 500 Fifth Avenue, New York, New York, 10010
W. W. Norton & Company, Ltd., 10 Coptic Street, London WCIA IPU

1 2 3 4 5 6 7 8 9 0

CONTENTS

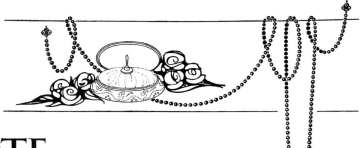

AUTHOR'S NOTE AND DEDICATION

Directly or indirectly, knowingly or unknowingly, a great number of people and organizations have contributed to the creation of this book over the past twenty-five years or so. In particular, I wish to acknowledge my indebtedness to the late Sir Kenneth Clark, who together with Professor Janey Ironside of the Royal College of Art, persuaded me to research this subject much more thoroughly than I would otherwise have done. I also wish to thank Professor Bernard Dupaigne and members of the staff of the Laboratoire d'Ethnologie, Musée de l'Homme; Professor Milton Diamond, Dept. of Anatomy & Reproductive Biology, University of Hawaii; Dr. Helen E. Fisher, Research Associate, American Museum of National History; the staff of the reading room and archives of the British Museum and the Museum of Mankind; the staff of the picture library of the Victoria and Albert Museum; the Guildhall Library; the New York Public Library; the Smithsonian Institute; the Musée National des Arts Africains et Oceaniens; La Chambre Syndicale de la Couture Parisienne; the Library of the Metropolitan Museum of Art; the National Gallery; the National Portrait Gallery; and the Museum of Modern Art. Also I thank the countless village people, many from remote regions of the world, who have borne my curiosity and pertinacity with forbearance. Thanks to the Chairman and Principal of the Sydney College of the Arts for their generous financial settlement, and that received from the NSW State Crown Solicitors Office, who acted on behalf of the NSW Police Department,

which made this book possible. Thanks to my solicitor, barrister, QC, and their staff who handled my legal wranglings against the police and other authorities with wit and sedulity, and to all those students and members of the staff who stood by me when I was fighting in the courts to be allowed to lecture on this subject as I saw fit. I am grateful to the numerous travel agents, airline pilots, hotel managers, bus drivers, tour guides, historians, typists, editors, journalists, photographers, artists, layout specialists, and a great number of other individuals and organizations from around the world without whose help and encouragement this book would never have been written. I am also indebted to my current partner, my many friends and professional acquaintances, my ex-wife, my three tribal "wives" and three long-term de facto partners, my parents, my brothers, my three children, their partners, and their numerous progeny. And it is to this generation who have not yet been irrevocably tainted by our restrictive and prescriptive ways, and all other as yet uninhibited children from other cultures around the world from whom hopefully a new generation of creative geniuses will emerge, that I dedicate this book in the hope that it may help them expand their notions of the possible, and serve as a beacon to light the way to an even more beautiful, varied, and emotionally fulfilled future.

PREFACE

I first became interested in the subject of this book in the early 1950s while studying fashion design at a small East London art school. One afternoon, while searching for ideas to enliven a rather dreary dress design project, I chanced upon a recent edition of *National Geographic* in which there were a number of exciting and colorful photographs of New Guinea tribal warriors in full war paint, resplendent in feathers and shell adornments. They greatly influenced my fashion drawings and design ideas, which had been set with a mass-production market in mind. The design

lecturer, however, was not amused and went so far as to say that if I lived to be a hundred, I would never see such tribal ways influencing Western styles of dress, adornment, and beauty. How wrong he was.

A few weeks later, after my pride had recovered from this failure, I was rummaging through a local second-hand book shop, when I came across two volumes of *Peoples of All Nations,* a broken copy of *Women of the World,* another on *Manners & Customs of Mankind,* a copy of *Venus:*

die apotheose des Weibes by Frederick Fuchs, a copy of *From Nudity to Raiment* by Hilain Hiler, a copy of the 1930 German photographic masterpiece *Der dunkle Erdteil: Afrika* on many African tribal modes of body presentation and packaging, and a strange book—*Jak se Zeny Stroji* by Dr. C. H. Stratz, published out of Prague in the late 1890s—that contained a wonderful array of different types of human beauty and styles of traditional adornment, which made my heart leap with excitement and my body tremble with desire. My fate was sealed. I fasted for the rest of the week in order to buy these books and I have been collecting such publications ever since, along with photographs, magazines, original drawings, and all number of associated ephemera, pieces of ethnic jewelry, strange contraptions for distorting the body, an array of piercing equipment, decorative branding irons, ritual circumcision knives, and the like. My design studio is now full of such items—it's more like a museum than a place of work—but I still receive such inspiration and energy from the juxtapositioning of this collection of unique pieces of human creativity, that I would be lost without them.

In the mid-1950s I served a brief two years of National Service in the British Army, where I learned the art of wearing a Hussars plumed headdress and frogged jacket, a Grenadier Guards busby, a Cameron Highlander's kilt; how to burn the fuzz off a new uniform to give it the appearance of having been well worn and thus giving the wearer status; how to remove the stamped-on texture from army boots so that they would glisten when polished; and how to salute correctly—the other officer cadets with whom I shared the barracks were a mixed bunch and of an evening there was little to do in the way of entertainment other than trying on everybody else's uniform, or trying to improve one's own.

During that two-year period I also learned how to drive a tank, an armored car and a ten-ton truck, how to use a parachute, the art of camouflage and concealment, and the importance of rank within the establishment. I learned the value and meaning of military insignia and the use of symbolism in military dress, which became a catalyst on my return to civilian life, prompting me to think about the psychology of our multitudinous ways of body packaging and the motives behind various styles of embellishment. In the fall of 1956 I recommenced my studies, this time at

the prestigious Royal College of Art in central London, where I had been awarded a three-year postgraduate scholarship. While there I also won a traveling scholarship to New York and Paris, and it was during a visit to the Paris flea market that I chanced upon an extensive collection of rare Art Deco *pochoir* illustrations and early fashion publications, some dating from the sixteenth century. They included works by Watteau, Le Clèrc, Heideloff, Ackermann, Barbier, Erté, and the like, together with early travel books, anthropological studies, sartorial theories, art books, some erotica, and numerous closely related subjects, which has supplied many of the illustrations in this and my earlier publications.

My interest in ethnic modes of beauty and idiosyncratic styles of dress and body adornments was quickly revived and entered a new phase of intensity during the research and writing of my major dissertation, in which I explored the influence tribal art and styles of beauty had on Western art and design—a subject of particular interest in the mid-to-late 1950s because of the growth of a new form of Urban Tribalism as witnessed by the rebellious Teddy Boys and Skinheads, who were beginning to appear in many city centers and, of course, the leather-jacketed biker groups, such as Hell's Angels, whose influence had been captured on film in *The Wild One.*

I had the good fortune to meet and interview many leading fashion and costume experts and journalists during this exciting period of change, as well as having the freedom to use the reading room and archives of the British Museum and the Victoria and Albert Museum. It was through their expert help and guidance that I came across many marvelous reference books on the subject of human beauty—including a number that were then considered X-rated and were not on public view—which helped open my eyes to other previously veiled aspects of human physical beauty that I had not been shown while studying life drawing. I still treasure these works today and I feel they should be compulsory viewing for all budding students of human aesthetics, as their intricate detailing are at the very core of this fascinating subject.

Through my earlier involvement in the film industry and the theater—I was a child actor from the age of 10 to 18 years, prior to going to art school—and with contacts made through the Royal College of Art, numerous journalists, art historians, and the British Museum, I was introduced to many famous people who were involved in various aspects of human beautification and modes of adornment: the fashion historians James Laver, Doris Langley Moore, and Vyvyan Holland, the Russian Art Deco illustrators Erté (Romain de Tirtoff) and Sonia Delaunay, Peter Finch, James Mason, Michael Caine, Prudence Glynn, then Fashion Editor of *The (London) Times*, the author Lawrence Langner, the sexually ambiguous Quintin Crisp of *The Naked Civil Servant* fame, April Ashley who was originally George Jamieson, the fashion photographers Norman Parkinson, Henry Clarke, John French, and Helmut Newton, the actor Stewart Granger, Joan Collins and her sister Jackie, Vivien Leigh and later her ex-husband Lawrence Olivier, Audrey Withers, then editor of British *Vogue* and her successor Ailsa Garland, the fashionable hairdresser Raymond and his young usurper Vidal Sassoon, Ernestine Carter and Professor Madge Garland (two of the last surviving dragons of the fashion world), the couturiers Digby Morton, Victor Stiebel, and Norman Hartnell, the milliner Aage Thaarup, my future employer and mentor Michael of Lachasse, a very young Mary Quant, the even younger Yves Saint Laurent and Karl Largerfield, Shirley Conran and her then husband Terrance, the famed nude photographer Royce (Horace Nasbeth), the artists David Hockney and Peter Blake, the art forger Eric Hepburn, Cecil Beaton, Princess Margaret, the model Barbara Goalen and the then new face Jean Shrimpton, Ken Russell and his wife Shirley, David Bailey, Coco Chanel, Balenciaga, Richard Attenborough and his brother David, Sean Connery and Terrance Stamp who I again met quite recently during the filming in Australia of *The Adventures of Priscilla, Queen of the Desert*, in which I had a small part, and the indomitable Sir Kenneth Clark, who had

agreed with my RCA professor, Janey Ironside, to oversee my research.

At various informal meetings, Sir Kenneth and I discussed the subject of human beauty and the importance and complexity of the embellishments used

by different cultural groups throughout history to improve the social and sexual appeal of the natural naked human form. We also spoke at length of the effects such modes had on other forms of aesthetic expression, and on Western civilization as a whole, and we agreed that the enhancement and beautifying of the human form by various means appeared to be an inborn human trait—an essential part of our genetic makeup and an expression of our psyche, which was in no way frivolous as so many other theorists had suggested, but was as important a form of aesthetic expression as any other, and in addition was probably the oldest. Recent discoveries in prehistoric cave dwellings certainly support this view, with the evidence of the use of body painting and embellishments predating any wall paintings and carved figurines by many thousands of years.

Several years later, I again met up with Sir Kenneth, when he was in need of help to research material for a series of lectures he was planning to give at the Royal Society of Arts on "Aspects of Human Beauty"—a subject he subsequently incorporated into his books and television programs.

At one of our research meetings, after discussing the aesthetic merits of human beauty contained in the paintings of Ingres, Rubens, Botticelli, Raphael, and others, Sir Kenneth said that much as he admired such paintings, his own interests lay in classical styles of beauty as seen from a purely Mediterranean viewpoint, which had reached its zenith in the marble sculptures of ancient Greece. He explained that to a great extent the aesthetic appeal of such beauty depended on perfect symmetry, regular features, and an unvarying adherence to the prevailing classical ideals of shape, form, and measurable proportions. In turn, I explained that my inclinations and convictions had become firmly rooted in the notion that human beauty is a reflection of cultural perceptions and inherited ideas of aesthetics, and that such perceptions and aesthetics were not immutable as I had detailed in my original RCA dissertation.

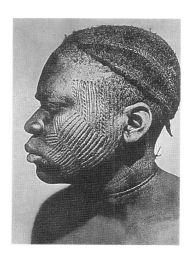

I went on to say that all human ideals and notions of beauty appeared to be inextricably linked to the varying forms of symbolism to which cultural groups appear to become "addicted" and which by ritual becomes an important aspect of their lives, and that each new generation learns

these notions and addictions in the same way as it learns all other cultural matters—thus human beauty exists only in the eyes of those with the specific knowledge and cultural heritage that enables them to perceive it. I also voiced my interest in the reasons why Western perceptions of human beauty have differed so greatly throughout history, and in particular why our current views embrace a far broader range of characteristics than has hitherto been the case. I amplified this by explaining that this was particularly noticeable in the growing acceptance of ethnic variations within my own world of fashion: by that time, I had become a well-known designer and design lecturer with many of my off-beat styles being featured in *Vogue* and *Harpers Bazaar* and selling in New York and Paris as well as London, while my students—Sally Tuffin and Marion Foale, James Wedge, Sylvia Ayton, Brian Godbold, Janice Wainwright, Wendy Dagworthy, and for a short time, Zandra Rhodes and Barbara Hulanicki of *Biba* fame, were beginning to revolutionize the fashion world with their young Carnaby Street style.

Through my work in the art and fashion industries and also as an actor and craftsman, I had come to realize that in a hi-tech industrialized world our aesthetic sensibilities had become closely linked to commercial interests, with the mass media, through its constant bombardment of advertising, having us believe that beauty, particularly human beauty, could only be had for a price. It had become separated from reality, departmentalized and made purchasable—hair treatments, cosmetics, face creams and lotions, nail polish, perfumes, the then new art of cosmetic surgery, and innumerable fashion items like narrow shoes, uplift bras, tight-fitting jeans were, and still are, essential items needed to achieve our notion of human beauty. We had begun to judge beauty not objectively or aesthetically, but by its sales potential and cost. If something was expensive and exclusive, like *haute couture,* then it was by its very nature seen as intrinsically more beautiful and desirable than items that were cheaper and more readily available.

This notion had also seeped over into other aspects of visual aesthetics. The appeal of, for instance, the *Venus de Milo* has been readily capitalized upon by manufacturers of cosmetic creams, deodorants, and vast numbers of other products from lawn mowers to chocolate cupcakes, which in turn has raised her perceived "beauty." Similarly, Frans Hals *The Laughing Cavalier,* the young women depicted by Renoir, Gauguin, and many others have, by being used for commercial gain, entered our visual consciousness and thus gained in aesthetic appeal—how many admire the beauty of the late-fifteenth-century Florentine youth painted by Filippino Lippi, which now hangs in the Uffizi but which has not had the good fortune to grace the cover of a box of chocolates, or the young Florentine woman painted by Piero del Pollaiuolo although it too graces the wall of another major Italian art gallery, the Poldi Pezzoli, Milan. They are little known and seldom receive much attention or adulation, not because they are not beautiful but because we place much more emphasis on familiar aesthetic images that have accredited sales appeal.

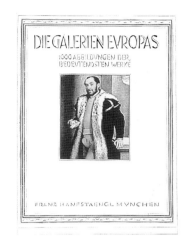

At one meeting with Sir Kenneth, I raised the question of the belief in many cultures that male beauty, or "handsomeness" as some theorists prefer to call it, rivals, and is sometimes thought superior to that of the female and that in such cultures male beauty is not seen as being in any way deviant or sexually suspect. I repeated my belief that the adornment and beautification of the human body by both males and females by different means is of great cultural and psychological significance—as vital a tool in our evolution as language—and is the foundation from which all the other arts had developed, which could well be why so many art historians "seem" to disdain fashion and other changeable styles of body art as it clearly raises a doubt as to the true origins and value of aesthetics and the ladder of its evolution.

Although Sir Kenneth did not agree entirely with all my propositions, he did concede that in much of the Western world, he too had noticed a growing acceptance of a number of cultural differences of a distinctly non-Western origin. This, he said, allowed for far greater freedom of choice in our search for human perfection than appeared to have been acceptable in, say, ancient Greece. Subsequently, in his books and television programs, he examined in some detail many of the points we had discussed, noting his agreement with the view current among his colleagues that other notions and perceptions of human beauty, together with the classical forms, now constitute the cornerstone of the Western ideal, and that this ideal could be further enhanced by a huge variety of adornments and styles of beautification that undoubtedly add to the overall aesthetic appeal of the human form. This acceptance of some styles of nonclassical beauty and of the legitimacy of all manner of adornments marked a major shift in the hitherto narrow view of what was or was not regarded as beautiful about the human body.

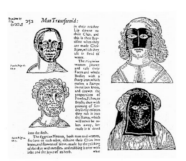

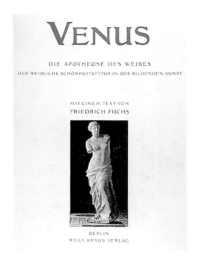

Sir Kenneth encouraged me to pursue my research of beauty and adornment in places such as Japan, Polynesia, South America, and Africa and among other non-Caucasian peoples. *The Quest for Human Beauty* is in many ways a direct result of Sir Kenneth's encouragement of my research, which has also been an important motivating force in my professional career as a designer, author, and academic—a career that has allowed me to travel to and live in many exotic countries, to work with many beautiful and talented people, and to see the wide variety of human beauty and modes of adornment that exist. Sir Kenneth's encouragement also acted as an inspiration to me while I was fighting in the courts to be allowed to lecture to university and college students on the aesthetic and physical differences of the human body— not as a form of obscenity or pornography, as was often suggested, but as a way to show design students the myriad techniques used to embellish and beautify, rather than to hide, our uniquely human characteristics and sexual differences.

As I was able to demonstrate during this legal battle, our current perception of human beauty is, thankfully, no longer as restrictive or prescriptive as it was in the past. I was also able to show that it is now widely accepted throughout the industrialized world that all humans, of whatever race, religion, education, or social background, have a natural right to show to advantage more of their physical attributes that has hitherto been the norm, with no feature of the male or female body being regarded as inherently obscene, except by the most bigoted, regressive, or authoritarian members of society.

This alteration to our perception of human beauty has, of course, been influenced by a great number of recent changes in the industrialized world, particularly in the areas of mass communications, advertising, and the performing and visual arts. These changes allow vast numbers of people to see, via satellite television, videocassette recorders, printed material, films, exhibitions, and so forth, the fascinating array of beauty and adornment that now exists, even in remote parts of the world. Many of these images have also shown how, over the millennia, the diverse racial groups of the world have been able to capitalize on their differing physical characteris-

tics, and in the process helped to evolve a wondrous display of idiosyncratic modes of human beauty, which are astonishingly complex and refined. Thus it is that today the unique array of human beauty is more accessible than ever before. It is there for all of us to admire and enjoy.

This book is a celebration of this wonderful pagent of human beauty, and of our newly acquired right to openly enjoy that which in the past has often been censored. As with several of my previous books, both the illustrations and text may shock some readers: I do not believe in limiting the illustrations used, nor do I believe in limiting discussion to only those parts of the human anatomy that have traditionally been sanctioned by society. Instead, I aim to show that there is no part of the male or female body that is not worthy of embellishment, admiration, and display. It is my belief that those parts of our bodies that we customarily hide are just as important, in an aesthetic sense, to our cultural identity as are those areas that we parade with pride. And it is my earnest hope that we are at last able to accept our millions of years of inherited development, so that we can take pleasure in all forms and styles of human beauty, free from preconceptions, prejudices, and notions of "morality" or "respectability": the magical quality of this beauty should be such as to elate the soul as well as to make our blood boil with desire. I hope, too, that we will continue to be allowed to enjoy and participate in this pageant of beauty in all its varied manifestations; we must insist that we have a right to do so and that no one has the right to stop us.

The illustrations I have used to convey my message are much more telling than words can ever be. I thank all the illustrators, photographers, painters, printmakers, gallery owners, publishing houses, agencies, and individuals, who by their generosity have contributed to this

wondrous array of human beauty, so enabling me to rightfully place the emphasis of this book on the illustrations. The text here is intended to highlight the changing ways of life and the attitudes of the peoples concerned, and to illuminate and draw attention to the philosophical

and journalistic observations with which each change in the perception of beauty has been surrounded.

It is my ardent hope that having once read this book and perused the illustrations you will agree that in the realm of human beauty neither sex has a monopoly, nor has any race, creed, or color, and that, in truth, diversity is of the essence, with the greatest aid to such diversity being the human imagination. This inventive genius, together with our quest for perfection, is an essential part of our humanity, and produces a legitimate form of aesthetic expression that is worthy of taking its place alongside all other artistic manifestations as a true reflection of our sensibility and creativity. Long may this unique human trait survive and thrive.

Julian Robinson.

Traditions of Adornment

Long before there was any form of written history, men and women were already going to elaborate and often painful lengths to change and beautify their natural naked bodies in their quest for a mate, to gain tribal prestige, to protect themselves from evil spirits, or to appease their gods.

Since that time, no feature of the human body has been spared these attempts at modification, enhancement, and beautification, and scant regard has been paid to the time, the cost, or the suffering involved. Individuals, and sometimes whole communities, have altered the shape, color, texture, and size of almost every feature—waist, hips, nose, eyes, teeth, hair, ears, head, breasts, skin, hands, fingers, finger and toenails, nipples, lips, navel, genitals, shoulders, wrists, neck, legs, feet, ankles, rib cage, cheeks, pubic region, silhouette, and so on—in order to achieve a socially desirable and sexually appealing appearance.

Even today, throughout the world men and women subject themselves to mutilation and other ordeals for this elusive, ephemeral, and often questionable "improvement." They willingly submit to a regime of distorted or broken bones, a constricted blood supply, restricted breathing, poisoned skin, debilitating diets, exhaustive exercise, regular purges, and complicated surgery, frequently suffering an agony that in any other context would be condemned as torture—all this to achieve an appear-

ance that will be the envy of their peers, that will be admired by members of the opposite sex, or that will clearly and visibly mark them as members of a particular tribal or cultural group.

In some parts of the world, people have slaughtered large numbers of rare animals so as to obtain "magical" substances in this quest for beauty. Others have spent fortunes on exotic and rare plant materials. And entire communities have willingly submitted very intimate parts of their bodies to traditional and sometimes bizarre forms of modification: some of these rituals being carried-out for reasons of religious faith, tradition, cultural initiation, group bonding or sexual attraction.

During the past five thousand or so years humans have also worn a great number of unusual, costly, cumbersome, impeding, and sometimes dangerously constricting garments, not out of modesty as one might first suppose, but in order to display wealth, social position, lineage, place of origin, authority, and even the wearer's distinctive sexual characteristics. People have worn huge pannier skirts that prevented the wearer from passing unassisted through a doorway, cartwheel neck ruffs of the finest lace supported on intricate metal frames that prevented the wearer from eating or drinking, sleeves that were so tight they inhibited every movement, steel and whalebone corsets that crushed ribs and impeded breathing, high-heeled shoes and chopines that distorted feet and posture, tight skirts or trousers that made it impossible to sit down, and numerous other strange impediments, including elaborate wigs, flamboyant hats, huge bustles, thigh, calf, chest, and shoulder padding, and decorated codpieces.

Today, in this same quest for beauty and an admired social identity, men and women of the Western world have their genitals tattooed or pierced, diet to the point of anorexia, drink their own urine, ingest the eggs or cut-up sections of live tape worms so that they become infested, have parts of their intestines surgically removed so as to reduce the waistline and lower their calorie intake, or have their buttocks, breasts, thighs, or nose reshaped. Some parents give their female children inhibiting growth drugs so that they do not grow too tall, and force their feet into tight, narrow shoes to impede their natural development and to reduce their eventual size.

In other parts of the world, where traditional ideals and symbols of beauty differ quite markedly from those of Western society, cultural groups call on the aid of other techniques, which include using animal waste products like cow urine and dung, to help beautify their hair and skin. Some mark their bodies with welts or branding irons, or distort parts of them with tight bindings and compression boards. And, although such notions of beauty are at variance with our own, the intention is the same: to obtain the approval of their peers, the respect of their elders, and the attention of members of the opposite sex. In some countries, such as with some tribal groups in Cameroon, West Africa, the Sudan, Mongolia, Nigeria, the Amazon, and on some Melanesian islands in the Bismarck Sea fatness is equated with beauty, so at puberty young women are placed in a specially constructed communal "fattening house", where they are fed an enriched diet. Later they will proudly display their corpulence, using modes of adornment that highlight, rather than conceal, their intimate female features. In other societies, it is the male who is considered the more beautiful of the sexes; he spends much of his time adorning himself, sometimes in very explicit and provocative ways, openly preening and posturing in the hope of being chosen for a liaison or for marriage.

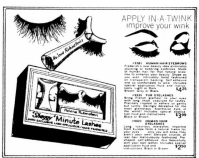

Other cultures believe that the body without its traditional marks of civilization and symbols of beautification—such as tattooing or decorative scars (a traditional pattern of raised bead-like keloid skin markings, shiny cicatrization scars, or the like)—is not worthy of attention; the natural, unadorned body is merely animal. It is the tattooing or scars that make a body human, beautiful, and desirable. I have traveled to areas of the world where white teeth and pink lips are despised as being "like those of a dog", where only the eldest son is allowed to marry and where the younger sons, if they are attractive enough, are promoted to the status of symbolic women so that they can be married, or "pair-bonded." In other areas, very distinctive features, such as a broad nose, are much admired as a symbol of race; for emphasis, the nose is broadened during childhood, and then on reaching maturity is decorated with boar's tusks and cassowary quills or the like. In yet other areas, the genitals of both men and women are by tradition enlarged and decorated in such a way as to

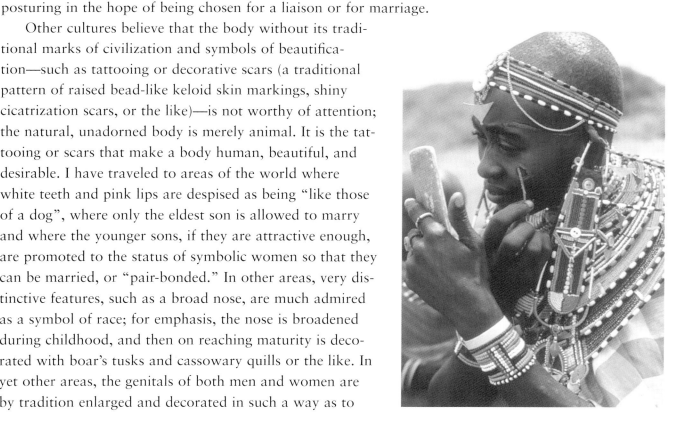

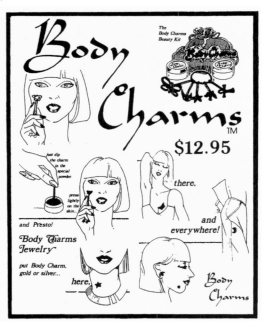

leave no doubt that they are the most beautiful physical feature, intended to be the center of attraction for members of the opposite sex and the envy of members of the same sex.

In one country I visited, I found that I offended local custom by wearing a t-shirt and shorts; it was customary for the body of a mature male to go unadorned on most occasions, except for a little paint and pig fat. The people wanted to know what I was hiding, and why I wore so many clothes on nonfestive occasions. In that society, the males wore garments only during ritual courting ceremonies, to arouse the curiosity and ardor of the single females. In another area, I discovered it was only the village prostitutes who habitually wore concealing garments, using them as a form of sexual lure. Clients of these women made several attempts to procure some of my garments to help enliven their humdrum sex lives.

In another community I found that, although the young men devoted much of their time and energy to making themselves attractive in the eyes of their peers, it was nevertheless the custom for marriageable young women to be courted by a mature man, who displayed the symbols of his wealth and social position upon his person in an impressive but rarely ostentatious manner. This was a demonstration of his ability to pay for and support another wife, even though he might already have six wives, including the elder sister of the young woman he was currently courting. In yet another community, I found that a nubile woman was not regarded as attractive until she could display on her person symbolic love tokens from many suitors who had been successful in gaining her sexual favors. The more tokens a young woman was able to display, the more beautiful and desirable she became in the eyes of her peers—"Who could possibly love a woman, or think her beautiful, when no other males have desired her?" seemed to be the local logic.

In fact, everywhere I went while researching this book I found that the prevailing notions of what was beautiful or sexually attractive about the human form varied greatly, and it came as no surprise to find that few societies were in agreement about what are the most attractive human physical characteristics: whether it is the male or the female who is, in general, more beautiful, or, in some instances, whether it is the individual's ability to display his or her tribal allegiance, wealth, or social position. I discovered, too, that what was often regarded as beautiful in Paris was not much admired in the upper Amazon; what was found beautiful in the upper Amazon failed to impress in the highlands of New Guinea; what delighted the highlanders of New Guinea was not deemed beautiful by the Maasai of Kenya and Tanzania; the sort of person the Maasai considered beautiful was not considered so by the Akha, Karen, Yao, Lisu, or Shan, who inhabit northern Thailand and neighboring areas; and beauty as perceived by these varying groups is not so perceived by the majority of people who live in London or New York.

Even within Western culture, the display of painting and sculpture in great art galleries and museums clearly show that our own notions of beauty have varied greatly from one generation to another. It is also apparent that, although by tradition we are a clothed rather than merely an adorned society and that in normal circumstances we have a marked phobia about nakedness, we have, in our arts at least, not completely lost our admiration for some aspects of the naked human form. Nevertheless, this culturally generated phobia about what parts of our bodies should or should not be displayed is keenly observed; various body parts are "redesigned" so as to conceal the more intimate details of both the male and female reproductive organs, which are often glorified in the art forms of other cultures.

The great paintings and sculptures show, though, that our ancestors were not always as puritanical or as conservative about their modes of self-presentation as many people are today. These paintings also show that at some stages of our history our ancestors preferred a certain plumpness and opulence in the female form and fashions of adornment, and that at other stages a leaner shape and less ornate style of adornment were preferred. Similar variations are evident in the array of male depictions. We can also see that long hair, plucked eyebrows, long necks, or padded codpieces were sometimes the center of interest; at other times small, high breasts, slender sloping shoulders, curved hips, or padded calves and thighs were the features most admired.

The German painter Albrecht Dürer discussed this phenomenon early in the sixteenth century, pointing out that such variations simply show our range of choices, with one

choice being in no way inferior, in an aesthetic sense, to another. In relation to the question of whether plumpness or slenderness might be more appealing, he said: "It would be quite possible to make two different figures, neither conforming with the other, one stouter, the other thinner, and yet we might scarce be able to judge which of the two excels in beauty."

Since the time of Aristotle, many painters, historians, and philosophers have mused on this subject of human beauty. From the vast quantity of theories generated, it would be reasonable to assume that there is no consensus on the subject, except that in general in the Western world we do not seem to admire the male or female bodies in their natural, naked state. Our admiration is reserved for the fully or partially clothed person, or for the naked form only after it has been embellished in some way, with civilized marks or modes of adornment, and redesigned to remove or refine certain features to make them more socially and morally acceptable. Such refinement is somewhat in the ancient Greek tradition, although it fails to embrace the essence of the Greek philosophical beliefs, which unconditionally accepted all forms of nakedness and sexual practice.

As Kenneth Clark notes in *The Nude* (1956), we also find ourselves disturbed by such natural phenomena as "wrinkles, pouches and other small imperfections," which were always eliminated in the classical Greek works. He goes on to observe that "by long habit we do not judge the body as a living organism, but as a design," but that our ideas of how that design should be changes as our lifestyles and circumstances change. Hence we are continually redefining our ideals of how the human body should really look, as can be seen from the enormously varied depictions in Western art since the time of ancient Greece. Because of our religious and cultural traditions we are not accustomed to observing the naked body as it really is, in all its various shapes, as was the norm in ancient Greece. In general, we see only those naked shapes depicted by artists, and in more recent times by photographers who specialize in the subject and who tend to portray only those individuals whose bodies have well-defined erogenous features—features that tend to be exaggerated so as to heighten the body's erotic appeal. As a result, we have come to believe that the naked body is an object upon which the eye will always dwell

with pleasure. Of course, this is rarely the case, as anyone who has studied at art school or who has visited a nudist camp would testify. As Kenneth Clark observes, "In almost every detail the body is not the shape which art has led us to believe that it would be." He adds that in the Western tradition the naked body is no more than the point of departure for the artist's experimentation and inventiveness, resulting in images that are continually changing as the artist's ideas, as well as our own ideas, ideals, expectations, and lifestyles, change.

Even so, each new experiment is, I believe, still aimed at arousing in us the urge to procreate, nakedness having been used in our culture for generations (intentionally or not) as a symbol of carnal pleasure. As Kenneth Clark so aptly states, "No nude, however abstract, should fail to arouse in the spectator some vestige of erotic feeling—even though it be only the faintest shadow—and if it does not do so it is bad art," based, I venture to add, on false values and an inhibiting moral code.

Although the nudes displayed in such magazines as *Penthouse, Mayfair, Club International,* and *Playboy* may seem sexier to modern eyes than the carvings of the Stone Age or the works of Titian or Ingres, there is little doubt that the artist and his contemporaries saw these naked forms at least partly with Playboy eyes. Thus many works that today may be acceptable to us were originally seen as erotic, even pornographic—just as some people today see any form of nudity as licentious by virtue of its inherent cultural symbolism.

Fortunately, it has always been well understood that the desire to clasp and be united with another human whom we perceive to be attractive—even if this union is only a fleeting fantasy—is so fundamental a part of our nature that our judgment of beauty, as well as many other aspects of life, is inevitably influenced by it. This instinct cannot be completely suppressed by force of law, nor by any imposed religious or moral attitudes.

In recent years, numerous commentators have observed that even our cultural judgment of what is known as "pure form"—form from which all human details and associations have been eliminated and that exists in its own right, without association with other objects—is nevertheless influenced by our subliminal sexual instincts. So, indeed, are almost all the techniques and decorative trappings used to adorn and decorate the human body. In *Skin to Skin: Eroticism in Dress* (1982)

Prudence Glynn states that in the Western world, nearly all clothing styles and adornments carry symbols of sexual association; such as the association of a white wedding dress with virginity, or of tattooing with prostitution, or at least questionable virtue. The labia and symbolic rendering of pubic hair are also a common motif used in the design and decoration of women's dress and in jewelry, and many authorities see a man's necktie as a form of phallic symbolism. Even the much-loved symbolic heart shape, which is used in all forms of design and displayed *ad nauseam* on all kinds of merchandise, has its origins deep in our subconscious—its shape has very little to do with the organ that pumps blood around the body, rather it is a deeply etched memory in our primordial brain of our female ancestors' genital display, or so I have been told by such experts as Helen Fisher, Desmond Morris, and Professor Milton Diamond, among many others.

Thus, one of the difficulties encountered when discussing human beauty is that, whether we like to admit it or not, such natural instincts and cultural forms of symbolism cannot be ignored, as they generally are in a discussion about, say, an abstract piece of sculpture—although most experts concede that such works gain much of their creative force and aesthetic appeal from the sublimation of erotic feelings and our addiction to sexual modes of symbolism. The subliminal form of expression and our inclination to symbolism are also important in the appreciation of other art forms, such as classical ballet, poetry, films, and theater, and in the appreciation of such natural phenomena as flora and fauna—think of why, for example, a pink rose excites ardor, or why the scent of a lily is so intoxicating. The readers of the *Kama Sutra* would know, as did Havelock Ellis when he wrote his detailed *Studies in the Psychology of Sex* (1901–10).

In some societies, the sublimation of erotic feelings is far less important than it is in the Western world: those societies do not share our phobia about nakedness, or the horror we have of depicting many of our natural bodily functions. This lack of inhibition can be sensed from, for example, an ancient Greek vase, the sculptures that adorn Hindu temples, many Japanese *ukiyo-e* prints, and numerous carvings from Africa, New Guinea, and elsewhere. None of the cultures that created such works regarded what we term "pornography" as being in any way abnormal. In fact, many of these works of art form an essential part of their religious and cultural life and they not only depict but glorify the human acts that Western artists tend to judge unworthy of recording.

In general, it would seem that Western culture would rather ignore all forms of fornication and deviation, preferring to concentrate on the adornment and concealment of the physical details that so many other cultures prefer to celebrate in their near-naked state. This obsession has resulted in a state of mind that leads us to accept the human form as essentially a clothed or adorned one, thus rendering the naked human body incomplete, one lacking its natural and symbolic coverings. We also tend to regard beauty of clothing as a form of beauty of body. Goethe commented upon this transmutation when he wrote, "We exclaim 'What a beautiful little foot!' when we have merely seen a pretty shoe. We admire a lovely waist when nothing has met our eyes but an elegant girdle." Havelock Ellis went further, noting that it was quite early in our cultural development when "the tendency for beauty of clothing to be accepted as a substitute for beauty of body" appeared.

This theory was later developed by Lawrence Langner in *The Importance of Wearing Clothes* (1959): he went into considerable detail about the advantages to our society of being traditionally clothed and stated that without such clothing and all the psychological consequences that have flowed therefrom, our civilization would never have progressed as far as it has. It is clothes, in Langner's view, that make it possible for governments to obtain obedience, religions reverence, judiciaries a respect for law, and armies discipline. He also observed that it is the effects of clothing that have altered our path of sexual selection, changed our notions of beauty, and brought about the triumph of brain over brawn.

In the realm of painting and fine art in general, our admiration for such depictions as those by Velázquez and van Dyck has certainly as much to do with dress and adornment, and all the associated intricate detailing, as it has with any natural beauty the wearer might possess. It would also be fair to say that in paintings of the nude our admiration is usually reserved for the human body only after it has been "redesigned" and "refined" to make it acceptable to our established moral code.

None of this is intended to suggest that erotic art does

not exist in the Western world: it does and always has, as evidenced by the somewhat risqué frescoes Raphael painted for Cardinal Bibbiena's bathroom in the Vatican or the mass of eighteenth- and nineteenth-century illustrations by artists such as Rowlandson and Beardsley. But until very recent times, such art has not been widely accepted or openly displayed. And even today, despite our proclamations of self-determination and freedom of thought, censorship laws still operate to restrict the display of certain erotic images.

This reliance on censorship to protect our visual and moral sensibility is a reflection of our society, one that greatly influences our attitudes toward what is or is not considered beautiful about the human form. To a large extent, our notions of human beauty are based on a *melange* of beliefs, conventions, convictions, traditions, and modes of symbolism that are taught to us by the society in which we live. Some experts argue that these notions are influenced only minimally by our genes, and that human beauty is undoubtedly culturally determined, with any fixed, universal notion on the subject being an invention of misinformed theorists or cultural egotists, who believe that by some kind of divine right their own ideas and ideals must be superior to those of all others.

Having spent many years researching this particular question, and having traveled extensively throughout the world and lived with numerous tribal groups, it is my belief that each cultural group really has invented the ideals and symbols it needs to reflect its natural peculiarities: Alexander von Humboldt put forward this notion in *Travels to the Equinoctial Region of the New Continent* (1806): "Nations attach the idea of beauty to everything which particularly characterises their own physical conformation, their natural physiognomy." The fashion magazine *La Belle Assemblée* amplified the notion in 1808: "In countries where the women naturally have full bosoms, they have persuaded the men that this conformation is the highest degree of perfection; they have also worked themselves into the same belief. On the other hand, in countries where the bosom is less full, beauty has been made to consist in this scantiness, which becomes more and more desirable."

Charles Darwin also noted this tendency to admire one's own physiognomy, this time in relation to male beauty, when he wrote in *The Descent of Man* (1871), "The men of the beardless races take infinite pain in eradicating every hair from their face as something odious, whilst the men of the bearded races feel the greatest pride in their beards." He adds that "The women, no doubt, participate in these feelings."

Darwin and others have also speculated that it was possible that a woman's choice in such matters could well be influenced by the social position and wealth of the men who courted her, which of course the men displayed in the amount of time they spent grooming, in their mode of adornment, and in the artifacts with which they surrounded themselves. Such display, in the Western world and elsewhere, certainly adds to a man's allure and could in many respects be considered a form of masculine beauty. It is further enhanced by posturing and gestures of dominance, as explained by Desmond Morris in *The Human Zoo* (1969) when he likens an admired man to the most admired male baboon; that is, as the leader of the troop and by virtue of this, the prime breeding male. "To be admired," he writes, "you must clearly display the trappings, postures and features of dominance. For the baboon this means a sleek, beautifully groomed, luxuriant coat of hair; a calm, relaxed posture when not engaged in disputes; a deliberate and purposeful gait when active. There must be no outward sign of anxiety, indecision or hesitancy." With a few superficial modifications, the same holds true for an admired man: the luxuriant coat of fur becomes the expensive suit, which must outshine that of his rivals; he assumes postures reflecting his admired position; when he is put under pressure he asserts himself and becomes more impressive than his rivals; he must rise above them in the eyes of members of the opposite sex, matching his psychological state with his physical posture; and he can emphasize his authority with symbols of wealth and power, such as an expensive car, a penthouse, a yacht, or a private jet.

In fact, the perception of a man as attractive, admired, or even beautiful involves a combination of many factors. The right physiognomy is but one—as indeed it is with feminine beauty, although we often have difficulty accepting this fact. In this regard, Darwin said words to the effect that people of each tribe admire their own characteristic qualities: the shape of the head and face, the squareness or otherwise of the cheekbones, the prominence or depression of the nose, the color of the skin, the length and texture of the hair on the head, and so on. He concluded that in terms of natural selection within a particular society "these and other such features could hardly fail to be slowly and gradually exaggerated" and suggested that over time "such preferences could become inherited."

Darwin also referred to Lubbock's *Origins of Civilisation* (1870), which, he said, "showed that in the old times high

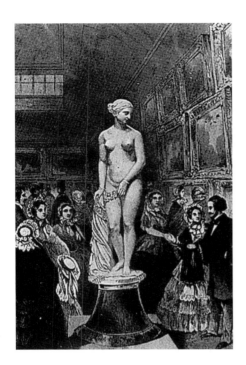

honour was bestowed on women who were utterly licentious." Licentiousness, like so many other admired feminine traits, has, according to Lubbock and Darwin, thus become an important ingredient in our perception of feminine beauty. Darwin continued by saying that women had long been selected for such "beauty," their beauty having become by common agreement a symbol of carnality, which is why women in the Western world are perceived as having become more beautiful, according to general opinion, than men. And this is why they add to their natural beauty with cosmetic and other sexually oriented embellishments. Darwin went into some detail about the importance of the physical differences between the sexes in bringing about an actual state of sexual arousal. These differences, he theorized, had in many cases become more pronounced through natural selection: the more pronounced the difference, the greater the promise of sexual fulfillment and the greater the attraction to members of the opposite sex. Thus such secondary sexual characteristics, which in our own case also include differing styles of dress and adornments, form the basis for today's notion of beauty, which, from a strictly biological point of view is, I believe, exactly what nature intended, as beauty ensures the random mixing of human genes in unpredictable and unplanned ways by instigating and encouraging random sexual activity. In addition, it also keeps suitors in constant attendance, thus aiding survival of any progeny.

Being sexy, or rather, the wish to be more sexually attractive than we may actually be, is also at the root of much aesthetic creativity, as the hormones and other body chemicals aroused by sexual activity, or the thought or wish for such activity, have a flow-on effect—they work on the creative mind like any other stimulating drug, leading one into a world of fantasy and creativity, and fuelling a desire for even more sexual activity. My own experience while working with many creative people and my research of the work and lives of many others shows that they were far above the norm in their sexual appetites—many were quite profligate and the scandals that surrounded their love affairs are legion. It would appear from studies, such as my own and others, that in some way sexuality or perversely, in some cases, the frustration of sexual activity by celibacy, fuels our aesthetic sensibilities and drives both them and us into all sorts of experimentation. In painting, the results are there for us all to see, while in the realm of beauty it motivates us to fantasize—if only I were a little taller, shorter, slimmer, blonde, blue-eyed, long-necked, or in some other way more attractive, then maybe, just maybe, I would meet the partner of my dreams. So we use our creative urges to right that which nature seems to have been remiss in providing.

Human beauty is, in fact, an expression of this inventive and aesthetic nature, a celebration of our humanness, a reflection of our inner spirit, which transcends all thinking and analysis—a biological imperative sculpted into our soul by some seemingly godlike life force, about which we can do little except accept its reality and validity. It has a quality that makes it both real and illusory, a metaphor for our attitudes, fantasies, traditions, hang-ups, and lifestyles that also gives us a sense of personal and collective identity. It is an essential part of our very essence and a reflection of the mystery of the human condition, which is etched deeply into our innermost consciousness and carries important physiological messages that take it beyond reason. It is as if it has been encoded into our genes as a natural predisposition, which for one reason or another each cultural group seems to perceive slightly differently. Many primal people regard their form of human beauty as a special gift of the gods created by an important cosmic vibration that marked their tribe out as being one of those especially favored and therefore deserving of respect. Others see it is a manifestation of *maya*—an illusion conjured up by the commercial interest of the material world. Conversely, there are those who believe that it is entirely rational and only resides in complete symmetry resulting from the right proportion between the component parts, which gives a balance to the whole, a congruity and harmony, forgetting that a slight imperfection, if wisely used, adds considerably to the allure of such beauty. And they also forget that the power of the imagination is such that, for instance, no breast, or nipple, or other physical feature is ever as beautiful as the one we see in our mind, and that therefore a veil adds considerably to our perception of such beauty—a notion noted by that master poet of erotic psychology, Robert Herrick, who also correctly suggested that "a sweet disorder in the dress" is more alluring than almost anything else—two psychological

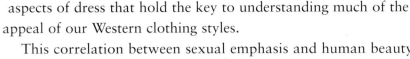

aspects of dress that hold the key to understanding much of the appeal of our Western clothing styles.

This correlation between sexual emphasis and human beauty has many supporters. In *Culture des Idées* (1901), Remy de Gourmont wrote that the human notion of beauty "is not an unmixed idea, it is intimately united with the idea of carnal pleasure." Sigmund Freud also dwelt on this point, stating, "I have no doubt that the concept of beauty is rooted in the soil of sexual stimulation and signified originally that which was sexually exciting." The mystic Yatri in *Unknown Man: The Mysterious Birth of a New Species* (1988) believes that human sexiness had a tremendous evolutionary advantage for human development and was a dominant factor in the formation of early societies that allowed civilization to progress much more quickly than it may otherwise have done: "non-stop erotic behaviour is evolution's stroke of genius to create conditions for curiosity, excitation, stable groups and co-operation." He observes that "The powerful, non-stop sexual urge stimulates a constant flow of hormones to and from the brain, accompanied by greater enhanced electrical activity. This in turn stimulates a whole sense of inquiry, curiosity and alertness." This point is also taken up by the Anglo-Sri Lankan mystic Babagee Attman, founding member of *The Free Will Society*, and numerous other mystics and eastern gurus, together with many Western theorists who have studied Eastern sexual prac-

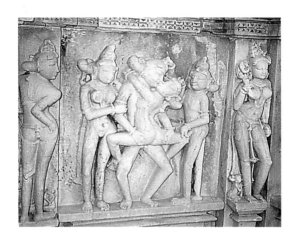

tices and who have long sung the praises of the power of "raw" Tantra, Taoist, and Kundalini sexual energy— which Attman refers to as "the sex-sensual pathway to health and happiness"—and he also sings the praises of the flow-on beautifying effect such activity and energy has on the mind, body, and beauty of participants. As Attman pointed out to me when I met him and his co-founder of *The Free Will Society*, the Australian Ray Burton in 1996: "such energy is entirely self-replenishing, and as it puts one in touch with the cosmos it should be enjoyed as an essential part of our daily ritual."

A similar theme was also discussed by Frederick Turner in *Beauty: The Value of Values* (1991) who believes we actually receive a chemical reward from our brain which is akin to a narcotic drug, for our mere appreciation of beauty (but without the side effects of drugs we choose to ingest). Other specialists have shown through a variety of experiments that regular indulgence in sexual activity brings similar chemical rewards and can be viewed as an indicator that the participants have a healthy mind and body—a theme that echoes the beliefs of Havelock Ellis and John Carl Flügel and, in more recent times, that of Desmond Morris and Helen Fisher in *The Sex Contract: The Evolution of Human Behavior* (1982) and *Anatomy of Love: The Natural History of Monogamy, Adultery, and Divorce* (1992).

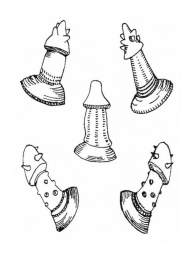

Fisher's first book offers a fascinating theory of our origins and development over the past four million or so years: She convincingly suggests that human beauty and sexuality have played a considerable role in the survival and progress of the human race. Apparently, it does not matter if you are the richest man in America, the most powerful woman in business, the brightest in your class: if you fail to pass on your genes to the next generation you are a loser as far as Nature is concerned. According to Fisher, human beauty evolved to aid our forebears in their desire to breed, and by a process of natural selection this form of sexual attractant, which we call "beauty," played a crucial role in the survival and development of our progenitors: it also had a flow-on effect in helping to develope our intelligence and aesthetic sensibilities.

Fisher studied baboons in the wild and extensively researched our primate cousins to see how beauty might have evolved. She was confident in her postulation of the close link between beauty and sexuality. It appears that when a female baboon is in estrus she advertises the fact with a distinctive attractant: "The skin around her genitals becomes swollen with blood and blossoms below her tail like a huge pink flower", and she exudes a pungent, sexy scent. During the early days of being in heat, the female excites the younger males into copulation by presenting her pink-petalled attractant to them. As ovulation approaches, formidable contenders vie for her sexual favors.

Studies of nubile human females have elicited similar conclusions but unlike other primates, they usually achieve their sexual objectives by the symbolic flaunting of their distinctive secondary sexual attributes, evolution having endowed them with a number of unique characteristics (the flaunting of their primary sexual characteristic is

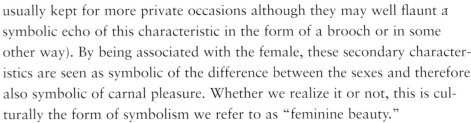

usually kept for more private occasions although they may well flaunt a symbolic echo of this characteristic in the form of a brooch or in some other way). By being associated with the female, these secondary characteristics are seen as symbolic of the difference between the sexes and therefore also symbolic of carnal pleasure. Whether we realize it or not, this is culturally the form of symbolism we refer to as "feminine beauty."

At puberty, human females retain the higher pitched voice and the hairless face and body of childhood, (a phenomenom usually referred to as a form of *neoteny*) with the exception of those parts of the body where special growths of hair denote sexual maturity. Human breasts also appear to have developed where they are to transmit the same message—they have no physiological function that could not be carried out without the subcutaneous deposits of fat that surround the mammary glands. These fatty deposits play no role in nursing and in some cases are a cumbersome impediment. Fatty buttocks do not seem to have much practical use either, but they appear on almost all women and, like breasts, are admired for their distinctive feminineness. They undoubtedly act as powerful allurements for members of the opposite sex and may well be a biological signal to the male that a female so endowed is fit and ready for mating and possible pregnancy—it has been well established that a minimum proportion of twenty to twenty-five percent body fat is required for the onset of regular menstruation, and this is why some cultures introduce fattening houses for their young nubile females. Some cultures teach their young women how to emphasize their distinctive gait as an attractant, which also helps to emphasize the appeal of breasts and buttocks. Many also flaunt their distinctive facial features; in fact, young women everywhere seem to use almost identical ways of flirting with their eyes, lips, and other facial features, which represent another innate sexual attribute much glorified for its distinctive feminineness, and hence beauty, and which is emphasized by use of a wide variety of embellishments. Its power is such that many poets have found this aspect of feminine beauty irresistible and tens of thousands of words have been written in its praise, thus underlining what is an essential part of Nature's reproductive strategy.

Poets have also long sung the praise of the sweet scent that young women exude at times of flirting, and Fisher mentions such scent in connection to our primate cousins at times of courting and mating. Ancient Asian writers also commented upon human scent as being Nature's own aphrodisiac, and in the *Arabian*

Nights there are instructions for adding to that scent with perfumes in order to excite one's lover into the realm of ecstasy, while in *The Perfumed Garden* it is said that such a combination excites one's lover to the generative act. Havelock Ellis sung the praises of the natural body scent of women and the use of enhancing perfumes, and, as he says, there seems to be a good biological reason for this, and one which I believe undoubtedly influences our perception of human beauty. It seems that while our other senses relay their signals to the emotional center of the brain via an indirect information-processing route through the cortex, the nose is directly wired to this emotional center, which is deep inside the brain's primordial core. This inner region is responsible for generating our most intimate feelings, so when we meet someone to whom we are instantly attracted, someone who makes our blood race and fills us with amorous desire, the cause may well be the odor molecules secreted by the body, which act like love potions. We, on the other hand, don't quite know what has happened, so our brain immediately rationalizes the situation by telling us "Isn't he/she beautiful. Look at his/her lovely body/buttocks/hair/lips/legs/eyes" etc., transforming the appeal of the scent into a vision of beautiful and/or intelligent masculinity/femininity—just another of Nature's reproductive strategies.

In *The Naked Ape* (1967) the zoologist Desmond Morris says that "if our ancestors' hairy covering had to be discarded then there must have been a very powerful biological reason." Being hairless also seems to be part of Nature's reproductive strategy—it has allowed our bodies to become much more sensitive and sexual—a point taken up by Elaine Morgan who, like Morris, speculates that we could all well have lost our fur covering during an aquatic phase in our evolution. In her book *The Aquatic Ape* (1982), Morgan brought forward a number of factors supporting the aquatic theory, in addition to that of losing our fur covering, including the proposition that most water-dwelling mammals seem to indulge in far more sexual play than do those who have always dwelt on land, and that a number of aquatic mammals have also developed better vocal facilities and bigger brains. Maybe this is why we humans are so

vocal, so active, why we indulge in so much sex play, and why sexiness seems to be such an important ingredient of our perception of human beauty. Most specialists agree, for instance, that sexual activity between adult humans is far more frequent than is necessary for procreation, but without such regular sexual contact very few couples would stay together for very long. And it is also this sexiness that seems to fuel our aesthetic sensibilities and drive us to experiment within the realms of painting, sculpture, opera, poetry and so on, to extol our undying love and admiration for members of the opposite sex. It is also one of the main motivating forces behind our modes of beautification, compelling us, as it were, to be forever seeking out and experimenting with new and different ways to attract a mate and create envy in the eyes of our peers and competitors. From an aesthetic point of view, however, it is not necessary to fully understand all of the evolutionary phases through which our ancestors have passed, but to accept that our comparative hairlessness and the adipose layer we have under our skin adds considerably to our perception of our human beauty, and that given the opportunity, the human animal does appear to have an affinity with water. Our bodies also seem to incorporate a form of aquatic streamlining which is often glorified in the Miss World and Miss Universe pageants, and on beaches everywhere.

It is, I think, also relevant in our attempt to understand our obvious complex attitudes toward human beauty to note how many cultures associate feminine beauty with a watery origin, and how they venerate the beauty of mermaid-like creatures. Mermaids are involved in many myths and legends

about human origins and the origins of human beauty, as for instance in that of the Mende of Sierra Leone. The American cultural historian Sylvia Ardyn Boone, in her study of the culture of the Mende entitled *Radiance from the Waters: Ideals of Feminine Beauty in Mende Art* (1986), writes that for the Mende "the female face and body are beauty incarnate. Woman is the most beautiful thing that God has put in the world; she is God's finest handwork"— God, in this case, is Ngewo, ruler of the cosmos. It is against the standard of feminine pulchritude that other creatures and objects are judged. If, for instance, a man is really handsome, they say with pride "He is like a woman." The sight of such a handsome man or a lovely women is considered one of the great pleasures of life and their presence brings a surge of satisfaction and contentment to the whole community. Beauty is an essential part of the definition of what it means to be a Mende woman, and it is a concomitant belief that every woman has an inherent beauty— the very fact of being female makes her attractive. Regardless of how plain we may perceive her to be, by virtue of being Mende and female she is a beauty in the eyes of her peers.

The Mende, however, believe that beauty doesn't just happen. It has to be worked at—the most is made of each individual. They start by reshaping a newly born baby's head to their ideal even before the umbilical cord has been cut—pressing and manipulating the bones so that the shape of the head is as beautiful as it can possibly be.

The ideal of all Mende women is to be as beautiful as Tingoi, a mythical mermaid—a spiritual ideal to be yearned for but one they know can never be attained. They say "There is no one more beautiful than Tingoi"; rather, she is the standard to be aimed for. It is through this myth that the Mende affirm that, try as they might, they do not expect to ever achieve perfect female beauty in this life—such perfect beauty "is divine, unearthly, from paradise," and thus can only be imaged and aspired to. But, as Boone observed, "The Mende still long for the ideal, even just some piece of perfection, some small part," which they strive to achieve by perfecting the beauty of their hair, breasts, hands, legs, eyes, or

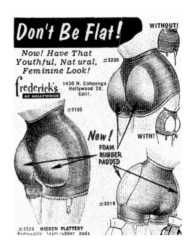

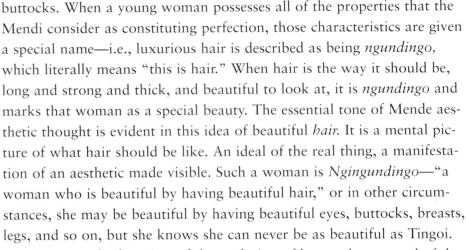

buttocks. When a young woman possesses all of the properties that the Mendi consider as constituting perfection, those characteristics are given a special name—i.e., luxurious hair is described as being *ngundingo*, which literally means "this is hair." When hair is the way it should be, long and strong and thick, and beautiful to look at, it is *ngundingo* and marks that woman as a special beauty. The essential tone of Mende aesthetic thought is evident in this idea of beautiful *hair*. It is a mental picture of what hair should be like. An ideal of the real thing, a manifestation of an aesthetic made visible. Such a woman is *Ngingundingo*—"a woman who is beautiful by having beautiful hair," or in other circumstances, she may be beautiful by having beautiful eyes, buttocks, breasts, legs, and so on, but she knows she can never be as beautiful as Tingoi.

A more orthodox view of the evolution of human beauty and of the survival of our species is that proposed by Helen Fisher, who agrees with the importance of the look of sexiness as a survival strategy in humans— the look of sexiness denotes healthiness, the ability to successfully bear children, and a number of other important pieces of biological information. Fisher also believes that the look of sexiness is an important female characteristic and that it is only the human female who actively seeks the sexual attention of males throughout her menstrual cycle. The reason for this, she says, appears to be that early in human evolution there was no regular form of "pair bonding"; females reared their young as best they could. As life became more complex, the over-burdened females needed help: "Everywhere there was an untapped work force, a cornucopia, a gold mine—proto-hominoid males." All the females had to do was to learn to woo these males with something the males liked; those females who were more sexually active than the norm proved to have greater success than their less active sisters. With this success came extra attention, which included bodily protection and often gifts of food. The conse-

quence was that the offspring of these more sexually active females had a greater chance of survival, thus "passing on this genetic anomaly to a greater percentage of the next generation." Natural selection had begun in favor of sexier females—the "look" of such sexiness became an important ingredient in the perception of female beauty.

Male beauty on the other hand seems to have evolved somewhat differently—as anybody who has studied zoology or seen the wondrous display of animal species would

fully appreciate—a phenomenon which is usually referred to as *dimorphism*. In the animal world, it is quite normal for there to be considerable divergence in visual presentation, visual preferences, and visual messages between sexually mature males and their female counterparts, and this can be seen in all species, including our own, with the female in particular making very specific demands upon her suitors. And it is the visual manifestation of these demands that, for want of a better term, we call masculine beauty or "handsomeness", although, I should add, all such characteristics are not necessarily related to sexuality and breeding, but have to do with survival in a general sense. Nevertheless, most experts agree that nature and evolution has made all males of whatever species a breeding experiment from which the females may choose, and in other species the power of her choice has created many very strange, wonderful, and often bizarre visual forms, of which the peacock's brightly colored display feathers are possibly the most noteworthy.

In the human species the male has also developed physical differences from the female that are at the root of his beauty—a difference in head size, for instance, in the growth of facial hair, width of shoulders, and general body shape. A difference in muscle growth and the distinctive shape of the male genitals are all of considerable importance, as are the firmer male buttocks and more powerful legs, together with a difference in voice tone, countenance, and general bearing, which all bespeak his ability to support and defend any offspring—traits that are formalized, emphasized, and displayed differently by different cultural groups.

Many attempts have been made to measure and collate the natural differences between various groups of peoples, and between males and

females. For instance, in the mid-1930s the American cosmetic manufacturer Max Factor invented a device for measuring the different forms and details of female beauty, which involved comparing many complicated shapes and measurements in what he called a "beauty calibration"—the result was a Hollywood ideal of beauty used to grade potential female movie stars. However, it has been my experience that

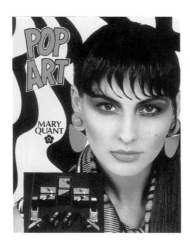

throughout the world most women actually glorify in their natural cast of features and physical differences, using every device and technique available to them to look more attractive, noticeable, alluring, and the like according to their natural physiognomy. Women of numerous cultures have long tattooed their bodies, scarred their faces, filed, removed, or splayed their teeth, inserted plugs in their lips, stretched their earlobes, and pierced their noses to achieve their essential and traditional mode of sex appeal and beauty. Some women of the Western Pacific even tattoo the inner lips of their vulva to enhance their physical looks. Kalahari San bushmen and a number of other tribal groups regularly massage their infant daughters genitals' so that they will grow to their full potential and dangle enticingly by the time they are teenagers—a mark of beauty to a potential husband that speaks eloquently of sexual compatibility. And, in cultures where permanent body modifications have not been fashionable, women have donned every imaginable type of temporary allurement for sexual display. In the Western world they have even invented a complex ritual of exaggerated modesty so that they can exploit more successfully the frisson of desire engendered by a display of previously concealed erogenous zones: with many new styles of display being specially invented to exploit this "immodest" invention.

It seems, too, that in recent years we in the West have developed a curious attachment for intimate forms of apparel, such as corsets, stockings and suspenders, underpants, bras and slips, and for high-heeled shoes, see-through blouses, form-fitting jeans, and tightly clinging dresses with which to increase the attractiveness of women and to act as a kind of aphrodisiac for males who appear to many to have lost some of their potency, possibly due to our changing ways of life. We also surround ourselves with the mating calls of pop singers. Films and television series rehash lovers' problems and lovers' delights. Romantic novels and opera, jazz, country-and-western music, and rock-n-roll songs labor the ecstasy of passionate love. Paintings depict our ancestors' passion for visually enhanced modes of beauty, and today's photographers glorify many naked forms and Nature's more intricate allurements. We laugh at sexy jokes. Play sexy games. Exchange sexy stories and watch sex on X-rated videos. And we flirt with each other in the office or in a restaurant, parade for each other on the streets, and court each other at bars and parties or in dance halls and disco clubs.

This, then, is our heritage. It seems to have become as indelible a part of our makeup as our genes, and it constitutes a major part of our perception of beauty. And, although in strictly biological terms, Nature's undoubted aim for such "beauty" is to aid human reproduction, it does not mean that nowadays we always use our own beauty solely to advertise our reproductive qualities. Indeed, for many people, their capitalization of their beauty has little to do with any desire for procreation.

Human beauty can, of course, be seen from a purely aesthetic and subjective standpoint, as discussed for instance, by William Hogarth, in *The Analysis of Beauty* (1753). For Hogarth, beauty was a matter of line and shape, with some lines and shapes being inherently more beautiful than others. Scottish philosopher David Hume, on the other hand, believed that beauty was perceived differently by different people—it was not really tangible or measurable, being "only in the observer's mind"; each person "perceived a different beauty" and therefore beauty only existed "in the eye of the beholder." Thus, in their own ways, both Hogarth and Hume confirm beauty's subjective nature, although not all theorists and philosophers come to the same benign conclusion. The nineteenth-century philosopher Arthur Schopenhauer, for instance, did not believe in the aesthetic beauty of the female sex, particularly those by whom he was surrounded: "It is only the man whose intellect is clouded by the sexual impulse that could give the name the 'fair sex' to such a strange misshapen race," he declared, adding, "The whole so-called 'beauty' of the female sex is bound up with this sexual impulse" and thought

"I Grow Hair"

To Prove It, I Send a Trial Package
Free By Mail.

Before and After Using This Magic Compound.

it would be accurate to describe women "as the unaes-thetic sex"—an obviously misogynist attitude.

Darwin, following the ideas of Hogarth and Hume (but not Schopenhauer,) expressed a similar rationale about the subjective nature of human beauty, concluding that there was no "universal standard of beauty" within the human species, since it was essentially a matter of different races perceiving beauty in different ways. He theorized that, if perchance such a standard were invented, "we would for a time be charmed: but we should soon wish for variety; and as soon as we had obtained variety, we would wish to see certain characteristics a little exaggerated beyond the then existing standards." It should be understood, however, as Darwin and others have also explained, that "beauty," whether in humans or in any other species, is much more subtle than mere sex-appeal *per se*—it is, in fact, the visual manifestation of a number of important biological messages, not the least important being the tens if not hundreds of thousands of years of evolutionary difference between the races, which in one way or another enabled each of them to survive and thrive in their own particular environment. These differences, I believe, should be honored for their uniquely human qualities, as it is this range of differences that clearly sets us apart from our close cousins among the other primates. But, like our cousins and the other animals with whom we share this planet, all of our different forms of "beauty" speak eloquently of health and vigor and fertility and of the promise of the survival of any genes invested. Beauty is pregnant with power.

In order to capitalize on this powerful biological gift, cultures have gone to extraordinary lengths of embellishment and adornment. There is seemingly no end to this human inventiveness, designed to trigger our adulation and infatuation. But the information projected, like all other cultural output, is not causeless, mindless, or disembodied. As Barkow, Cosmides, and Tooby observed in *The Adapted Mind* (1992), cultural manifestations are "generated in rich and intricate ways by information-processing mechanisms situated in human minds. These mechanisms are, in

turn, the elaborately sculptured products of the evolution process." Although beauty and all of its human trimmings may well only be admired "in the eye of the beholder" or "the heat of the loins," the reason that particular physical features are seen as beautiful has sound and informed biological reasons, reasons that—although they may have become embroiled in our varying cultural conventions to aid the survival of particular groups— are not in the wider human sense arbitrary or inconsequential. They are in fact powerful weapons used to ensure the propagation of the species and, possibly, the varying cultures that make up our essential diversity. This diversity—both biological and cultural—is essential to our survival as a species.

It has also been postulated that aspects of neoteny play a considerable part in our perception of beauty, particularly in the female where young features are often regarded as more beautiful than those of a more mature woman. It is also suggested that in strictly biological terms beauty may well reside in averageness—a notion proposed by Donald Symons in *The Evolution of Human Sexuality* (1979). He says averageness is the best way for a breeding pair to judge both health and fertility, but in our mainly urban existence, surrounded by a barrage of advertisements and information, averageness seems to have lost its mass appeal. In fact, social anthropologists, such as Robert Brain, writing in *The Decorated Body* (1973), have asserted that our current Western modes of beauty are far from being based on averageness. They are, in fact, not even products of natural evolution but of astute marketing and industrialization. He adds that we in the industrialized world now live in what can best be described as a "beauty culture"— a culture that in many Western countries has virtually replaced traditional religion. This beauty culture has its own ideology, rites, temples, sanctuaries, and high priests, uniting men and women in a way that no other cultural invention has ever been

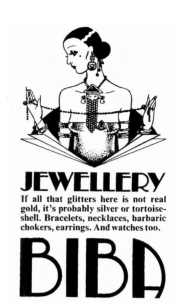

JEWELLERY

If all that glitters here is not real gold, it's probably silver or tortoise-shell. Bracelets, necklaces, barbaric chokers, earrings. And watches too.

BIBA

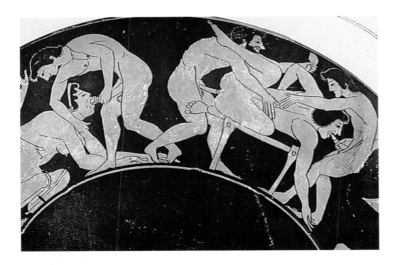

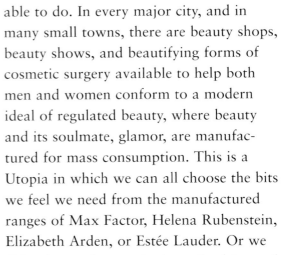

able to do. In every major city, and in many small towns, there are beauty shops, beauty shows, and beautifying forms of cosmetic surgery available to help both men and women conform to a modern ideal of regulated beauty, where beauty and its soulmate, glamor, are manufactured for mass consumption. This is a Utopia in which we can all choose the bits we feel we need from the manufactured ranges of Max Factor, Helena Rubenstein, Elizabeth Arden, or Estée Lauder. Or we can be completely "made over" by the modern equivalent of a fairy godmother, who, with a touch of her magic wand—or lip gloss—can turn an ugly duckling into a swan, or a homely maid into an enviable icon. It is a culture in which individuals who have little natural beauty are advised to use the vast range of beauty products available, plus a new array of clothing, adornments, and other aids to the greatest possible advantage, to camouflage their physical faults, and to make the best of their "good" features. The end result will be a perception of beauty. Failing that, a traditional display of wealth, social position, and even power and authority is essential: If you can't be beautiful, be well-dressed or drive an expensive car. These appurtenances still inspire widespread admiration and thus also tend to have an aphrodisiac effect. As in many other cultures, this can be construed as an alternative mode of beauty, albeit a rather specialized one.

These observations are, of course, at odds with the ancient Greek belief in the beauty of the perfect human form, an aesthetic masterpiece based on a passion for mathematics. In every branch of Hellenic thought we encounter a belief in the perfection of measurable proportions, which ultimately amounts to a mysticism far removed from commerce. This "faith" found expression in idealized sculptures of both men and women, and over the centuries these sculptures have greatly influenced our own aesthetic judgment. Significantly, though, we have neglected to promote the male form as one of great beauty; the ancient Greeks revered it even more so than they did the female form.

The Ancient Greeks also attached great importance to nakedness and normal bodily functions, celebrating acts that we often find pornograph-

ic. They believed that this conquest of inhibitions distinguished them from the Barbarians and was a liberating
force, the sign of a truly mature civilization. Their confidence and pride in their nakedness—at its zenith during
their great Athenian festivals and the original Olympic
Games—can only be fully understood in terms of their
philosophy, fundamental to which is a sense of human
wholeness and wholesomeness. They believed that nothing that pertained to the whole person could be isolated
or ignored, and when in their sculptures they set about
redesigning the human form, it was not with the idea of
removing those areas of the anatomy that seem to embar-
rass so many people today. As Aristotle put it, "These
artists give us knowledge of Nature's unrealised ends,
completing what Nature could not bring to a finish."
They refined those areas of the body that they thought
would gradually have been refined by Nature.

Our ancestors, however, while embracing the ancient
Greek aesthetic ideal, failed to comprehend or accept
many aspects of the Greek cultural beliefs, including the beliefs in nakedness and wholesomeness, the enjoyment of sexual activities in all their
forms, and the depiction and glorification of these activities. Instead, the
Judeo-Christian cult of the "sins of the flesh" became prevalent throughout Europe, and everywhere nakedness and sexuality in almost every
form were suppressed. And where nakedness was portrayed in images,
the offending genitals were either removed or covered. This dichotomy
between our aesthetic heritage and our religious and moral beliefs is at
the very root of the love-hate relationship we currently have with our
bodies; it is also a contributing factor to our continually changing concepts of how we should present ourselves to the world.

Since the fall of the ancient Hellenic culture, however, and the imposition of the Judeo-Christian belief that the flesh was evil and was to be
hidden from all prying eyes, together with the effects of an inclement climate, resulted in the adoption of an all enveloping mode of dress. It was-
n't long, however, before they began to experiment with a wide range of
body adornments, that together with accessories and an assorted array of
embellishments were soon enlivening both the male and female form in
an unending array of different styles, creating a unique mode of body
packaging. Even when artists produced naked images that expressed our

ancestors' continuing interest and admiration for the naked body, what they depicted were rarely completely unadorned. Often the models were embellished in various ways and more importantly they also appear to be wearing the ghosts of contemporary garments which not only shaped their waistlines, lifted their breasts, padded their shoulders, and made their feet and legs appear more elegant and appealing according to the fashion of the day.

These idealized depictions also recorded in great detail our ancestors love of jewelry, hairstyles, decorative lace edging, intricate embroidery, a wide range of accessories such as shoes, belts, stockings, gloves, shawls, ties and cravats, wigs, hats, veils, parasols, fans, muffs, the use of cosmetics, and numerous other items of adornment and embellishment. This occurred despite the fact that our ancestors' Judeo-Christian belief condemned avarice and the open flaunting of wealth, or so we are told by theologians. Nevertheless, these depictions, together with the written evidence of the period, clearly show how, over the intervening years, they gradually created an outer mode of packaging—or second skin—to which we have become accustomed and to which we now apportion much of our notion of beauty. In fact, for many people, their second skin is regarded as an extension of their individual bodies—and a comment made about the attractiveness or otherwise of their garments and embellishments is interpreted as applicable to them personally as if these articles really were physically an integral part of the body they were adorning. Even when this is not the case, clothing and adornments have nevertheless become an essential part of our psyche, as indeed are the wide variety of modes of adornment employed by other cultural groups elsewhere in the world. The only difference being that in many ethnic groups, beauty is not seen as an individual attribute so much as a cultural endowment and is therefore part of the cultural rather than the personal ego. As Elizabeth Nyabongo, a leading fashion model in the early 1960s put it, "Beauty is not one's own, but a reflection of one's culture."

Our adorned and decorated bodies are, in fact, a vivid reflection of our varying ways of life, openly displaying our attitudes, lifestyles, religious and political beliefs, creativity, wealth, social position, and the technology that surrounds us. Our clothing styles and modes of adornment have become one of our most enduring gestures of social evaluation, personal identification, cultural enunciation, and artistic expression. In many cases, this is the only visual medium used by ordinary people to make an aesthetic statement. It is also the medium through which each new generation seeks to establish its identity, its members seeking out those styles that clearly differentiate them from all previous generations and from the millions of other people with whom they share their world.

These forms of adornment are also the measure by which we judge other people. Many of us find it difficult to comprehend or accept the aesthetic merit or logic behind any form of apparel or adornment other than that which we currently admire within our own society. This is particularly true of the myriad forms of beauty admired by cultural groups in nonindustrialized countries, and we must realize that our own ideas are often generated by the xenophobia that insulates us from others. This xenophobia is based on our attitudes toward the unfamiliar and what we perceive as the painful and often inhumane methods employed to achieve what others consider a beautifully decorated and socially desirable body. We forget that many of our own methods of beautification rival in gruesomeness those used at the most primitive of puberty rites. The American painter Wes Christiansen expressed the problem in his essay entitled *Ancient Maya Body Modifications*, which was published in *Modern Primitives: An Investigation of Contemporary Adornment & Ritual* (1989): "We must be careful to remove the bone in our own noses before criticising another's duckbill lips."

In fact, the evidence shows that although our progenitors and others went to excruciating lengths in order to change and beautify their bodies, they appear to have done so willingly. The evidence also shows that such activities were certainly among the earliest human forms of aesthetic expression and, with dancing, chanting, simple forms of music, cave paintings, and early ceremonial rituals, formed the foundation upon which the arts of all civilizations have been built. Succeeding civilizations

evolved their own unique ways of decorating and adorning, and thus celebrating the human body. Whether painted, tattooed, scarred, or in some other way embellished, our ancestors' bodies had the power to attract, enchant, captivate, seduce, and delight. Unadorned nakedness was never so appealing.

Thus, each morning as we prepare ourselves to meet the world, we are performing a universal and time-honored ritual—we symbolically as well as actually transform our bodies, obscuring our natural, naked state behind some form of embellishment. Depending on our cultural heritage, or personal whim, this may mean putting on a printed silk dress with a belted waist, a business suit with all the formal trimmings, a feathered headdress, a necklace of sharks' teeth, an ivory labret and earrings, or simply daubing a few marks of paint on the face and body. So important has this human preoccupation become that not to be adorned in the mode of one's peers marks one out as inferior—many cultural groups go so far as to believe that such a person is no better than a mere animal, and not worthy of consideration.

This is why, in this age of central heating and air conditioning, when we could all so easily go naked, we continue to adorn ourselves as we do, and why so many anthropologists, psychologists, sociologists, and art historians now believe that our varying styles of body packaging have become an essential part of the human psyche. These styles not only set us apart from the animal world and from each other, they also represent humanity's unique creativity, which is at last being accepted as worthy of further aesthetic study. It behooves us to see that this study takes place before many of the more unusual modes of adornment disappear, to join those others that have already so dramatically reduced our vocabulary of the possible.

It is society's loss that many traditional ways of beautification and adornment, which for centuries have been used by cultural groups in the

more remote areas of the world, are now rapidly disappearing as a result of industrialization and inhibiting new laws, such as those enacted in Nigeria that forbid traditional forms of tribal marking on the face and body, or the wearing of the traditional *caché-sex* pubic jewelry by young nubile females. In Indonesia many tribes, such as the Iban and Jalé, are forbidden to mark themselves with their traditional motifs. The groups affected, who lose their forms of visual identification, become lost forever.

This trend is increasingly prevalent in parts of South America, Asia, India, Polynesia, Irian Jaya, as well as in Africa.

While researching material for this book, I encountered many cultural groups who nowadays adorn themselves in the style of their forebears only for tourists and anthropologists. The ideals of the industrialized world are rapidly spreading through these remote areas—especially via satellite television, videocassette recorders, and tourism—affecting the way of life and the sensibility of all, regardless of the color of their skin, their religious beliefs, or their cultural heritage. Thus the so-called global village is coming into being.

I have also observed how many businessmen from small communities in such countries as Zimbabwe and Sri Lanka now shave and prepare their hair in the Western style, and wear a traditionally cut business suit on even the most informal of occasions, thus signifying their membership in the world-wide community of commerce and advertising their newly acquired wealth. And, in reverse, many women of the Western world wear garments, jewelry, and cosmetic products that originated in, say, Turkey or Mexico, thus signifying their spiritual membership in a different community, one in which the exotic and the natural differences between people are still admired.

Many younger Western men have also begun experimenting with non-European modes of attire and beauty products, although such products are generally sold as aids to cleanliness and hygiene— real men, we are still told, are not interested in beautifying themselves. Nevertheless, perfumes, cleansing creams, and other aids for men are selling well, and many men from all walks of life are now reclaiming the right to wear more decorative and alluring styles of attire than have been the norm in the West for the past two hundred years or so. Additionally, new developments in synthetic hormones and cosmetic surgery have enabled many of these men to totally remodel their physical selves. The results often blur the distinction between races and between men and women, thus creating new standards of beauty.

In recent years, the media have featured many ethnic modes of

beauty—through television travel documentaries, for example. This has helped to change our concepts of what is or is not beautiful about the human form; it has also taught us much about various techniques used for bodily embellishment. Events such as the Miss World and Miss Universe competitions, in which the physical attributes of individuals from around the world are compared and judged, have also been widely publicized. Until recently, the winner was invariably of Caucasian descent, but this white monopoly seems to be waning and winners of these and similar events are increasingly of African, Asian, Indian, and Oceanic origin.

This development has greatly influenced the way many women in the Western world now wish to appear. Traditionally, the Western mode of dress has concentrated the observer's eye on those areas of the female anatomy in which Western women were believed to excel—face, hair, shoulders, hands, upper areas of the breasts, waist, and ankles. Other areas of the body have generally been kept covered and, prior to this century, were only displayed at specific times, when it was deemed "fashionable" to do so. However, the growing popularity and accessibility of air travel, coupled with the media's interest in change and the new, have allowed other parts of the female anatomy to emerge gradually for display, particularly the legs, the buttocks, and the full round of the breasts. This has resulted in young women becoming more adventurous in their modes of beauty and body presentation, and new, sexier styles and more experimental modes of presentation are gaining wider acceptance.

The twentieth century has also seen a dramatic change in attitudes toward the use of facial makeup, perfume, and decoratively trimmed lingerie. Today, of course, we are accustomed to such habits, and it may seem strange that decorative lingerie, lip gloss, or Chanel No. 5 could be thought of as immoral. But the use of beauty aids and pretty underclothing was relatively new during the first two decades of the twentieth century, and a great number of moralists regarded such items as fit only for courtesans, divorcées, and women of questionable virtue, therefore creating connotations of sin and licentiousness. It is widely known that the lips of a female redden during sexual arousal, becoming engorged with blood and mimicking the changes taking place in the genitals. During our evolution, it appears that this display has gradually focused on the front of the body: not only do the lips redden, and the facial cheeks and ears blush,

but the soft skin around the eyes also changes color. This is why the wearing of lip gloss, blusher, and eye makeup is now so prevalent and appealing; it undoubtedly affects the wearer's own perception of her beauty as well as that of the observer. Yet less than eighty years ago the use of such beautifiers was seen as a sin and condemned by religious and social authorities.

It may also surprise some readers to learn that the wearing of any form of decorative underclothing, especially "bifurcated" undergarments, such as today's underpants or pantyhose, under the traditional plain linen petticoat, was a hotly debated issue during the nineteenth century, clerics and moralists condemning such garments as being "against the laws of God," "man traps," "lust provoking," and "the invention of the Devil in his quest to seduce men into sins of the flesh" because of their association with "dancers," "actresses," and the *demi-mondaines*, who had been among the first to wear these items of forbidden apparel. Interestingly, though, such garments were not criticized if they were loose fitting and left unseamed at the crotch, held together only by a tape at the waist. The practice of leaving the legs as two separate sections was also the original method of design for men's trousers. Until the twelfth century, trousers were a form of thick loose hose, sometimes with the two legs in different colors, and they were worn under a long cloak-like garment so the open crotch seam was of little importance.

If we look back at our history, however, we find that our concepts of appropriate attire, for both men and women in search of beauty and admiration, are not at all like those of our ancestors. In England, during the reign of Edward I, for instance, men who could afford to purchase the latest expensive imported European style—a shorter padded cloak called a doublet—were permitted to display their naked genitals in the manner of their European cousins. If their genitals were not of sufficient size or if they were the wrong shape to make a distinguished display, these men could wear a *braquette*, which was a glove-like device made originally of flesh-colored leather and tailored to fit the well-padded penis and

scrotum. Some fifty years later, in 1348, when a number of British merchants adopted this style of dress, a law was passed that restricted the right to wear this fashion to the aristocracy; lesser mortals, regardless of their wealth and natural physical endowments had to be content with padding their front crotch area so as to simulate a continual erection, which at that time was perceived as a splendidly alluring male characteristic. The law, however, was impossible to enforce and the contemporary English commentator Chaucer remarked in *The Parson's Tale* that many male garments "were horribly scanty—too short to cover their shameful members." This fashion eventually gave rise to the codpiece, a brightly colored, bejeweled, padded protuberance much favored by men of fashion during the reign of Henry VIII.

At other times, in their quest to be found attractive and desirable, our wealthy male forebears wore layered doublets to increase their bulk and high-heeled shoes and wigs to increase their height; they also wore colorfully embroidered waistcoats, lace collars and cuffs, satin knickerbockers, fine silk stockings with frilled garters, very ornate lace and embroidered gloves, tightly laced steel and whalebone corsets, crotch, thigh, and calf padding, facial makeup and patches, vast quantities of

jewelry, specially made phallic-shaped shoes called poulaine, and many other adornments to display their riches, sexual prowess, and prestige. Our wealthy female forebears used a variety of adornments, which also do not conform with our current notions of acceptability, often wearing very sexually oriented styles that drew attention to their erogenous zones. For example, between the fourteenth and eighteenth centuries, it was periodically fashionable for young women in the royal courts and wealthy homes to display their entire breasts and rouged nipples, a fashion referred to as *vespoitrinement à la Venice*. The clergy condemned such display as "an intolerable crime," "a pernicious scandal," and "the zenith of human rebellion against the laws of God."

Of course, many such women felt themselves above the edicts of the clergy—after all, had not God decreed that they were the elite of society, able to conduct themselves according to their wishes? And their wishes includ-

ed the art of being beautiful and the enjoyment of the flesh. Nor were they beholden to their marriage partners. As Thomas Wright pointed out in *Womankind in Western Europe* (1869), women of the upper echelons of society were often independent beings, owning their own lands and living lives of luxury and sensuality according to their own dictates. They had not been seized by their husbands and forced into servitude.

They were 'free spirits', who, although married, were frequently seeking either an affair of the heart or simply an affair of lust. Wright also noted that it was the women who invariably made the first advances to the man of her choice, and who determined the pace of the courtship and, of course, their perceived beauty was of major importance in attracting prestigious partners.

Many of these courtly women were remarkably promiscuous and used numerous aids to enhance their allure and their chances of a sexual conquest. One such "aid" was wearing various forms of breast padding; another was the practice of decorating the pubic hair with colored ribbons and semiprecious stones. Yet another was to wear a tightly laced leather corset without any other form of underclothing so as to emphasize the bustline and *derrière* and to display a trim waistline—a slim waist signified a nonpregnant state that acted as a challenge to one's suitor.

For most ordinary people, though, liaisons of this kind were rare, unless they happened to be young and attractive and the chance of being chosen to enhance court life arose. There are numerous accounts of insatiable sexual appetites at royal courts—the courts of Versailles, the Habsburgs, St. Petersburg, and Hampton Court were notorious, and new maids awaiting seduction and energetic, attractive young men were always welcome. At some courts it was the practice to employ an experienced *éprouveuse* to test the beauty and physical attributes of young recruits, and even to test their sexual aptitudes and abilities before they were groomed in courtly ways. This process of selection and elevation for certain members of the lower classes increased the allure of aristo-

cratic modes of beauty—masculine or feminine—among ordinary people. It was often from this class that exceptional and/or beautiful women came. Nell Gwynne is one famous example. Lord Nelson's mistress Lady Hamilton who had started life as an artist's model, is another. The nineteenth-century *demi-mondaine*, Cora Pearl, who amassed and spent many fortunes, is another. Lillie Langtry, mistress of the Prince of Wales (later King Edward VII), is another, as were the thirty or so young ladies who formed King Ludwig's for ever changing harem in the early nineteenth century, and whose portraits now hang in the *Nymphenburg* palace as symbols of his Bavarian virility. Another was Mademoiselle Lantêlme whose photogenic beauty attracted the attention of the American press baron Alfred Edwards. A little later another American press baron, William Randolph Hearst, befriended the Ziegfeld chorus girl Marion Davies, and he spent millions of dollars on her and millions more in an attempt to make her a Hollywood movie actress. In more recent years there have been numerous scandals involving young showgirls and leading politicians and royalty, and others involving billionaires. And then there have been Playboy centerfolds whose unblemished beauty has been their entry ticket into an enviable lifestyle, thus continuing the belief that one's face and, of course, other essential physical attributes, can be one's fortune.

These attitudes also helped to popularize the *Directoire* style after the French Revolution, when it became fashionable for men to display their physical charms, rather than their inherited wealth, in drop-fronted form-fitting trousers and shortened jackets, and younger women wore no more than a single layer of muslin, often draped directly onto the naked body in what was known as the Grecian style. Most historians now

regard this mode of feminine attire as one of
the most licentious to be found in the annals
of Western dress. Nevertheless, to some
extent it did allow the ordinary people to
compete with the more affluent, since the
minimalism of clothing styles leveled a playing field formerly dominated by the accou-
trements of wealth.

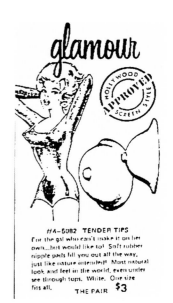

From a historic perspective, however,
our ancestors' needs and notions of beauty
were really no different from those that
exist in many places in the world today:
the differences that do exist are simply
matters of convention, symbolism, and tradition and, as we know, these conventions,
symbols, and traditions change as society itself changes. But to put all of
the foregoing into perspective, we need to understand a little about the
workings of our inner brain and why it functions in the way that it does,
and to this end I quote from Fisher's *The Sex Contract: The Evolution of
Human Behavior:* "In my view human beings have a common nature, a
set of shared "unconscious" tendencies or potentialities that are encoded
in our DNA and that evolved because they were of use to our forebears
millions of years ago. We are not aware of these predispositions, but they
still motivate our actions. I do not think, however, that we are puppets of
our genes, that our DNA "determines" our behavior. On the contrary,
culture sculpts innumerable and diverse traditions from our common
human genetic material; then individuals
respond to their environment and heredity
in idiosyncratic ways that philosophers
have long attributed to free will." Fisher
goes on to say that, nevertheless, what we
generally decide to do is indeed genetically
influenced. It seems to me, however, that
we are at a crossroad between our genetic
inheritance and the power of our brain,
each of which pulls us in opposite direc-
tions. It is true that we have an inner need
that is genetically determined and that has
not yet adjusted itself to our newly invented

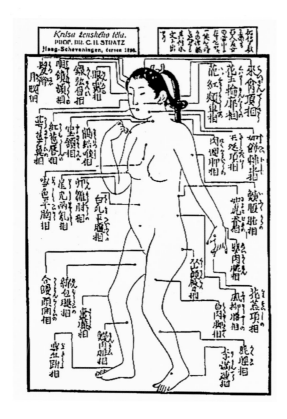

industrialized existence. And we have a brain that has by and large been taught to disregard these inner needs and instead to enjoy all the pleasures that our industrialized life has to offer—a change that has affected us both mentally and physically, and one that we will need to resolve. One way we can do this is to come to terms with ourselves as we are. We must understand our needs as individuals, and we must be honest about our faults as well as our good points. We must learn to appreciate our differences, both culturally and individually, and to make the most of our opportunities. And we must accept, as I have tried to explain throughout this book, that try as we might we cannot turn the clock back to some idyllic bygone age. We are alive now and we should enjoy our opportunities and differences now. And as for the subject at hand, this means we should accept that change and difference are at the very core of our appreciation and enjoyment, particularly in regard to human beauty. They are also an essential part of our humanness and an essential part of Nature's survival strategy. We should enjoy them while we can and we should make sure that our current trends towards a global village don't destroy our inherent differences and biodiversity. Being an optimist I am sure this won't happen, for we humans are very resilient and inventive, and I am positive we will find ways to survive and thrive, just as we have done in the past.

MARKS OF CIVILIZATION

During his voyage on the *HMS Beagle*, Charles Darwin noted in his diary that, although he had come across many unclad peoples, some living in the most inclement climates, these peoples were seldom unadorned. Numerous other explorers and travelers have commented upon this phenomenon, which, along with the mass of evidence collected from excavations of early human encampments, has led most anthropologists and social historians to conclude that after food and shelter our ancestors' preoccupation was the embellishment of their bodies.

In his detailed study of the origins of clothing and adornment, *From Nudity to Raiment* (1929), Hilaire Hiler asserted that protection from the elements was "to little or no extent the motive for attaching foreign substances to the body." He also commented that "the tribes of central Australia wear no clothing although they often suffer from the cold," adding that it was well known that they did apply various forms of decoration to their bodies. Hiler wrote, too, of African safari porters, who, when carrying heavy loads through the heat of the day, wore all the clothing they possessed, including coats and breeches borrowed from the "white man." In the cool of the evening, though, he said, the porters removed all their clothes, so as to relax in their nakedness. It appears that the clothing was probably worn during the day to

impress the local people with the symbols of power of a foreign culture, and as a clear mark of the wearer's "civilized" status. Hiler also mentions Darwin's observations of the people of Tierra del Fuego standing quite naked while sleet lashed their bodies; when Darwin gave one of them a length of cloth, instead of using it to protect his body or modesty, "he tore it up into small pieces and distributed them amongst his companions, who immediately employed them as ornaments."

Hiler and others, such as John Carl Flügel in *The Psychology of Dress* (also published in 1929), suggested that people ornament themselves for a variety of reasons; as a form of identification; to set themselves apart from the natural untamed world; as a way of exercising their imaginations and satisfying their egos; to display prowess as a hunter, or wealth as a trader; to mark themselves out as members of the family of an important chief or of having inherited wealth; as a symbol of cultural identify; as an extension of the bodily self; to protect themselves from the "evil eye" and other spirits; as having participated in a "rite of passage" and thus as a mark of being civilized; to distinguish between the sexes and to attract members of the opposite sex; as a way of identifying themselves with particular animals; and to establish some form of hierarchy. Protection and modesty are the result rather than the cause of such forms of ornamentation.

It has taken until recently, however, for theorists to begin to comprehend that differing kinds of beautification, body marking, dress, and adornments can bestow psychological as well as physical benefits on an individual or a community. And even now the actual workings of this phenomenon are still not fully understood. Medical evidence clearly shows that for whatever reason, and for female hospital patients in particular, a new hairstyle, or access to makeup has a markedly beneficial effect. These "marks of civilization" provide the wearer with a sense of personal control that is often stripped away in the hospital setting. Researchers have also observed how human males and females respond in different ways to both their own and others' modes of body presentation: certain styles can promote aggression; others attraction; and yet others subservience—a phenomena of which I was acutely aware during my years as an actor and a professional designer and about which Lawrence Langner speaks eloquently in *The Importance of Wearing Clothes.*

Langner, Hiler, and others also drew my attention to the importance of early carvings, such as the limestone figurine known as the *Venus of Willendorf*, which dates back nearly 30,000 years and is one of the earliest of human depictions. The actual figure, although only a little over 10 centimeters high, reveals important modes of adornment: a bracelet is indicated by a row of dots on the forearm, and the hair appears to have been decoratively curled or braided. Significantly, the facial features are absent, suggesting that they were of little importance. *The Venus of Lespugue*, which is of similar antiquity, features a form of fringed apron worn low across the hips—not as a means of hiding the buttocks, but seemingly as an adornment that emphasizes them. Among a number of fragments of figurines of around the same age, one, a fragment of carved mammoth ivory, has generated much discussion because of the manner in which the hair is presented: some authorities believe that it suggests a form of braiding; others believe that it represents a kind of wig. Either way, it is undoubtedly an attempt on the part of the artist—or the model—to improve on nature, and it and the two Venuses clearly show that the adornments and civilizing symbols that are applied to the human form have a much longer history than most people realize.

The cave paintings done by prehistoric humans also add to our knowledge of our ancestors' adornment and its connection to civilization: they reveal ceremonial clothing made from animal skins, and masks with animal horns. Some caves have been found to contain quantities of shells, toggles,

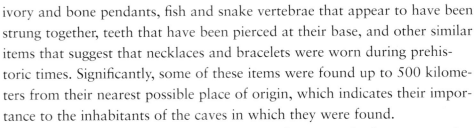

ivory and bone pendants, fish and snake vertebrae that appear to have been strung together, teeth that have been pierced at their base, and other similar items that suggest that necklaces and bracelets were worn during prehistoric times. Significantly, some of these items were found up to 500 kilometers from their nearest possible place of origin, which indicates their importance to the inhabitants of the caves in which they were found.

Other such adornments may have come from even further away and were obviously the fruit of long treks or trading. Bone and ivory needles with eyes, and fine scraping tools of great antiquity, have been found—these latter having been used to scrape the inside of animal skins to remove excess thickness and fat so that the skins would be more flexible. The needles would have been used for joining skins together, to create various items, including a form of ceremonial wrap or dress. Single skins also appear to have been worn, tied over the shoulders or around the waist, as a trophy in the case of a successful hunter or to denote status when worn by a chief or a member of his family. This is probably the origin of our addiction to furs as a status symbol and a symbol of authority.

The invention of the needle had a significant bearing on the development of Western-style beauty: it allowed certain types of body covering to be constructed, and this in turn, along with the use of fire, allowed cool areas of the northern hemisphere to be successfully inhabited. Such a visible and impressive innovation created a sense of superiority among those who were able to acquire these coverings, and in the process created a hierarchy that would eventually be able to rule by virtue of its habiliments—the remnants of which still exist in the robes of office of dignitaries, such as judges, dukes and monarchs, that continue to elicit obedience from many people.

But, even more important, such modes of covering eventually altered the path of sexual selection: the covered human body focused our male ancestors' attention on the face and upper torso of their female counterparts; garments also drew the female's attention away from a potential mate's physical characteristics and toward his qualities as lover, husband, father, or breadwinner. Langner pointed out that it was significant how rapidly Western culture developed after this invention of "clothing," and how different

that development has been from what took place in cultures that merely adorn rather than cover their bodies.

In numerous cultures around the world that didn't develop the art of clothing other characteristics have long been more important than the face, hair, and upper torso promoted by Western culture—some have body ideals that rival the sculptural forms of ancient Greece; others extol particular attributes, such as the fatty buttocks prized by the Hottentots and the San bushmen of the Kalahare desert: a characteristic that, it is believed, may well have helped such peoples survive in harsh desert conditions. Many also tend to mark their bodies in very specific ritualistic ways, and they reserve their notions of beauty only for those who have been so marked.

In his book *The Masks of God: Primitive Mythology* (1959), the American mythologist and philosopher Joseph Campbell wrote that our human urge to embellish ourselves and thus to improve the normal sign stimulus of our bodies is found in evidence from many millenniums ago. Cosmetic substances, for instance, for heightening the lines and features of the face and eyes have been discovered among the earliest remains of the Neolithic Age. He goes on to say that many of the things we do to our bodies are directly connected with the essential transition through various rites of passage into adulthood "to aid in the much needed reorganising of the common childhood imprinted inheritance in such a way as to conduct the energies of the psyche from the primary system of reference of infantile dependency into the sphere of the chief concern of the local group"—i.e., to make a dependent child into a responsible adult. Campbell goes on to observe "throughout the world the rituals of transformation from infancy to adulthood are attended with, and effected by, excruciating ordeals. Scourging, fasting, the knocking out of teeth, scarification, finger sacrifices, the removal of a testicle, cicatrization, circumcision, sub incision, biting and burning are the general rule" as indeed is clitoridectomy, branding, certain forms of tattooing, teeth filing, lip stretching and the like—the natural body being transformed by such ordeals into an ever-present recognizable sign of the new social status of the individual.

It was Campbell's belief that it is every society's responsibility to provide its young people with ceremonial rituals so that they can be transformed into respected adults. As he stated to the journalist Bill Moyers,

the problem with our modern society is that it has not provided adolescents with the much needed rituals by which they can become adult members of our tribe or community. "All children need to be twice born in order to learn and function rationally as adults in the present world, leaving childhood behind." Like Campbell, I believe that if they don't have some form of recognized and respected ritual, they will invent one, which may well include rioting, killing, taking drugs, promiscuous sex, or some form of body marking or mutilation, that may well conflict with the mores of their culture.

Until very recent times, in clothed societies such as our own, such transitions were marked by new styles of clothing and adornments to symbolize the new social status of the initiate—i.e., the wearing of one's first pair of long trousers or high-heeled shoes, the gift of a wristwatch, gold bracelet, and the like, or of a Confirmation dress, the wearing of lipstick, facial makeup, etc. But these traditions have by and large been forgotten in most industrialized cultures, as young children wear such adornments for no "earned" reason. Children also have their hair styled in adult ways, have a key to the front door and can stay out all night if they wish. There is, in fact, no longer a real transition from childhood into adulthood, so it is little wonder that many young adults refuse, or are unable to take on the adult role. Why should they? Where is the benefit for such a transition? Under the old system, the transition gave access to certain adult rights, now they get these rights as children. Biologically though, we still seem to need to mark ourselves in some way to claim the right of being "seen as an adult" as if this need has been encoded in our DNA. Géza Roheim speculates that this need is, in part, due to our natural neotenous retardation. In *Psychoanalysis & Anthropology* (1950) Roheim postulates that our natural prolonged period of infancy not only affects the way we look, but that the human need for civilization itself originated in our delayed maturity. It also appears that we need some form of ritual to visibly mark our progress from childhood to adulthood, and this may well be why so many young adults

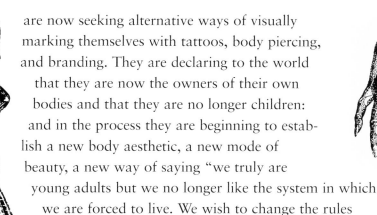

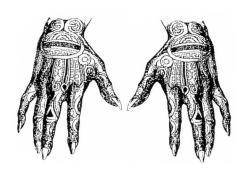

are now seeking alternative ways of visually marking themselves with tattoos, body piercing, and branding. They are declaring to the world that they are now the owners of their own bodies and that they are no longer children: and in the process they are beginning to establish a new body aesthetic, a new mode of beauty, a new way of saying "we truly are young adults but we no longer like the system in which we are forced to live. We wish to change the rules and change this oppressive industrialized way of life."

Our western ideal of beauty, therefore, must be seen in the context of its evolution as a product not only of nature but also of changes in modes of civilization and culture. Many of these are brought on by rebellion and rejection on the part of one section of our culture against the views, ways, and ideals of the majority, which may eventually lead to a fundamental transformation in our civilization.

Those who study genetic inheritance tell us that all animal species have a fixed idea what their desirable partner should look like, and some species have gone to extraordinary lengths to display their particular superiority and what we call "beauty." It is along these lines that each human culture adds their own particular "marks of civilization" so that its members know who is who when they come to choose a mate—its "marks" are intended to confine its members to their own cultural "species." This is why those not so marked are considered to be "little better than animals." In the television series *The Trials of Life* (1990), David Attenborough explains that when strangers in the wild meet, the first question they must resolve is whether they belong to the same species. This they do by displaying their "identity cards," nature having provided each species, even those that genetically vary only very slightly, with very distinct differences, which are particu-

larly noticable at times of courting. Birds throughout the world have developed myriad ways of displaying this difference, in their song, in their modes of behavior, in their plumage, and in other ways, too. The male bower birds for instance have developed a strategy for attracting a mate by the display of brightly colored objects, which they collect from the surrounding area, with each species of bower bird having its own particular aesthetic taste—one species preferring blue objects, another red or green. Each species also builds its own individual style of "show-case" in which to display its treasures, with the strongest, most fit, and most able male invariably having the best location and the finest selection of "treasures." It is with him most females mate, because, in bower bird terms, he is the fittest and therefore the most "beautiful."

The strategy of the peacock, like that of many other male birds, is to show his fitness as a potential partner by using his special display fan of tail feathers, which by the process of female choice during their evolution have become quite wondrous—an extreme case of sexual selection that also carries many important pieces of biological information. When a mature male peacock displays his fine "fan" (these feathers only develop during the breeding season and are shed immediately afterward) he is not only calling attention to his natural beauty but is also saying something very profound about his physical state and the superiority of his genes. As A. Cronin explained in *The Ant and the Peacock* (1991) such extremes are "a sign of the owner's innate resistance to disease and parasites, and an advertisement of its ability to gain sufficient resources to be able to 'afford' this flamboyant trait," adding that any disadvantages experienced by such extreme displays are "offset by the advantage of its attractiveness to potential mates," which invariably leads to more offspring and thus a greater chance for the survival of his genes.

In the world of the primate, being fit and healthy and relatively free of parasites is also of great importance when seeking a mate, as is perfect symmetry, regular features, and the display of the distinctive physical differences between the sexes, all of which can be considered an essential part of primate "beauty." For the male mandrill, a certain shape and coloration of the female hindquarters is his ideal. For the female mandrill an erect mandrill penis, which is proudly displayed and which is

permanently spotlighted in brilliant red and
enhanced by scrotal patches of vivid blue
and white, appears enchanting, as does the
shape and coloration of the male mandrill
face, which approximate his genital region
as a form of sexual echo. But there is an
important difference when it comes to
comparing the mating rituals of mandrills
and our notions of love and beauty and
humanness. For the mandrill, the physical
ideal appears to be totally instinctive while
in humans it is colored and shaped by
thought, tradition, and culture.

In fact, all primates other than humans pursue their same ideal,
which is at the height of its enchantment during ovulation and is sig-
naled by changes of color and scent. For humans, however, ideals of
beauty have become inextricably entwined with our minds and culture
and our differing marks and modes, and these must be learned. They
have become an important symbol of our cultural notion of our ideals
and differences rather than being perceived from a purely aesthetic
standpoint. We know that these ideals are learned because of the discrep-
ancies that exist between cultures, and even within our own society.

What is not generally realized, though, is that a very large industrialized community such as our own, is, in reality, an agglomeration of
many different cultural and social groups that inevitably overlap—some
complement the ways, notions, ideals, and traditions of those with which
they overlap; others conflict. Each group has its own ideal of human
beauty, and of the ways in which such beauty should be adorned so as to
make the most of its characteristics. This makes it very difficult for those
of us who live in the midst of such an agglomeration to properly appreciate and understand. As if it wasn't difficult enough to sort out all of
these different modes and marks, our lives are further complicated by the
invented notions of the beauty industry, which constantly replaces certain ideals with an updated commercial model. This model is often based
on a different cultural mix from its predecessor, so that consumers who
wish to copy this new style will have to buy new products. Such cre-
ations are a form of disposable artifact, invented for the sole purpose of
selling products and then being superseded by other disposable ideals—
thus generating a neverending demand from consumers for an ever

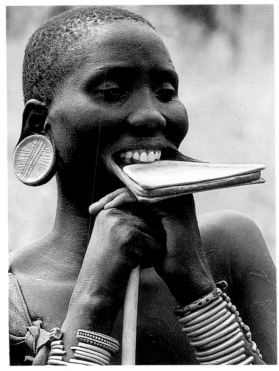

changing array of beauty and fashion merchandise.

This process of continual change also greatly influences that other important human relationship—the one we each have with ourselves and the reflection of ourselves as seen in a mirror. A growing number of commentators believe this relationship is the most important one we have. The image we see bedecked and adorned, or absolutely naked, helps us to affirm, reaffirm, define, and redefine who we actually are, our place in society, and our general notions and perceptions of human beauty. This is very important, particularly for those of us who live in a large urban community, where the look of our dress, Cartier watch, Hermès tie, Reebok sneakers, Givenchy belt, or Burberry coat has much greater purpose than their practical use, or where a slight fullness of the hips, a chipped fingernail, or badly trimmed hair can put us out of the running for a promotion or a date.

The social nature of our varying modes of attire and adornment and our cultural ideals of beauty are, however, best seen in small communities, such as exist in the South Seas, the highlands of New Guinea, the desert regions of northern and central Africa, or the jungles of Brazil, where homogeneous groups have withstood the onslaught of more powerful cultures and where they still use ancient methods to mark their bodies according to their mode of civilization—what many refer to as "rubbing our ancestors' culture into our bodies," and it is in such places where we can truly see the essence of the marks of civilization—the peoples of one village or valley are always quite distinct from the next.

I have visited many such communities, and what I find most striking is the extent not only of the differences of their applied marks of culture, but also the extent of the physical difference between people from one community and people from the next. In the late 1940s, Clellan Ford and Frank Beach visited a number of such communities in order to document some of these differences. From them, we learn that some tribal societies such as the Abelam, Chukchee, Gandee, and Wageo preferred a plump female form, whereas a slim female body was preferred by many neighboring tribes. And while the Azande and Ganda preferred long, pendulous breasts, upright, semi-spherical breasts were preferred by the Maasai and Manus. Additionally, these and other more recent surveys have documented the great variety of adornments and modes of decoration in each community, including, I might add, the increasingly common practice of wearing an assortment of genital jewelry among members of the tribal community of San Francisco and Los Angeles. And it is also of interest to note that a growing number of contemporary social commentators now regard many American women, including several of Hollywood's most renowned beauty icons, as being simply an amalgam of hair dyes, cosmetic surgery, liposculpture and silicon implants, the art of facial makeup, costumes, and good public relations—a manufactured product who proudly displays all of our commercial "marks of civilization," and thus is a true reflection of our consumer society.

One of these social commentators, Ted Polhemus, from the television series *Bodystyles* (1988) and author of several books on the subject, suggested that since beauty as we perceive it is not a reflection of any real biological body, but rather of the socially invented body, it is always, in strictly biological terms, a somewhat bizarre and freakish innovation. Within the social system itself, however, such modes are always perceived as being entirely "natural"—it is only other societies' beauty ideals that seem bizarre. But, theorizes Polhemus, this is simply a tribute to the extent to which a society is capable of imposing its own perception of the natural upon everything within its social construction of "reality." Of course, random genetic variations generally ensure that for any given style of socially invented beauty, some individuals will be born with characteristics that approximate this invention, and thus, by a fluke of timing, these individuals will be celebrated as the great beauties of their time.

If, however, the socially invented ideal body were somehow to be stripped of all of its symbolic powers and were to revert to its original biological function, concentrating our attention only on the genitalia and the act of copulation, humanity would be stripped of one of the most important factors that differentiates it from other primates. It would also lose a vital source of creative energy. As Polhemus points out, although the loss of the symbolic power of our styles of beauty might at first glance not seem like much of a loss, "closer examination reveals that such a happening would be catastrophic. We human beings are what we are because we live in social groups, each with its own culture, its own rules of behaviour, its own beliefs and values, its own vision of itself and of how life ought to be lived. Without all this we really would be just a bunch of wild animals."

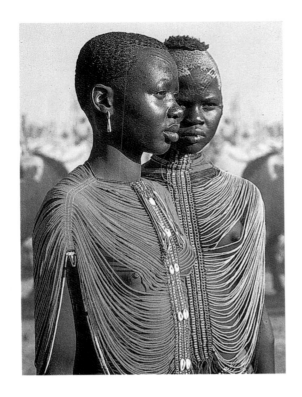

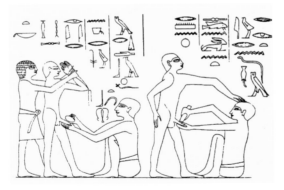

From the sixteenth to the nineteenth century, many third world cultures were decimated by western plundering and colonization. During this latter phase, the new ruling minorities of each annexed country prohibited the indigenous people from adorning and decorating themselves in their traditional manner or from living their traditional lifestyles. Of course, the phraseology used to explain such events was always religious and "civilizing," but in fact it was cultural genocide, with the energy of the conquered being diverted into benefiting the conquerors and, over time, many of these cultures vanished, their differences killed by the oppressors' xenophobic laws.

Something similar happens within societies during times of great social change; for instance, during the French Revolution, when the proletariat finally freed itself from inherited aristocratic tyranny, the furbelows of the court of Versailles, which had originally been symbols of privilege, but which had become symbols of oppression, were swept away and replaced by the austerity of the *Directoire* style, and anyone who persisted in displaying the mark of the previous regime was liable to summary execution. Less dramatic was the revolution of the early 1960s, when the so-called baby boomers, by virtue of their numbers and spending power, affected Western civilization: not only the way people looked and what they wore, but also their ideals and dreams, the food they ate, the music they listened to, their mode of entertainment, and many aspects of everyday life.

Such is the power of dress and adornment that it is one of the symbols by which we recognize each period in our history, even though we often fail to understand what we see. And, despite the transient nature of the varying styles, each style always seems admirably suited to its wearers. Could you imagine, for instance, Julius Caesar in anything other than a toga, or Henry VIII in any form of attire other than a bejewelled tunic, padded hose, and protuberant codpiece? Or who could imagine the Empress Eugenie wearing anything but an elaborate crinolined confection, or a flapper of the mid-1920s in anything other than a short, beaded dress? Conversely, can you imagine living your current lifestyle dressed in the costume of James I or Louis XVI?

Our understanding of our adorned inheritance is further complicated by the subjectivity of our perception and the way we currently clothe and adorn ourselves. We believe that our current ways are the result of a logical evolutionary process and are therefore perfectly suited to our lifestyle. We also view our current style as an extension of ourselves—our visible skin, so to speak—and a sign of our individuality within our particular social group. This very personal response makes it almost impossible for us to be objective about unusual styles and different modes of embellishment.

We belong to a clothed society and the act of covering our bodies in a certain way is so much a matter of habit that we scarcely think of this social convention having a reason or a beginning. Originally, though, all humans went naked. Since the days of the great Mesopotamian and Egyptian civilizations, scribes and philosophers have detailed the fact that all humans of whatever rank, race, or creed, whether wealthy or poor, educated or illiterate, beautiful or plain, were born naked and were complete in their natural, naked state. They reasoned that if their Creator had intended them to completely cover their gender-signalling areas, He/She would have arranged for them to have been born with at least a fur covering or a fig leaf. The fact that they, like us, had only a thin covering of skin, which, although fragile, served to keep their blood in and water out, indicated in evolutionary terms that this must have given these people, and our even earlier progenitors, some special advantage as a species that enabled them to survive and thrive.

Why then have so many human societies discarded this obvious evolutionary advantage? Why do they insist on dressing and adorning their bodies? And why is it that the very thought of being naked, except in our most intimate moments, embarrasses us, so that we call on our lawmakers and religious leaders to protect us? This embarrassment is obviously unnatural, in a biological sense, but perhaps the fact that we are born into a traditionally clothed society, rather than simply an adorned one prevents us from accepting our naked bodies as they really are.

Western civilization's phobia about nakedness is inculcated in each new generation, not only by keeping our

children clothed on almost all occasions but also by teaching them that only a clothed person is a complete person, the garments being an actual extension of their bodies—their visible skin. Everywhere in the industrialized world the emphasis on enveloping the body is overwhelming, and our children learn at every stage of their development that it is by means of their attire that they can identify both themselves and others. They learn, too, that these garments contribute in no small measure to the wearer's overall attractiveness and beauty and that they have distinct sexual connotations, being tantamount to secondary sexual characteristics, with women's clothing always being thought of as being more beautiful than that worn by men. Whenever I ask a group of young children to imagine the most beautiful woman in the world, they have invariably described her in terms of clothing and adornments—i.e., wearing beautiful jewelry and lovely flowing silken dresses, a new hairstyle, beautifully painted nails, and high-heeled shoes—answers almost identical to those given to Dr. Leo Spiegal in 1950 and published in *The Journal of Genetic Psychology*. In "The Child's Concept of Beauty: A Study in Concept Formation," he concluded that the children he asked appeared entranced by the shimmering images of fairy tales, the heroines of our collective unconscious, in their dresses of spun gold, cloaks of fur, and a fabulous array of precious jewels. It seems that "the emphasis on the envelope of the body is so overwhelming one has the impression that children consider beauty something one puts on and takes off with clothes and cosmetics, and not an inherently intrinsic part of the body."

Many design students at colleges and universities where I have lectured have been of the same opinion and they were horrified at the thought of seeing, let alone drawing, the naked human body. The idea of designing baubles with which to decorate their pubic hair was absolutely abhorrent to them—many had an unnatural phobia about nakedness and failed to appreciate its inherent beauty, a phobia, that, despite our claim of being free and open-minded, is still widely held in the industrialized world.

A phobia about nakedness was not however evident in the Mesopotamian, Egyptian, Minoan, and Greek civilizations, in all of which there was open acceptance of nakedness for all strata of society. The various modes of adornment that were used were not motivated by an attempt at concealment or by an attempt at sexual segregation or differentiation but rather, they were viewed as merely an extension or addition to other forms of embellishment. From the writings of the Sumerian, Assyrian, Babylonian, Hittite, and Egyptian scribes, and from carved and painted images, we can see that their styles of beauty and adornment were quite different from our own, or those of any other social group today, although the rationale was often similar—to display wealth and social position, to gain prestige within a social group, and to attract members of the opposite sex—to be considered what we call "beautiful."

The ordinary people of these early civilizations wore very little body covering. The very wealthy, about whom much has been written, wore a simple oblong-shaped wrap-skirt made from animal skins, a mixture of skins and pelts, or coarsely woven fabric made from a mixture of animal and vegetable fibers called a *kuanakes,* a shorter version made from a kind of semi-coarse linen fabric called a *schenti,* a shoulder wrap of much finer linen called a *haïk,* a decorative and semitransparent one called a *kalasiris,* or one of a number of similar wrap-style garments made of animal skins, a form of bark fabric or linen, cotton, and, a little later, silk, embellished with patterns of color and gold thread, according to where the wearer lived and his or her ability to pay. Such wraps were worn by either sex but were relatively expensive, so they were worn only by the social elite. The vast majority of people, however, appear to have been able to afford little more than the simplest of loincloths, some wore even less. Basically, this appears to have remained the case until Minoan times, although over the years the wraps worn by the elite became more complex, more colorful, more decorative, and more costly, with certain colors and patterns gradually becoming reserved by law for people of inherited wealth or members of the ruling class.

Wigs were also worn, although they were not intended to imitate natural hair. They were decorative and often indicative of rank: members of the ruling class employed a number of different styles according to the occasion; some were decorated with colored braids, threads of gold, and precious stones. The wigs worn by men and women were very similar, although if a man had a beard or wore a false beard his wig was often made somewhat smaller than his wife's so that he would not be totally swamped by artifice.

The beards of the ancient Babylonians were much cherished as a sign of virility and prowess, and men lavished great care on them, decorating them with rows of elegant curls made stiff with perfumed gum. To the ancient Egyptians and Assyrians, the beard was also a sign of social rank—the prerogative of the ruling class—the actual rank being signified by the beard's length. Long beards that curled up at the ends were strictly reserved for the gods.

MADO SE MAQUILLE

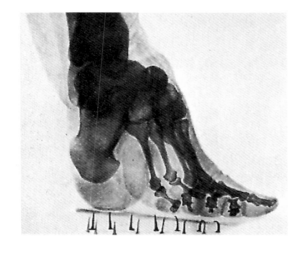

A great variety of perfumes and cosmetics were also employed; they were imported from all over the known world, including India and the Far East. Kenneth Clark believes it was during this period, some time toward the beginning of the second millennium B.C., that human beauty as a work of art (as we currently perceive it) was finally conceived— "with the sculptors inventing a style of beauty that was not to be equalled until the mid-Grecian era." He goes on to say that this invention showed "how completely the love of beauty filled the minds of Egyptian artists and, presumably, their patrons." The images to which Clark was referring, in his book entitled *Feminine Beauty* (1980), were associated with funeral rituals; they expressed the belief that the journey to another world must be made as pleasant as possible, that death was an occasion for much joy and celebration, and that the dead person should be surrounded with beautiful objects and sculptures. Clark continued, "This obsession with beauty reached its zenith in the entourage of Amenhotep IV— Akhnaton—where a sculptor of genius, who seems to have been called Imhotep, portrayed a group of human beings so exquisitely beautiful that we could scarcely have believed in them were it not that the same sculptor did heads of other members of the court which are revelations of spiteful ugliness."

One of the beautiful images from ancient Egypt to which Clark later referred and which embodied many of the then "marks of civilization" is that of Queen Nefertiti, who is considered by many a timeless beauty. Her beauty, however, was not entirely natural. For instance, as a very young child her head would have been bound so as to artificially elongate it—an ancient practice still evident today in some remote areas of the world. Her eyebrows appear to have been completely plucked and, as was customary at the time, her head would probably have been shaved so that she could wear an ornate wig, or under the wig her hair would have been elaborately arranged by using heated curling irons and special oils. She also made extensive use of cosmetics and perfume, using kohl to mark out an arched eyebrow line and to reshape and elongate her eyes. Kohl would also have been used on her eyelashes, probably mixed with a little spittle or other body fluids to make a smooth paste. Ground malachite would have been used on the soft areas around her eyes; red fucus or shell purple would have added a blush to her cheeks; and carmine dye or a special extract of seaweed would have reddened her lips. Like the Greeks, she probably also used finely ground pumice stone mixed with fresh urine to soften the skin of her hands, arms, legs, and feet and to whiten her teeth. And on special occasions her hands and feet may have been decorated with complex henna patterning, as is still common in parts of northern Africa today.

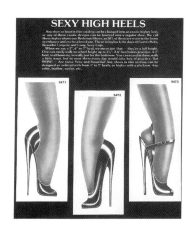

It is not recorded whether Nefertiti had her body hair plucked out in the oriental style, as did the Minoans and Greeks, or whether it was removed or modified in some other way. Her nipples, which were openly displayed, may well have been gilded. Her fingernails and toenails may also have been colored—they were certainly well shaped and immaculately manicured, as was the custom of the time. Her front teeth had not been removed, chipped or splayed, nor had her facial skin been scarred. This was a practice reserved for the neighboring Sudanese and therefore not appropriate for an Egyptian of royal blood. And it appears from the shape of her ears that she did not conform to the practice, prevalent among the elite of many later periods, of having them bound flat during childhood to make them less noticeable. Instead, Nefertiti's ears appear to

have been made more pronounced: this would have been achieved by wearing a wig during childhood, over her head binding; thus, her protruding ears could well have been regarded as a sign of royal birth and, by association, beauty. Her feet and ribcage may well have been bound during childhood to improve their shape and to reduce their size; this was a sign of not having to work, or even walk. (This practice of signaling aristocratic birth was much employed among many races, for both boys and girls, until well into the eighteenth century.) And there is little doubt that Nefertiti wore the most expensive and prestigious jewelry and adornments, which by their rarity would be perceived

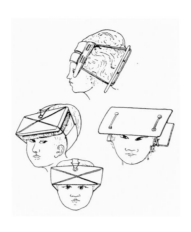

as even more beautiful than others of equivalent aesthetic merit.

Obviously, such modes of beauty did not come cheaply—in terms of time or money—or without some measure of pain and deprivation. The maxim that the more painful, time-consuming, and expensive such rituals are, the more exclusive, prestigious, and beautiful they are perceived obviously applies. This is further amplified by the funerary mask of the young Egyptian king Tutankhamen, which clearly shows he had ⅜" circular ear piercings (the beginnings of what would have been an arduous period of earlobe stretching, as was the custom in ancient Egypt). Like Nefertiti, he would also have had his head bound as a child to give it the correct aesthetic shape. He, like many other aristocrats and men of great privilege may well have undergone other aesthetic "improvements" like hand, foot, and waist binding. In fact, for all forms of human beauty, whether male or female, there appears to be a very close correlation between expense, pain, and the availability of time. This was observed by many early explorers, who recorded that almost all tribal communities that had not previously come under the influence of foreign habits devoted a great deal of time, resources, and personal dedication, including deprivation and pain, to achieving a socially and sexually accepted body—that then became their symbolic mode of beauty.

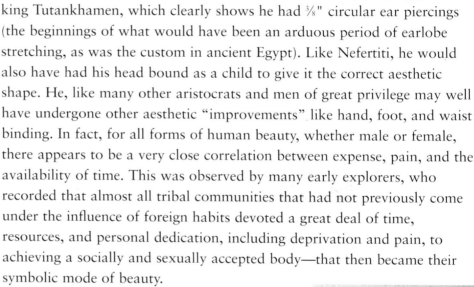

It appears that the choice of which parts of the body a particular society traditionally decorates, exaggerates, modifies, or mutilates is never random, nor are the methods used, based as they are upon symbolic beliefs about the body that such groups hold as essential to their culture. In all societies, even today, particular areas of the human body will be stressed or altered in one way or another. Each grouping of individuals mark out its members as different from its neighbors, and there is a consistent trend throughout the world toward emphasizing those physical attributes that are already noticably

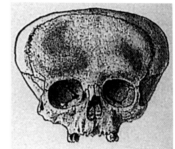

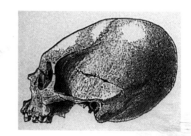

different, thus making them even more noticable and making them an essential part of their cultural markings. And, since members of such groups tend to admire those features that are most distinctive for their group and that have been enhanced, conversely, this emphasis would tend to make these features less appealing to their neighbors, who will

prefer, and thus emphasize, some other feature.

In general, the tradition in the Western world, for instance, was to admire a woman primarily for her facial beauty, her hair, her delicate hands, feet, and ankles, her shapely breasts and the narrowness of her waist, all of which are emphasized by means of clothing. Since the beginning of the twentieth century, the list has come to include long legs—these attributes having evolved quite naturally in the United States and other New World countries such as Australia, South Africa, and New Zealand. They then adopted very un-European styles of dress to display their legs to advantage, forcing European women to follow suit.

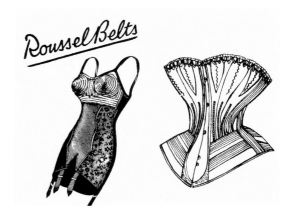

Other cultures have developed other distinct notions of both masculine and feminine beauty, placing the emphasis not so much on their clothing styles, but on their natural figure shape, their skin color, *derrière*, the shape of the head or the back of the neck, or tattoos and scar formations applied to various parts of the body. Some anthropologists believe, for instance, that the Chinese bound foot originated in those areas that bordered on China's warlike neighbors the Tartars. The feet of females in these areas were naturally smaller than those of the Tartar women and in order to make the young Chinese females, particularly those of wealthier families who did little or no manual work, less appealing to the Tartars, a system of foot-binding which was probably already in use amoungst the aristocracy as a means of displaying wealth and priviledge (as indeed was the practice in parts of Europe during the Middle Ages) was extended, spreading throughout all classes of the Chinese, and thus becoming one of their cultural

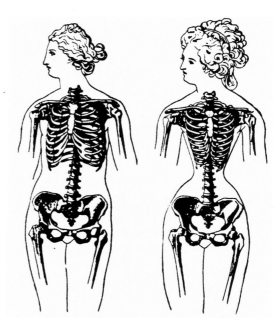

"marks." Thus, due to these cultural marks, these young Chinese women would be less likely to face kidnapping. An eighteenth-century explorer noted that the Tartars had great contempt for the small stature of Chinese women, "particularly those who had small feet." They preferred women who "gave their foot its natural length" and who were thus much more active and productive. In turn, the Tartar women tended to emphasize this different physical characteristic, adding to the length of their feet "by wearing long curved shoes which the Chinese, in derision, called 'Tartar junks' from the resemblance they bear to these vessels."

As often happens with such customs, over time the original reasons became lost. In much the same way, the tightly laced corset (which had to start early in an individual's development in order to curtail growth of the ribcage and waistline) became a symbol, or civilized mark of beauty and prestige in Europe during the sixteenth to nineteenth centuries—a style of body modification that not only narrowed the wearer's waist but consequently increased the appeal of both the hips and bustline. Obviously, a woman with small, bound feet cannot walk very far without assistance so

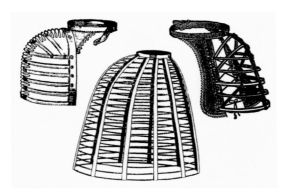

she is quite unsuited to manual work; the same applies for a woman with a tightly laced corset, whose ribcage may have been crushed and distorted, or who may have had to have ribs surgically removed to achieve the perfect shape. In both cases, this inability to perform manual tasks greatly increased the woman's visual appeal and social value, clearly establishing a claim to prestigious birth, or at least a wealthy family background. Traditionally it was also an indication that she had probably been well trained in the arts of fine living and sensory pleasure, and was thus a willing showcase for the display of wealth—both great attractants to those whose symbolic understanding of beauty was attuned to this form of ostentation.

In complete contrast, it is believed that the wearing of lip plugs by both male and female members of various cultural groups in Africa and South America, and among a number of Eskimo tribes, evolved as a device to ward off

evil spirits and as a means of establishing a cultural identity. The tribal groups who originally wore these lip plugs
are thought to have had slightly more protuberant lips than
their neighbors. Soon those with larger lips began to
emphasize this characteristic, eventually adopting the habit
of wearing small lip plugs, which would make them more
attractive to members of the opposite sex within their own
communities and less attractive to those in other communities. They were thus less likely to marry out of their group
or be kidnapped by their neighbors. With the growth of
the African slave trade in the sixteenth century, those who
wore lip plugs proved to be virtually unsalable and therefore not worth abducting—a good enough reason for more
communities to adopt the practice and for the size of the
lip plugs to be gradually increased, with those in the most
plundered areas becoming very conspicuous indeed. In
such areas it is now the size of the lip plug, not the facial
or physical features which, in the female in particular, are
perceived as being the true mark of beauty.

Changing male and female genitals in some way is also
closely linked with tribal and religious traditions, allegiance, beliefs, and notions of beauty, and hence, they too are marks of
civilization, no matter how barbaric such practices may appear to some.
In a special issue of *The Truth Seekers* (July 1989), which was devoted to
many such genital changes among numerous tribal and religious groups
around the world, no logical reason could be found for their origins
except that of conserving tribal energy by reducing sexual activity. They
detailed the practice of both male and female circumcision (more correctly called excision for females), removal of a testicle, infibulation,
sub-incision and the like, which were widespread and certainly
were practiced by many ancient cultures including the ancient
Egyptians—some Egyptian mummies dating back over
6,000 years show signs of having their genitals changed in
some way or other, either while alive or as part of burial
rites. My own research on the subject shows that such
practices have belonged to many cultures, so I must conclude that it is their detailed differences that are their particular marks of civilization, not just genital mutilation *per se,*
although the general intention of conserving tribal energy by

reducing the individual's pleasure during sexual activity could well be a common theme. The common belief that the male foreskin is often removed for hygenic reason doesn't seem to have any rational basis, and no evidence could be found of cultural groups pulling out children's fingernails in order to keep their hands clean, which , if hygiene was of importance would surely have been the first to go.

Genitals, both male and female, have also been tattooed by various tribal groups and, today, among communities like the "modern primitives" in Los Angeles and San Francisco, genital piercing and the attachment of various forms of jewelry—studs, bars, rings, chains, and the like—is commonplace. In southeast Asia such piercings were, until very recent times, an acknowledged tradition as I discovered on my first visit to an inland village in the center of Borneo (now Kalimantan, Indonesia). I found myself the butt of many jokes as the local males assured me that without any penis studs, rings, bars, or some other form of adornment, I would never be able to satisfy a woman and none of them would find me attractive. This, in fact, proved to be true. However, I was not willing to undergo such an important modification in order to avail myself of a temporary village "wife." Later in Los Angeles I was pierced and so adorned with several studs, rings, and bars, but only after having first studied the range of possibilities available.

While in India, I discovered the technique used by various mystics for lengthening their penis and scrotum by hanging weights upon them while meditating. The Karamojong of Uganda and several tribal groups in the Sudan also hang heavy stones from the ends of their penises in order to lengthen them and also endowing them with the appearance of a semi-erection. The women of the group find this attractive and alluring, thus such a modification should also be seen as a specialized mark of civiliza-

tion. In the Middle East I came across the practice of wearing a tight leather strap, called an Arab harness, which over time and by regular and prolonged engorgement that can last for many hours helps to thicken the male shaft as well as helping to develop the glans to its fullest potential. This thickening of the penile shaft is also a recent fashion innovation among body builders in the West; it is achieved artificially by injecting fatty tissue extracted from another area of the body into the base of the penis shaft to improve their silhouette when posing in competitions, but so far little thought has been given to the full development of the natural shaft or glans as a normal part of male development using well-proven natural practices—only if it creates work for specialist surgeons and makes advertising money for the mass media does it seem to be a legitimate subject for discussion on television, or in a magazine.

According to Professor Milton Diamond of the School of Anatomy and Reproductive Biology at the University of Hawaii, and author of *Sex Watching* (1988), the size of the male penis is unquestionably of aesthetic importance as it is such an obvious mark of humanness—it is, in fact (even in its general underdeveloped western form), far larger than it needs to be for the act of procreation. As those who study other species of primate are well aware, the penis size of most other primates in proportion to their body size and weight is less than half that of the human male. Human penis size could only have come about by female choice during our evolution—choice that in other species resulted in quite different physical manifestations such as the spectacular growth of display feathers or antlers and therefore could well be considered an essential part of masculine beauty, with the larger the male penis, the more masculine and beautiful he will be in most woman's eyes.

In one of his many ethnographic papers, Diamond details the efforts made by many traditional South Pacific cultures to improve on their genital allurements—the female genital area of traditional Hawaiians from a very young age were massaged with mother's milk and *kukui* (a local nut oil) and regularly pressed and molded into an attractive shape by an aunt or grandmother who was the holder of the aesthetic secrets of feminine beauty. The Marquesas islanders orally stretched the young female's inner labia and they, together with several other island cultures, also molded the children's buttocks. The children of the Society and Austral Islands have their genitals regularly massaged so they will grow big and strong and be able to function well during lovemaking, which, according to Bengt Danielsson in *Love in the South Seas* (1956), is an art for which much practice is needed. Young Hawaiian males had their foreskins lengthened and strengthened by ballooning the penis skin. Diamond explains that "the penis foreskin was blown into daily by an aunt or grandmother to balloon it and separate it from the glans which," he says, "guaranteed health and efficient coitus in later life." This procedure and that relating to the female was diligently carried out on a daily basis "to make the genitals more beautiful and to be a form of religious blessing" with which lov-

ing relatives were desirous to bestow on their offspring and which must be seen in the light of all other forms of physical adaptation as truly a mark of their civilization.

In the quest to mark themselves out as being civilized and not mere animals, other cultural groups change the color or shape of their teeth or drill and inlay them with foreign substances. Others pluck out their eyebrows or eyelids, or train their children's eyes to be slightly crossed. Some insert seed pearls or other small round objects into the skin of their foreheads or penis shafts, mark themselves with welts or branding irons, remove every trace of their body hair, including that from around the pubic region, or wear *cache-sexe* aprons or conceal their facial features with veils to stimulate sexual curiosity. Still others ensure that their female children have a prominent navel and well-formed protuberant nipples; they may soften the skin by exfoliation and massage, or roughen areas by the use of sharks teeth to give textural interest. Some cultures even indulge in ritual sex, sending out a call for others to join in when approaching orgasm in order to maximize the beneficial and beautifying effects of hormones and other body chemicals. Some remove all body fat by liposuction and exercise, wear nose ornaments made from precious metals, or artificially broaden their already broad noses by continual manual manipulation that deforms the bone structure and then decorate their broadened noses with quills or pigs tusks. And I think that it is also worthy of note that in the early nineteenth century, when the white woman arrived in Africa and elsewhere with her strange manner of dress and exalted position *vis-a-vis* the local men, the local women tried to copy her, to improve their own status and try to capture some of her perceived beauty. Aubrey Elliott, in his book *Tribal Dress, Beadwork and other Tribal Arts* (1986) on the Zulu and other Southern African tribes, observed that "during the nineteenth century many Xhosa women would have come into contact with the British pioneers who came to farm the frontier lands of the eastern Cape. The dress of these 1820 settlers clearly had its influence on tribal wear," especially in the bulky turbans and exotic hairstyles that, no doubt, were an imitation of the European hats of that gracious age. They also adapted other modes of dress and adornment, as did many other tribal peoples throughout this period of colonization—a practice that continues even today.

Yet other cultural groups, by tradition, stretch their already large ear-lobes so that they can be decorated and draped enticingly for others to admire. Others stretch and distort the neck with wide and heavy neck-bands or tightly bind their upper arms or thighs with braids made from jungle fibers. Some people in the West wear tight trousers and undergarments that can cause infertility and skin fungus. Others have their leg bones broken to be lengthened or shortened as desired. Some have their toes shortened, narrowed, or removed so that they can wear smaller shoes. Others have their fingers narrowed to give them an aristocratic appeal and some still wear tightly-laced corsets, which, as mentioned earlier, may require the surgical removal of the bottom two ribs to achieve the silhouette required. Some wear nipple rings and forms of constricting genital jewelry, which often requires multiple piercings. At one time there was a fashion for duelling scars among European aristocrats, and today sporting scars are much admired in some circles.

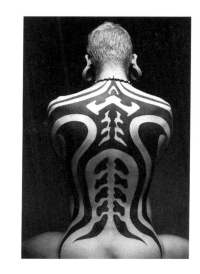

In some cultures various forms of scar patterning are made upon the face and body; a symbol of civilization and of allegiance to that particular cultural group and the scarred person's social standing within that group—i.e., when a girl reaches puberty or when a boy has passed through an arduous initiation ceremony and become a warrior. Tattooing is often used in the same way with both forms of marking being used as a mark of their culture, and anybody not being so marked is considered uncivilized and thus subhuman—"little better than an animal." Interestingly, scarification is used only among people with dark skins, which show this mode of adornment to advantage. Tattooing, on the other hand, is better seen on paler skin, among the Berbers, for instance, and several other tribal groups of the northern Sahara as well as throughout the South Pacific. The tattoos of such people helps to differentiate them from their darker skinned neighbors, emphasizing their paler skin—all of which is culturally taught to the younger members of each society who then in their turn carry on the traditions of their forebears. Such outward marks and symbols are important among traditional cultural groups as they signify an individual's social standing and how that individual is to be treated.

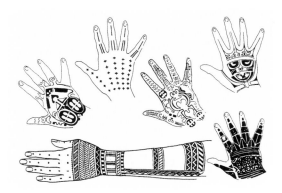

Tattooing is one of the ancient body arts, known to the Egyptians more than five thousand years ago. Queen

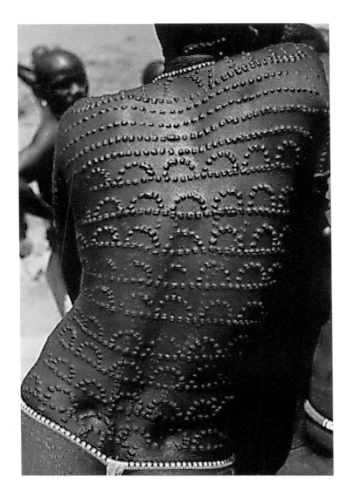

Nefertiti could well have had a small tattoo somewhere, as have many people in more recent times, among them George V, his brother the Duke of Clarence, Tsar Nicholas of Russia, and the famous American beauty and heiress Consuelo Vanderbilt, who became the Duchess of Marlborough, and Lady Randolph Churchill (nee Jennie Jerome, and mother of Sir Winston Churchill). Julius Caesar also commented upon the practice of tattooing among the Franks, Gauls, and Picts: he stated that many Britons "stain themselves with woad and bear on their bodies colored scars ingeniously formed in the likeness of various animals." With the arrival in Rome of captive fair-haired, blue-eyed, and tattooed concubines from Northern Europe and the British Isles, the art of tattooing and hair bleaching became quite fashionable, until it was condemned in the fourth century by the hierarchy of the Roman Catholic Church on the grounds that it had become "a symbol of base sexuality" and "disfigured that which was fashioned in God's image." As with many other ancient forms of personal adornment and marks of various civilizations, the art of tattooing was subsequently suppressed throughout the Holy Roman Empire; it was "rediscovered" by Renaissance traders in the fifteenth century, by the northern Europeans during their eighteenth century Pacific explorations, and on mainland Japan in the mid-nineteenth century by the American Matthew Perry.

The art of tattooing, although considered painful by Western standards, and therefore somewhat masochistic, is in fact very straightforward and I can vouch that it is not nearly as painful as it looks. These marks of civilization consist of making tiny punctures through the outer layer of skin and injecting dye. The punctures are usually made by a sharp instrument, such as a piece of splintered bone, a metal needle, or slivers of bamboo. Sometimes an impregnated thread is passed under the skin, or the skin is cut and dye is rubbed into the wound. Once the wound has healed, the resultant design is seen through the healed skin. The dye used is traditionally some form of carbon, such as soot, ground charcoal, or lamp black, which turns dark blue when placed under the skin. In Polynesia and other areas of the South Pacific the colorant is punched through the skin by means of a cluster of wood or bone splinters and a small mallet. In parts of Northern Africa textured tattoos, known as *kolo,* are traditionally used. These are made by cutting parallel lines with a sharp razor blade-like instrument into smallish areas of the skin and then aggravating and coloring the cuts so that they heal with a slightly raised, textured surface. In Japan a variety of colored substances and sharp metal needles are used for the traditional multicolored tattoos, called *irezumi,* which is the method generally used in the West.

Of the more traditional dark-blue forms of tattooing, probably those found in the Polynesian Island and among the Maoris of New Zealand are the most famous and most intricate. Some of the most ancient patterns took up to ten years to acquire, the body needing time to recuperate between tattooing sessions. Simple patterns were first applied to indicate sexual maturity; additional "social information" was added subsequently, such as when a young male became a warrior, was wounded, or made a kill, or, in the case of females, upon marriage, the birth of their first child, and so on. The great chiefs and their families often had their entire faces and bodies covered with designs of great intricacy and beauty. Upon contact with white explorers, Maori chiefs signing deeds of land sales frequently drew their face patterns on the documents of transfer as a form of signature, thus legitimizing such cultural marks as legal symbols.

Regardless of their actual social position, Maori women were always intricately tattooed, particularly on the lips and chin. An untattooed face was regarded as decidedly unattractive. Even in recent times, untattooed European women tourists have been described as most unappealing by Maoris because they lacked the symbolic facial beauty and mark of being civilized that only tattooing can bestow.

In Japan the love of *irezumi* reached its height during the Edo period (1615–1868) when wealthy merchants were not permitted to wear elaborately decorated kimonos, fine silks, brocades, ornate embroidery, or gold jewelry, these adornments being reserved by sumptuary laws for the nobility and the ruling classes. The merchants could, however, express their wealth, independence, and membership in the wealthy classes by wearing an expen-

sive and elaborate "secret" tattoo under a plain kimono; this they could display when bathing with friends—a national pastime—or when visiting the pleasure district.

The Japanese merchants were frequent visitors to the houses of courtesans, where for an hour or two they could wear the forbidden silk and brocade kimonos while indulging in the pleasures of the flesh. This is why the *ukiyo-e* prints and erotic drawings of the period rarely depict an unadorned naked body: the couples are always wearing elaborate kimonos, even in the throes of sexual excitement; the clothing merely added to the erotic appeal of such depictions and practices. It seems that, traditionally, the Japanese had scant regard for the naked and unadorned human body, regarding both sexes as unattractive, or so I was told while living in Kyoto during a research program on the art of *irezumi* and other forms of Japanese body arts. Sexual allure comes with the decorated human form. This is why *irezumi* is still popular: the colored tattoos render the naked skin aesthetically appealing. There is now an *irezumi* museum, housed in Tokyo's largest university where finely decorated human skins are displayed as works of art, and it has become established practice for a devoted collector of *irezumi* to literally buy the skin off a person's back by making a down payment of many thousands of dollars to the tattooed person while they are alive and completing the purchase after their death. It is said that finely tattooed Maori heads were purchased in much the same way in order to preserve and display the fine aesthetic quality of such work long after the original owner had left this world.

I have also seen a number of preserved examples of African tribal scarring patterns, as well as a wide variety of pattern types on living warriors and their wives. Many of these scar patterns are in fact a sort of bas-relief tattoo, in which the skin is pierced with a narrow hooked blade or thorn

so as to lift it up, whereupon the top edge of the raised section is cut with a small blade. The resulting cut is rubbed with a mixture of fruit juices and ground ash, or similar irritating mixture, so that the wound becomes inflamed and later heals as a hard scar in relief. Some are recut and inflamed several times, or a small pebble or pearl is inserted under the skin to enhance the raised effect. The resultant scars are referred to as "keloid"— intentional raised scars used in controlled ways—and are used to outline, draw attention to very specific features, or sometimes cover a complete area of the body.

There are what we call ridge cicatrization scars and random lumpy scars called *abaji,* and random textured skin decorations, which some tribes refer to as *kolo,* made with the cutting edges of bamboo slivers or razor blades. Then there is the deeply cut *moko* scars of the Maori face carvers, *hleeta* of the Gaánda peoples of northeastern Nigeria, *kulemba* skin inscriptions of the Tabwa of southeastern Zaire, the *mkali* cicatrix scars of the Tiv of Nigeria, and random lacerations and flanged skin cutting used by the Aboriginals of Australia, all of which, together with many other forms of body marking, are imbued with pertinent cultural, religious, and magical meaning. Most forms of tribal scars are made in traditional designs or patterned groups on specific parts of the body as an individual passes through various stages of life—what might be described as written evidence of a person's "rites of passage"—thus denoting the precise social status of each individual. These patterns are also perceived as symbols of tribal beauty for those able to decipher the messages conveyed, and give a unique sculptured quality to the body, which is widely admired. Cicatrix scar patterns are also widely used—they are a controlled long flat shiny scar formed by carefully cutting the surface of the skin with the design required, easing the wound apart slightly and then inflaming the open cut with ground ash mixed with a little fruit juice or other irritant so that when healed a flat shiny scar forms.

In addition to its symbolic meaning, scarring can also play an important role in preventive medicine not realized by many Western observers: the body builds up its antibodies during the gradual scarring process, so that the mature adult is more able to survive in the harsh conditions of bush life. Leni Riefenstahl remarked on this in her study of the southeast Nuba, *People of Kau* (1976): "The cuts give access to germs and bacteria, which causes the human organism to develop antibodies. This produces a certain immunity and has a beneficial effect on the healing of subsequent injuries to which natives are often exposed." Biologically speaking, this may well be an important contributing factor to the perceived beauty of this form of body adornment, and gives a sound reproductive reason for continuing the tradition of using such civilized marks.

On maturity, tribal adults often add to their traditional patterning of scars; the additions are thought to be purely decorative, to mark them out as individuals worthy of the attention of members of the opposite sex but they may well add to the subliminal message of being healthy. In the 1950s, when the American anthropologist Paul Bohannan asked a member of the Tiv tribe if such additional scarring was painful, the response was,

"Of course it is painful. What girl would look at a man if his scars had not cost him pain?" This could be a further part of the subliminal message of these cultural marks. Women also suffer pain during the final, more intricate stages of their scarring, but Leni Riefenstahl explains that, despite the pain, a young woman rarely cries out since this would involve loss of prestige: "The extent of her self-control can only be gauged from an occasional tremor on her face." She goes on to say that the rewards for such stoicism are high: "The new pattern that adorns her body renders a female highly attractive to the opposite sex and enrolls her among the most desirable women in her village."

People's appearance carries social as well as cultural information and messages. This is just as true of Western modes of dress as it is for those who practice tattooing and scarring; our own body presentations can be just as dramatic or unnatural looking as those of the ancient Maoris or other tattoo carvers and, in fact, they can be just as physically painful and time consuming. For instance, we insist that our children wear shoes that frequently distort the growth and shape of their feet. Women often force themselves into distorting high heels, which can also lead to damaged ankles, further disfiguring their toes, and hence then requiring costly cosmetic surgery. Most men in the industrialized world spend time each day removing every trace of their facial hair at the risk of minor cuts and abrasions. And both men and women follow often dangerous diets to change the shape of their bodies, eat sections of cut-up tapeworms or their eggs, drink their own urine, exercise to exhaustion, or undergo liposuction and cosmetic surgery to become beautiful according to our tribal ways, for we are tribal after all, even if we act as if we are God's chosen people.

In other cultures, decorative branding is also employed, as is the removal of finger joints and various forms of constriction, body manipulation, and body sculpting. The young women of the Alto Xingu in the Mato Grosso of Brazil, for instance, tightly bind their upper legs so that their thighs will swell enticingly. The young Trobriand Islanders wear tight bindings on their upper arms for a similar reason. And the New Zealand Maori developed an arduous and intricate method of body manipulation to achieve their ideal of the body beautiful, intricately molding it as a mark of civilization. In *The Coming of the Maori* (1949), Peter Buck describes how his body was manipulated during his childhood, a great deal of attention being paid to the growth of each part so that it would attain an accepted standard of beauty. "To achieve the perfect body various forms of massage were used," said Buck, such as "kneading the muscles with the fingers (*romiromi*), putting pressure into the spine with the feet (*takahi*) and stretching the legs by pulling (*toto*)." He adds, "I remember my mother looking at my legs approvingly and saying 'My hands made your legs what they are.'"

Other tribal groups seek to ensure that their female offspring will have a prominent navel as one of their marks of civilization. Others by a system of binding and massage ensure that their female children will have prominent nipples. Speaking of the children of the Society and Austral Islands, Bengt Danielsson in *Love in the South Seas* tells of the practice of bleaching and softening the skin of young marriageable people with extracts of leaf sap so that it is soft to the touch and will enhance their courtship and lovemaking—one of the more ephemeral marks of their civilization but, nevertheless, individuals not so marked were considered less desirable as partners and not as beautiful. "On these islands," he wrote, "love, or rather the love game, was an art which could and should be learnt" stating that "alongside beauty, sexual ability was the quality which these Polynesians valued the most highly and they celebrate its power whenever possible," their sensitized bodies adding to what was, in effect, a religious experience. Elsewhere I came across an anthropologist's observation that sensual feedback was one of the great delights of having the body scarred, especially when the scars are stroked by an ardent lover during lovemaking: the sensation, I am told, often compensating for the loss of the clitoris removed during traditional puberty rituals.

Some of the indigenous peoples of the Amazonian jungle use the teeth of the piranha to give areas of their skin a rough texture and also to sculpt out small marks, such as circles, which are then filled with color, an essential part of their traditional beauty. Other tribal peoples mark their bodies with a form of semi-tattoo or bleached tattoos to make themselves beautiful, for in their eyes, beauty, like sexuality, is one of the "great gifts of the Gods," which should be celebrated continuously. To be beautiful was to be divine and to be sexually active was even better, which I found out while living in Melanesia—where if one doesn't play checkers, bridge, or drink alcohol, what else is there to do? The spin-off rewards were truly miraculous—far beyond anything I had expected (and this could well be the origins of the religious notion of sexual activity). It is true that I had com-

pletely changed my lifestyle from that of central London—I was living on a small coral island in the Bismarck Archipelago with a young tribal "wife," away from all forms of industrial distraction. I was eating a plain, healthy diet of local food, without chocolate, dairy products, and the like, and I had freed my mind from all previous religious, educational, parental, and cultural forms of indoctrination, which I had found only enslaved my thoughts. By using a personal form of raw Tantra with my local "wife," I discovered over the period of only a few months the additional effects I had read about in the *Kama Sutra*, i.e., increased sexual activity really does increase one's normal energy supply and it helped my creativity. And it was this discovery that has been influencing my life ever since and that gives me the essential energy I need for my research, teaching, travel, and writing.

Many tribal people have known of this phenomenon for countless generations, and it is perceived as an essential part of both male and female beauty, of having a healthy mind and healthy body and of believing in an essential life force. But with the increasing influence of Western culture, the beneficial side effects of regular sexual activity are beginning to wane, along with many other tribal ways, including that of many of the wondrous styles of adornment and body packaging, which is a great pity as many of these methods appear to be very ancient, indeed possibly older than many of our own.

From reading the Bible we learn that although among the Israelites it was strictly forbidden to alter their appearance in any way, frequent reference is made to the use of black hair dye, kohl, perfumed oils, the wearing of ankle adornments and bracelets, and the use of razors for the removal of facial and body hair, and of women who walked with outstretched necks and wanton eyes. According to the eighteenth-century scholar James Stewart, during the time of Moses the Israelites had innumerable ways of wearing their hair and their beards, trimming and curling them in a style similar to that of the Assyrians and Babylonians. He also mentions gold and silver thread, pearls and other costly ornaments with which the women decorated themselves. Hair powders of different colors appear to have been used for special occasions, and Solomon's horse guards reportedly powdered their hair with gold dust so that it shimmered for the most important processions. From this it seems that there were just as many religious dissenters then as there are now.

Richard Corson (*Fashions in Hair*, 1965) refers to the early Franks, whom, he says, "are known to have shaved the chin and the back of the head while letting the moustache and the rest of the hair grow long." He also says that "it was esteemed a peculiar honour among the ancient Gauls and other northern tribes to have long hair as befitted their rugged way of life and was thus an important mark of their culture and civilized state, and, it was for this reason that Julius Caesar, upon subduing the Gauls, made them cut off their hair as a token of submission" thus denying their civilized state, so to speak, lowering their self-esteem, and showing that they were only fit for a life of servitude. Similar acts of cultural aggression by other conquerors, who ritually cut the hair of male prisoners to signify submission and loss of personal rights, or authoritarian zealots who advocated much the same, led many who turned to the cloistered life to shave off their hair so as to show that they had forsaken all earthly ornament and notions of personal ego and made a vow of perpetual subjection to their masters.

This attitude of submission by the cutting of masculine hair has been retained in most schools, institutions of punishment and correction, and the armed forces, and in fact among most businessmen, who generally also remove all evidence of facial hair, although from time to time various styles of moustache are permissible, as is the occasional well-trimmed beard, particularly if the wearer is of some monetary or hereditary importance, hence the beard sported by George V, Nuban Gulbenkiam, and George Bernard Shaw, and I can also recall the great impression a well-presented beard made in the army when worn by a man who had the power to override the normal clean-shaven rule. Our regimental sergeant major wore his flaming red beard with great pride and eventually on the strength of his beard alone became known around the world when he became a Yeoman Warder (Beefeater) at the Tower of London and was featured on tourist posters everywhere. He found, as I do know, that a

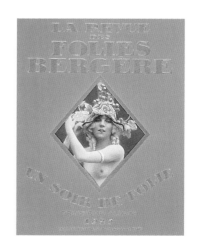

beard is still viewed quite differently by different racial groups, with some regarding a beard with almost religious veneration while others see it as a sign of a barbarian. Some groups see it as a symbol of great virility, and it elicits touching by unmarried nubile girls who seek a partner. But, although they might grow luxuriously on some individuals like RSM Crozier and myself, they are not entirely without problems and they certainly are not *au naturel*—i.e., they do take a lot of grooming, plucking, and trimming to look right and to be socially acceptable. There is, however, an old Maori proverb that says "There is no woman for a hairy man." This may be true for the Maori but for many other indigenous peoples I have found the reverse to be the case.

During Minoan, Greek, and Roman times the cult of male and female beauty and sexuality among the rich and powerful flourished. It seems that the upper echelons of Minoan society spent many hours each day beautifying themselves and they spent vast fortunes on jewelry of all types—rings, necklaces, earrings, diadems, decorative bandeaux, slides, pendants, and pins of all sorts, which were often given as gifts to one's lover. Many commentators believe that, through their various liaisons, Minoan women were actually dominant in society—this is possibly why the modish costume of the snake priestess, with her tightly laced corset and prominently featured breasts, became the symbol of the Minoan civilization, thus creating quite a different icon of beauty from that of the Egyptians or the Greeks who were to follow.

The ancient Greeks took the scepter of civilization and human beauty from the Minoans and were soon creating modes of beauty that are still widely admired today. They placed much more emphasis on masculine beauty, which many considered to be closer to aesthetic perfection than that of the female. They did however, honor both the male and female form in many fine sculptures, including that of the Venus de Milo.

The Greeks owned many slaves, which allowed them plenty of time for entertaining and beautification. Appropriate appearance, which was regarded by them as one of their most important marks of civilization, required not only great care of the body, correct posture, and a healthy lifestyle, but also continual and costly experimentation to achieve the

beauty and harmony expected of every person of wealth and position. Many also believed that regular love affairs and considerable sexual activity were essential for lasting beauty. Scholars have noted with wry amazement how much time some prominent Greeks devoted to sexual activity, a pattern that reappeared in the European courts of the Middle Ages—hence the term "courting," which originally referred to extramarital clandestine affairs—and, more recently, among the Hollywood stars of the 1920s and 1930s, about which much has been written.

The Greeks inherited their predecessors' love of jewelry, and the women spent much time choosing their bracelets, earrings, necklaces, diadems, and the like; adorning their hair; applying their makeup; and acquiring smooth, soft, supple bodies. They published their own literature on beauty hints—beauty for them was certainly seen as central to their lifestyle—advising their readers on the manufacture and use of face powders, rouge, cleansing creams, and creams that protected and softened the skin. The best creams, it would appear, were those made with the aid of human saliva and urine, and some households kept a young female slave (preferably a virgin) whose particular duty it was to keep to a very strict diet so that her saliva and urine would be clean and pleasant for the daily ritual of mixing the creams.

Perfumes imported from the East were also widely used by both men and women, and many are thought to have bathed regularly in ass's milk, which was believed to soften the skin and improve the complexion. Nails were well kept, and pedicure was just as important as manicure. Very finely crushed pumice stone mixed with fresh urine from their young virgin slave or small male child, was used to remove all body hair and the surface layer of skin. It is believed that most coarse hair was plucked out as it grew, especially from under the arms and the pubic region; for men, the plucking aimed to achieve an aesthetically pleasing shape, while for many women, the pubic and underarm hair was totally removed, or at least considerably reduced.

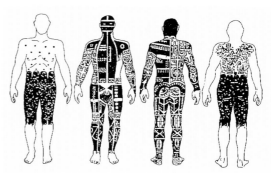

The Greek influence was very powerful during Roman times, although the Romans, like most other Europeans, never fully embraced the Greek philosophy of naked wholesomeness or the acceptance of liberal sexuality and

POITRINE

Ladies' Avon Shoe,   No. 30. Made of
$1.98.   the best materials,
fine Vici kid, with
the California stay in both back and front
seams. Six styles of lasts. Piccadilly toe,
laced and buttoned; opera toe, buttoned;
new common sense toe, laced and buttoned,
—all with the patent tips; also common
sense toe, plain. Actually equal to any
shoe sold for $2.50 or 3.

pornography. For a time, though, according to Pliny, many of the wealthier elite came very close to doing so. It appears that at one stage wealthy women who had a fine figure wore a semitransparent silk toga called a *coan*, which, Pliny said, "protected neither a woman's body nor her modesty and in which she cannot truly declare that she is not naked—and why? So that she may show as much of herself to the world as she does to her lover in the bedroom."

Lucian and others also speak of the Roman ladies' addiction to the use of cosmetics and aromatics: "all doctoring their faces with fantastic treatments—using a chemist shop of little jars; all vials of abomination with which to polish the teeth or blacken the eyebrows." Petronius refers to the women who "take their eyebrows, teeth and hair out of a little box," while Martial is a little more specific about fashionable beauty aids: "Whilst thou livest in Rome thy hair is colored on the banks of the Rhine. At night thou puttest off thy teeth like a garment, and two-thirds of thy person are packed up in boxes." In fact, it was not long before such luxuries degenerated into absurdity, requiring strict sumptuary laws to be passed to try and curtail the excesses. These laws might just as well have been written in water—the excesses continued until the collapse of the Roman Empire.

During the decline of this great Empire and its eventual division into two parts, each with a Christian capital, human beauty was seldom the subject of art, nor art a subject for beauty. The economies of both capitals were in tatters, and what money there was devoted by the faithful to works glorifying the new Catholic and Eastern Orthodox churches.

In the following century, the Eastern Empire, with Byzantium as its capital, prospered and gave birth to a new, heterogeneous civilization and an Eastern-style splendor that was echoed in magnificent mosaics and sumptuous fabrics, which were often interwoven with gold thread, and had baroque pearls and precious stones added to enhance their splendor. In the West, Rome was still in decline. However, toward the end of that period, which today we refer to as the Dark Ages, a new sensibility began to emerge. It was soon to produce one of the greatest indigenous styles in European history—the Gothic style. And among the many achievements of this style was a new mode of human beauty and adornment—new marks of civilization, so to speak—which, although entirely Western in its origins, nevertheless flourished under the influences of international trade, exploration, and colonialism, and the resulting interaction between a variety of cultures, lifestyles, and peoples.

THE SYMBOLS OF SOCIETY

We in the late twentieth century are all about change. We live in a dynamic, forward-looking, high-tech, inventive, wealth-conscious, fickle, fun-loving, you-name-it-we-have-it world. Every conceivable resource from the past is used to beautify the present, to make life easier, and to make a profit, regardless of the eventual consequences to ourselves and our planet. It seems, however, that with so much going on, the only thing that we can be absolutely certain about is that tomorrow is going to be different from today, because we will make it that way.

Life has become increasingly faster-paced and diverse during the past thousand or so years. Before that things changed relatively slowly. For most people who lived before the tenth century, life was more ordered than it is today: Everything had its place, and most activities were based on religious teachings and imposed social laws. It was widely believed by the educated elite that even Nature worked according to very strict predetermined principles laid down by God, which were fully understood and left

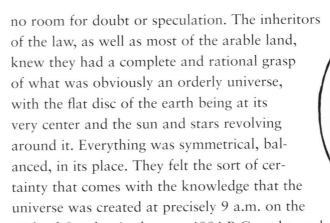

no room for doubt or speculation. The inheritors of the law, as well as most of the arable land, knew they had a complete and rational grasp of what was obviously an orderly universe, with the flat disc of the earth being at its very center and the sun and stars revolving around it. Everything was symmetrical, balanced, in its place. They felt the sort of certainty that comes with the knowledge that the universe was created at precisely 9 a.m. on the 16th of October in the year 4004 B.C. and was destined never to change. And they knew that God had created everything exactly as it then was: otherwise why would things be as they were? Those in authority were there by divine right, because God had ordained it and they fully exploited his so-called "will" to the utmost, being the arbiters of both life and death.

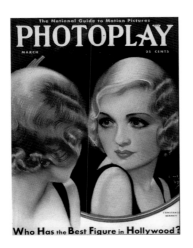

For many of us, coming from a somewhat more enlightened era, enjoying relative freedom, and experiencing change as a matter of course, it is difficult to imagine that being able to travel, own a house or a plot of land, change our style of dress, or use cosmetics or jewelry was once the prerogative of the royal courts, and that very strict laws were enacted to prevent even the very wealthy from copying the styles, fabrics, colors, accessories, and modes of beautification reserved for those of noble birth. We have become accustomed to the steady stream of television advertisements that tell us to buy, buy, buy; to the fashion pages of our daily newspapers that avidly promote the new and the different; and to the proliferation of fashion magazines and books that display seductive images of exotic modes of beauty, dressing, and adornment. We believe that these images could be our own if we had the courage, money, and inclination to experiment in our quest for beauty, social acceptability, and advancement.

It also takes considerable agility to visualize a time before the invention of the sewing machine, the motor car, moving pictures, air conditioning, electricity, mail-order companies, department stores, and cheap foreign labor; a time when every

garment had to made by hand, and no garments were ever sold ready-to-wear unless they were second-hand. In fact, if we look back, say, a thousand years to the garments worn by people of wealth and privilege we may well find it difficult to comprehend that they, like us, believed that they dressed and beautified themselves in the way they did because it was the correct and most appropriate way. And if we glance through the pages of this book we may find it difficult to believe that almost all the styles shown have for a time been accepted as the correct and most appealing way for people to adorn and beautify their bodies.

From about the middle of the twelfth century the gradual spread of trading and other influences from southern Europe, the Mediterranean, and the Middle East gave rise to the development of a new lifestyle. The Crusades brought plunder and new ideas to Europe and opened up the traditional trade routes of the Orient to Western merchants. Of course, not everybody in Europe and the British Isles benefitted from the influx of this newly acquired wealth immediately. Much of Europe was still feudal, ruled by those with inherited power and authority, whose ancestors had gained their wealth and their lands during the preceding millennium and who were supported by the Church hierarchy, an essential part of whose pastoral work was to prevent peasant uprisings, thus perpetuating the status quo.

During the Dark and Middle Ages, the courts of Europe had prospered and evolved a way of life that included dress and adornment that showed a certain opulence but little sophistication. This could not be said for the vast majority of people—the serfs—whose lives appear to have been monotonous and spartan, and whose style of dress was usually no more than a body covering of crudely woven fabric, simply made and without any form of decoration—a sack-like affair tied at the waist with a rope-like cord that could hardly be thought of as alluring.

CHOCOLATES WITH CREAMY CENTRES

Toward the end of the twelfth century, however, soon after the foundations of the first Gothic cathedrals had been laid, the situation in Europe began to change dramatically. Feudal life, with its roughness and violence, was coming to an

end. New forces were at work, influencing a wide area of activities and irrevocably changing the social framework. In southern Europe, cities, instead of courts, began to dominate both commercial and social life, eventually leading to municipal independence. The monotonous social life and spartan economy of the feudal world were beginning to be replaced by commercial enterprise and a growing egalitarianism. Relying on the principles of free labor and free trade, and organized into powerful craft guilds, the new bourgeoisie and the growing number of skilled artisans soon became influential in all aesthetic matters, and the cities in which they lived became the centers of social and economic activity. The community institutions of the city folk had become capable of eroding much of the arrogance and power of the aristocracy, replacing it with a new, more enlightened attitude and an independent lifestyle that was reflected in a novel array of ornamentation and attire. Thus, new forms of popular beauty were created to express the growing wealth and independence of the average citizen.

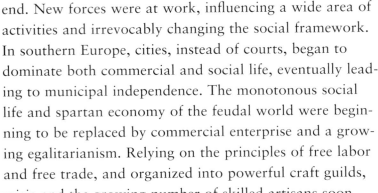

Many scholars regard the spread of the Gothic style, and the subsequent beginning of the Renaissance period, as one of the most fruitful and prolific periods of human history. In strictly European terms it undoubtedly yielded many human images of great beauty and inventiveness. During the period from 1250 to 1750 many great painters and sculptors in Florence, Rome, Milan, Venice, Paris, Vienna, and elsewhere boldly created myriad styles of human beauty, both masculine and feminine. At the same time, the artisans created a great many original styles of dress and adornment, embracing the aesthetics of the new architectural style and of the new painted images of Botticelli, Raphael, Michelangelo, da Vinci, Titian and others, demonstrating that during

periods of intense aesthetic experimentation there is no real division between the fine and the more decorative forms of expression. They are all part of the creative urge, with each form of expression borrowing from the other. In recent years, however, a form

of aesthetic conceit has evolved in our western culture which has created artificial barriers separating our styles of body art from the mainstream arts and regarding them as lesser forms of aesthetic expression. Such barriers do not exist in other cultural groups of the world who, like our ancestors, regard the body arts as an essential manifestation of normal aesthetic expression central to their culture.

Religious attitudes throughout Europe were also changing and Gutenberg's invention of movable type around 1440 enabled books to be printed in increasing numbers. This threatened the very foundations of the Church and its hierarchy, forcing a number of important reforms. Although European society remained fundamentally religious, much of the thinking began to change, influenced as it was by inventions of all sorts, the investigation of Nature, new ideas on the workings of the solar system, and the publishing of translations and illustrations of works from ancient Greece and the East. This, along with the steady increase in trade with the Orient, which introduced a vast array of new styles, accessories, adornments, jewelry, cosmetics, and perfumes, began to change the way that the bourgeoisie and the artisans wished to adorn and beautify themselves.

During the rise of the bourgeoisie and the artisans, sumptuary laws governing how individuals should dress and adorn themselves had been strengthened in a number of countries, such as England, Spain, France, and Germany, which had emerged as the most unified and powerful of the monarchic states. The strengthened sumptuary laws were enacted in order to create an obvious distinction between those of noble birth and inherited privilege and those of newly acquired wealth. For a time, merchants not only were banned from wearing the fashionable *braquette*, which would have displayed their virility to advantage, but also were refused the right to wear many of the fine silken fabrics, rich brocades, gold jewelry, exotic perfumes, fur trimmings, fancy leather shoes, embroidered hose, and lace-trimmed gloves in which they traded—the royal courts having decreed that only they had the right to purchase and wear such finery.

In 1482, for instance, during the reign of Edward IV, an edict was issued specifically restricting the wearing of cloth of gold or silk of purple color to all except the King, the Queen, the King's mother, the King's children, and the King's brothers and sisters. Doublets or gowns trimmed with velvet were limited to those of the rank of knight or above; damask and satin were limited to esquires and members of the King's bodyguard or above. Servants, laborers, and their families were not allowed to array

themselves in any cloth that cost more than a few pennies a yard, even if they could afford such luxury, and they were forbidden the use of any fur other than cat, rabbit, or goat. In 1509, this edict was modified to increase the cost of the fabric allowable for a servant of a lord or above: livery for servants had become fashionable as a means of further displaying the master's social status and wealth. Such a fashion grew in importance during the ensuing centuries—the results continue to be displayed at coronations and on important ceremonial State occasions.

A similar sumptuary law was passed in 1516. The king, Henry VIII, increased the range of restricted accessories that had only recently been imported. Even his successor, Queen Elizabeth I, sought to impose her will on the apparel of her subjects, decreeing that all vendors of imported apparel, fabrics, jewelry, lace trimmings, and similar forms of finery be forbidden to sell such items to any person not having an annual income of three thousand pounds—the average yearly wage for a laborer in those days was less than ten pounds. (Today, this would be the equivalent of saying only those who earned over a million dollars per year could purchase imported French fashions, Italian silks, or Swiss embroidery.) Queen Elizabeth I did, however, encourage both the male and female members of her court to indulge in all the latest frippery as a ploy to keep them occupied and away from matters of State—a ploy also

practiced by many other monarchs, which still operates today on an informal modified scale within powerful families and some organizations. As Mary Wollstonecraft so astutely observed in her landmark book *A Vindication of the Rights of Women* (1792), over indulgence in matters of dress, beautification, and fashion are very effective in cramping the normal activities of the mind.

Despite these restrictive sumptuary laws, and probably because they were impossible to enforce, there are numerous accounts of merchants in very ornate modes of dress, adorned with jewelry of great value: "their mills, lands, ships, and all their revenue swallowed up and completely consumed in habiliments." And there are reports of new fashions such as "slashing," which appear to have been invented to clearly demonstrate that, although restricted by law to certain styles of dress and to a maximum cost of fabric, the wearer could well afford to have his newest garment destroyed by having it meticulously slashed all over. Ironically, slashing became extremely popular among the aristocracy and was highlighted by pulling strips of more expensive, brightly colored silk—which were not technically part of the garment—through the slashed holes. This was one of the first reversals of the traditional system of the lower ranks copying their so-called betters. This demonstration of conspicuous consumption and contempt for the law was bitterly condemned by the clergy, as were numerous other fashions and modes of beauty such as that which in the 1580s had given women "a bummbe like a barrel" and made their "buttocks most monstrously round." This was an alternative to the Spanish farthingale, in which a series of wooden hoops were worn suspended from the waist by tapes, to give the dress a conical shape. The new fashion required a long sausage-shaped cushion to be worn across the back of the hips, just below the waist, which had "bends of whale bone to shape and beare out their bummbes" and was intended to replace the farthingale, which was the style worn by the enemy—at that time England was far from being friendly with Spain.

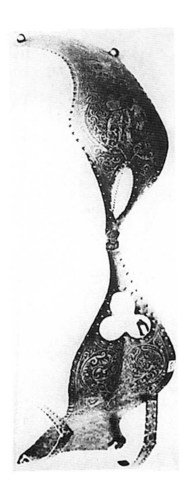

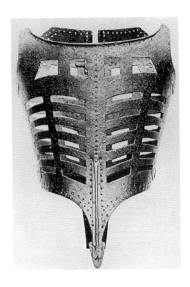

The clerics also condemned the very notion of beauty itself, saying it was the invention of the devil. They also condemned the use, by both men and women, of steel and leather laced-up corsets, which many had worn since early childhood so as to achieve a tiny waist and small rib-cage—it was said the "waisted figure encouraged lustful thoughts in the minds and loins of members of the opposite sex." The clergy were also outraged at the use, again by both men and women, of cosmetics and face patches, which were originally invented to cover up unsightly blemishes. They were further incensed at the sight of the male genitalia neatly packaged into a shaped codpiece, and of young virgins who openly displayed their breasts, often with rouged nipples. Regularly they chanted from Isaiah 3: 18–22: "...the Lord will take away the tinkling ornaments from about their ankles, the hand mirrors and the fine linen, and the turbans the veils, the chains and the bracelets, and the mufflers, the bonnets, and the adornments of the legs, and the headbands. The perfume boxes and sweet spices, the amulets and the earrings, the rings, and nose jewels, the changeable suits of apparel, the fine furs, the splendid shoes, decorative under garments and all their finery...." Of course, there was even greater condemnation for those who discarded all their attire in order to be painted nude.

From contemporary reports and the paintings of the period we can see that the railing of the clerics had little effect on the adornments and poses of the aristocrats or the favored models, or on the clothing styles of the *nouveau riches*. In fact, it was only by their mode of attire and embellishment that the *nouveau riches* were able to claim a respected place in society—they were not prepared to give that up in a hurry, and anyway the Holy Fathers were also indulging in their own display of sartorial splendor, bedecking themselves in such richness of fabric and quantity of jewels that they often outdid those they condemned.

The ladies of the Church were also busily adorning their necks with exquisite necklaces, their arms with gold and jewelled bracelets, their fingers with priceless rings. They had their hair dyed and curled, their cheeks and lips were often reddened with cosmetics, and they wore elaborate gowns made of imported silks, damask, or velvet, which due to their excessive length would trail along the floor—a habit strictly forbidden by law since all garments with a train were supposedly reserved for those of royal blood.

The condemnation of the clerics served to make such modes of apparel more desirable among the men and women of fashion: Once a style had been attacked as immoral, licentious, lustful, or depraved many members of society would openly compete with one another to see who was able to wear it most successfully. Costume historian C. Willett Cunnington stated, "We have to thank the Early Fathers for having, albeit perhaps unwittingly, established a mode of thinking from which men and women have developed an art which was supplied them with so much agreeable entertainment." He went on to allude to a variety of sexual styles of dress that were very popular during this period. Robert Burton, in his famous *Anatomy of Melancholy* (1652), also referred to such garments under the headings of "Artificial Allurements of Love" and "Causes of Provocations to Lust"; he said that, although the natural beauty of the feminine physical form was undoubtedly a very strong motivating force for inciting lust in the male, the use of a wide range of clothing, jewels, accessories, and beautifiers was far more potent. He concluded that one of the greatest of all "provocations to lust" came from apparel.

This theme was amplified by Cunnington, who wrote of the many varieties of such garments, which he said were responsible for "creating so many forms of agreeable diversions, so many satisfying substitutes for Nature's omissions, and so many novel means of exciting the sexual appetite." In his view, prudery, as well as gift wrapping, provides mankind with endless aphrodisiacs, which, of course, explains our reluctance to abandon them. Many others have also commented upon the role that prudery and its companion, modesty, play in our styles of dress and notions of beauty: the consensus is that they are both human inventions, and that without having first invented modesty it would be impossible to be immodest or to invoke the somewhat specialized allure of prudery. In fact, it is certain aspects of prudery coupled with immodesty that add so much excitement to our ideas of beauty and the way we dress.

The Church greatly assisted the effectiveness of this invention, by always being shocked by each new

Englands Vanity:
OR THE

Voice of God

Against the Monſtrous

Sin of Pride,
IN

Dreſs and *Apparel*:

Wherein
Naked Breaſts and Shoulders, Antick and Fantaſtick Garbs, Patches, and Painting, long Perriwigs, Towers, Bulls, Shades, Curlings, and Criſpings, with an Hundred more Fooleries of both Sexes, are condemned as Notoriouſly Unlawful.

With pertinent Addreſſes to the Court, Nobility, Gentry, City, and Country.

Directed eſpecially to the Profeſſors in *London.*

By a Compaſſionate Conformiſt.

Zeph. 1. 8. *I will puniſh the Princes, and the Kings Children, and ſuch as are Cloathed with ſtrange Apparel.*

Entred according to Order.

London, Printed for *John Dunton,* at the black Raven in the *Poultry,* 1683.

form of so-called immodesty and by always speaking out against change. In retrospect, we may find such condemnation amusing, but the measure of its success lies in the doubt that so many of us now have about our style of dress, what we may or may not do to make ourselves attractive, and our display of sexuality— even our thoughts of sex itself, as if it were in some way sinful, or, least not the delight it should be if we are to believe the ancient Greeks or the *Kama Sutra*. And, because religious and social laws have for centuries been so closely intertwined, the assumed immorality of sexual display and of the sex act itself (a myth that has engendered more misery and guilt than any other myth of Western life) has remained an important factor in the control of our society. It has also been instrumental in determining our attitudes about which parts of our bodies should be seen as beautiful. The naked female form, for instance, in our own society is generally regarded as more beautiful than the naked body of the male, by virtue of the near invisibility of the female sex organ, which, of course, is a form of distorted sexism.

The Greeks did not believe in such nonsense and proudly depicted both sexes completely naked, although, in keeping with Aristotle's theorizing, the sculptors removed any sign of the female pubic hair, as indeed did most of the women themselves, regarding pubic hair as somewhat barbaric—the women of the northern "barbaric" tribes were hairier than they. The sculptors also remodelled the male genitalia, reducing rather than increasing the size, possibly for the same reason or in agreement with the thinking about women's breasts: "when such a distinctive feature is naturally small its beauty is enhanced by this very fact." Freud, however, was of the belief that the male genitalia had not undergone the development of the rest of the human body in the direction of beauty and that therefore it could never be considered beautiful. On the other hand, Bernard Rudofsky in *The Unfashionable Human Body* (1972) stated that the chief obstacle to this distinctive male feature being accepted for display or being regarded as beautiful is not the belief that it is unattractive but rather that in general it seems too insubstantial to warrant such interest.

When discussing the aesthetics of the male physique, Remy de Gourmont in his *Physique de l'Amour* (1901) summarized European thinking of the time when he said that the male genitalia existed only for the perpetuation of the race and was not there to enhance the beauty of the individual:

> In the male, and precisely because of its erect attitude, sex is the predominantly striking and visible fact, the point of attack in a struggle at close quarters, the point aimed at from a distance, an obstacle for the eye whether regarded as a rugosity on the surface or as breaking the middle of a line. The harmony of the feminine body is thus geometrically much more perfect, especially when we consider the male and the female at the moment of desire when they present the most intense and natural expression of life. Then the woman, whose movements are all interior, or only visible by the undulations of her curves, preserves her full, aesthetic value, while the man, as it were, all at once receding towards the primitive state of animality, seems to throw off all beauty and becomes reduced to the simple and naked condition of a genital organism.

A little later, however, de Gourmont did agree with many of the Renaissance artists and the ancient Greek sculptors, whose philosophy professed that the proportions, shape, and silhouette of the masculine body were in an abstract, or mathematical sense, more aesthetically beautiful than those of the female. This is an important point, but one that over the years has been completely submerged beneath the clerics' attacks on the male nude in their determination to totally castrate all except the most inoffensive of nude male images.

The artists of the Renaissance, and many who came later, were, however, able to use this religious suppression to creative advantage in their depictions of both the men and women of the period. Like the designers of the garments that covered their patrons' bodies, they began to incorporate in their work a kind of sign language, the genitalia and other notable areas of the anatomy being transformed into symbols that appealed to the subliminal senses. Paintings, sculptures, and indeed the modes of allure

themselves were, through an elaborate system of coded symbols, used to draw attention to the wearer's varying physical attributes, to arouse sexual interest, and to inform the observer of an assortment of other pertinent information. Pink rosettes on a shoe, for instance, were a visible symbol of the pudenda, and the lace edging of the petticoat signified pubic hair. A glimpse of stocking was enough to remind the observer of the female ankle, calf, knee, thigh, and all the pleasures that lay above. A bow was placed to tempt the observer's imagination of what might be visible if it were undone, and again the possible pleasure that would transpire. The physical shape of the person would often be slightly exaggerated: men were made to appear much broader in the shoulders, while an object such as the hilt of a sword or later an upright object displayed on the front of a man (such as a necktie or its symbolic forerunner the *braquette*) needs little explanation. We must remember, though, that such symbolism was by no means new: the Romans, for instance, had always regarded the larger male nose as a symbol of the penis and an indication of its actual size, with many women preferring to be seen being courted by a man with a large and distinguished nose, which incidentally, increases in size with sexual excitement, being formed in part from the same spongy erectile tissue as that which it echoes.

Painters of the period used an array of colors around the eyes, lips, cheeks, neck, and ears of their portraits to symbolize, or echo, sexual arousal. At times they concentrated the eye of the observer on the slender waist of a nubile female, subconsciously challenging the male observer's virility and probably leading him into the realm of fantasy. Other paintings relied on the observer's voyeuristic tendencies, sometimes concentrating the eye of the observer on, for example, the ear as a form of erotic echo. Seeing this naturally evolved symbolism and recalling the notion that the Virgin Mary may well have conceived Jesus through her ear, the clerics banished the ears and the surrounding hair from sight—again giving rise to an interesting array of images and styles of ornamentation.

In addition to this symbolic portraiture, there was a lucrative trade in nude paintings and commercially inspired engravings of these paintings, such as Titian's *Venere Anadiomene* (1520–1522), which was copied by the expert engraver Benoist, whose nude print of the central figure of the

painting was selling well by the mid-sixteenth century—thus setting in motion a theme of feminine beauty in art that is still very active. This engraving can be seen as the first popular pin-up, the precursor to today's *Playboy* centerfolds.

The artists of the period also used their intimate knowledge of the risqué fashions of the moment, such as the "forbidden" pantaloons introduced to European fashion by the sixteenth-century prostitutes and courtesans of Florence and Venice (forerunners of the highly controversial bifurcated drawers of our great-grandmothers' day, which were originally outlawed by the clerics as being a "heinous sin" and "against the laws of God"). They hinted at the wearing of such pantaloons by the way they painted the skirts of fashionable women, making the fabric appear to fall in such a way so that the observer could almost "feel" the forbidden undergarment and the female thighs it covered. Such subliminal messages, are commonplace today, being widely employed by photographers, filmmakers, and advertising agencies. In fact, it seems we prefer subliminal eroticism, and in general are terrified, even revolted, by the sight of that part of the physical self that so delights us when partly veiled.

Havelock Ellis, Richard von Krafft-Ebing, and many others have had a great deal to say about this phenomenon, and in my own practice as a New Age sex therapist I had several young male patients who were addicted to the sight of the partly covered female body, but who became flaccid when they actually saw the naked feature that naturally and normally should have been the object of their ardent desire—a phobia made famous by the nineteenth-century British art critic John Ruskin who, seeing his first wife naked on their wedding night was so repelled by the sight of her pubic hair he was unable to consummate the marriage and it was later annulled. This unnatural state of mind about body hair and that of various body functions is today much encouraged by television and our *Playboy* society, whose main aim is titillation not consummation—in our current consumer society, there is more money to be made from titillation than from fornication, hence everything is sacrificed to this goal of moneymaking. Several young female patients also confided that they were horrified by the look of their own genitalia and could not even bring

A FASHIONABLE LADY
in DRESS & UNDRESS.

themselves to examine or show their genitals or pubic hair to their boyfriends, even in their most intimate moments—unlike the X-rated film studio I was also working in at the time. Young aspiring actresses like Traci Lords were only too willing to display their neatly trimmed and decorated allurements for the camera and, of course, audiences everywhere, including, as I found out later, the highlands of Papua New Guinea, where among the local people such displays are not normally considered erotic or arousing. But this unnatural reluctance was something my young female patients quickly learned to overcome after just one therapy session. Unlike the clergy, I believe that this area of the female anatomy should be glorified and honored as it was in so many ancient religions, and within the course of a few treatments all the young women who attended my therapy sessions became proud of their secret allurement and glorified in the photo sessions I organized to document their natural naked beauty.

Betty Dodson, author, artist, and sex therapist, in her books on sexual inhibitions and how to overcome them, and more importantly how to be content within oneself and to glorify in one's own sexuality (*Sex for One: The Joy of Self Loving*, 1987), states our cultural problems very clearly, and what, with a little effort, can be done about them. She tells how, when she was young and even when she was married, she was unable to accept the look of her pubic region and never explored her genitals, thinking in

some way or other that it was not normal to do so, and that they were extremely ugly and should always be hidden from view—a belief perpetuated by our culture to stop, I suspect, the spread of normal and natural sensuality. (One reason for this is that it is free and thus those in authority don't get their percentage cut.)

It seems that by educated tradition, and the force of the law, we are not able, even today, to accept ourselves as we really are. Instead we have

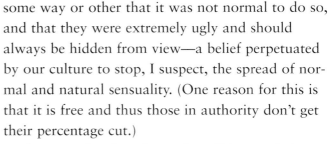

become devotees of signs, symbols, and subliminal messages about our sexuality, which we avidly display in our modes of dress, accessories, and cosmetics, using them to draw attention to, or emphasize those areas of our bodies which in normal circumstances indicate a state of sexual arousal, without any form of sexuality actually being involved—a subject I have dealt with in some detail in *Body Packaging: A Guide to Human Sexual Display* (1988). Suffice it to say that due to our inhibiting cultural tradition this preference is being capitalized upon by the videotape industry, multinationals, and others, as those who regularly thumb through the mass media publications, or regularly watch television and television commercials, would certainly know.

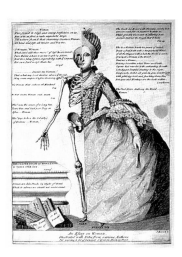

Unfortunately, we have also come to accept that, in a general sense, human beauty resides almost exclusively in the young nubile female—not in the mature woman nor in the male—with almost every aspect of her young face and body being displayed for the sale of something, except the genital area itself, which is rarely mentioned and never seen. Other cultures do not have this problem, some tending to glorify in those features that we hope will pass unnoticed. And although some aspects of this cultural tradition are beginning to break down as more people travel and see for themselves the love carvings so prominently featured in the great Hindu temples at Konarak and Khajuraho or more relaxed sexual attitudes of the South Sea Islanders, those who attempt to exercise personal choice in such matters when they return to their homes are often regarded as being either highly suspect, or even perverted—followers of the Marquis de Sade or worse.

Our history shows, however, that in the realm of human beauty, as in matters of sexual choice, nothing is ever permanent; and sexual attitudes and styles of dress and adornment in the sixteenth century were soon to change quite radically as the result of overseas exploration and

nternational trade. Scholars have long been aware of the influence exploration and trade have had on notions of beauty and consequently on costume and fashion. Such was the case in Italy and southern Europe during the Renaissance, but long before this there had been contact and trade with the Eastern world. At least two thousand years earlier, the Egyptian pharaohs had initiated a regular trade in luxury goods with the Orient, and this trade expanded during Greek and Roman times and during the most fruitful period of the Byzantine Empire. With the Crusades came an explosion in trade, plunder, and influence: the returning knights brought back not only perfumes, jewelry, and silken materials, which had always been avidly sought, but many new kinds of garments and a knowledge of how they should be worn. Soon many of the wealthier women and the courtesans were adopting oriental ways and styles—including the Muslim veil, Turkish trousers, plucked or decorated pubic hair, and the arts of love so beautifully detailed in the *Kama Sutra*. Some crusading knights even returned with wives or mistresses, male servants and masseurs, who by their novelty and charm were able to introduce new ways and new ideals to Western culture. This process of interaction and absorption continued for several centuries and expanded to include many cultures from elsewhere in the world. Nevertheless, many parts of Europe were still comparatively isolated: a number of the factors effecting change in southern Europe were quite different from those that were influencing the north.

From the beginning of the sixteenth century, the change from a medieval to a more modern society was beginning to accelerate in England and most of northern Europe, and by the end of Henry VIII's reign a degree of luxury had become evident in aristocratic apparel, rivaling in cost, if not in sophistication, the fashions worn in the Italian, French, and Spanish courts.

A new source of documentation of dress and accessories had also made its appearance, in the form of a collection of printed images depicting new styles of clothing, decorative motifs for embroidery, patterns of lace, and details of jewelry and accessories of all sorts. The first of

these publications appeared in 1520 and by the 1550s a number had been published in Venice, Paris, Antwerp, Munich, Vienna, and Frankfurt; London joined the fray a few years later.

This form of information was broadened still further in 1595 with the publication of *Habiti Antichi et Moderni di Tutto il Mondo* by Cesare Vecellio, cousin of the Venetian painter Titian, and a little later by John Bulwer's *Anthropometamorphosis;* "Man transform'd or the Artificial Changeling. Historically Presented in the mad and cruel Gallantry, Foolish Bravery, Ridiculous Beauty, Filthy Fineness, and Loathsome Loveliness of Most Nations, Fashioning and altering their bodies from the mould intended by Nature with a Vindication of the Regular Beauty and Honesty of Nature." This work also contained an appendix on the "Pedigree of the English Gallant and an account of all those Native and National Monstrosities that have appeared to disfigure the Humane Fabrick."

A new style of painting, quite different from that of the south, had also been evolving in northern Europe: the work of the earlier van Eyck, and of Memlinc, Dürer, Cranach, and Holbein was much admired and provided a prolific and detailed record of the fashions of the day, as well as an insight into the aesthetics of beauty during this period of great change. In particular, increasing emphasis was being placed on the face, hair, and hands of the patron, and styles of dress were often no more than extravagant frames for these much admired human features. Hints of pregnancy were also featured as they gave the woman being painted a special radiant beauty and an irresistible glow, which also added considerably to the husband's prestige. We must also be mindful that when we look at a painting or other work of art we "see" much more than the mere subject matter—our visual senses also perceive the beauty of the artist's skill and the inherent beauty of the medium itself which combines together in our mind's eye with our cultural tradition, our response to subliminal messages, notions of morals, religion, and rightness, preferences of coloration, patterning, priviledge, and more. In other words, a truly subjective evaluation which unfortunately often has an ingredient like xenophobia or some other tarnishing aspect.

A number of these paintings show us that life for the upper echelons of society was not quite as chaste as many historians would have us believe. In fact, life in most of the courts of Europe at that time was quite licentious, with ladies wearing extremes of dress as they vied for favors. One astute observer wrote however, that "the ladies at court do not choose their mode of dress to please the male courtiers, or even the King, but merely to raise their ardour, and to win the battle for admiration amongst themselves." Their promiscuity is legend. Many such ladies had entered into marriages of convenience but upheld the sentiments of the old "courts of love"—in which love sought obstacles, mystery, stolen favors, not the intimacy of married couples. This practice lingered well into the eighteenth century; Lady Mary Montagu wrote on the subject after a visit to the Court of Vienna in 1716, "The established custom of every lady is to have two husbands, one that bears the name and another that performs the duties"—a state of affairs much celebrated by the English artist Thomas Rowlandson in his numerous erotic illustrations, which were widely published for the edification and amusement of the educated classes later that century. Such affairs and the resulting passionate sex were greatly encouraged as beautifiers that gave a radiant, irresistible aura to a woman. The theory is that passionate sex stimulates the body's hormonal system, which is turn benefits the skin, the hair, and the facial features, and induces a desire for more sex—thus such affairs are self-perpetuating—although most historians and other romantic writers would have us believe that such love was in fact highly virtuous, chaste even. The hero is said to have only sought favor in his lady's eyes by overcoming all manner of obstacles and difficulties for the sole purpose of kissing her hand and being able to dream of an eternal life together without any carnal lust entering their thoughts.

During the seventeenth century, most of Europe was experiencing a turmoil of religious dissension and political unrest, which in England culminated in the execution of Charles I in 1649 and the establishment under Cromwell of a regime of strict puritan principles. The Dutch had won their independence from Spain, and the Protestant bourgeoisie gained control, introducing an era of unprecedented prosperity and international influence

for the bourgeoisie, coupled with very straight-laced moral ideas, especially about sexual matters. Soon they and the English began to colonize the Atlantic seaboard of North America, creating a new nation that for a time shared their puritan ideals. For economic and political reasons, Italy's supremacy was waning, while the growing strength of France's international position was matched by increased interest in its fashions and aesthetics ideals. By 1700 the hundred years of political strife that had beset Europe had begun to produce significant changes in the social structure; the middle classes were becoming increasingly affluent, and in general, it was their influence along with that of the aristocracy that once again began to change the direction of Western dress, aesthetics, and beauty.

Artists such as Rubens, Bernini, Vermeer, Velazquez, van Dyck, and Frans Hals began to experiment with new forms of expression—looking at the beauty of women with new eyes. It was Rubens, the oldest of this group, who created a new ideal. He rejected the established conventions of classical nudity, which had spread from Greece via Rome to the rest of Europe, and, by giving the women he painted a rather carefree plumpness, he opened the door for other painters' idiosyncratic ideals to become icons of beauty. Later, Watteau, Boucher, and Fragonard continued this trend of individual choice, although the choice they tended to portray was the image of the beautiful, successful, sensual, and shameless courtesans of the court of Versailles many of whom had come from humble origins such as

Louise O'Murphy who was the daughter of an Irish shoemaker. In contrast, English painters, such as Gainsborough and Reynolds, depicted what many experts claim is a more refined form of feminine beauty—a beauty of calculated restraint, privilege, and good breeding, which made a point of featuring the delicacy of many of the female physical features. As was stated at the time in a book aiming to advise its readers on feminine elegance, "A lady has the right to be proud of the advantages of small hands, slender feet and slim arms"

Soleimnization.
A New Matrimonial Ladder.

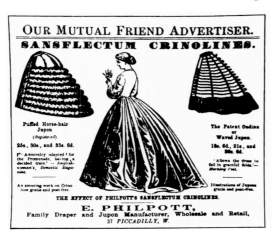

OUR MUTUAL FRIEND ADVERTISER.
SANSFLECTUM CRINOLINES.

Puffed Horse-hair
Jupon
(Register ed)
25s., 30s., and 33s. 6d.

The Patent Ondina
or
Waved Jupon.
18s. 6d., 21s., and
26s. 6d.

THE EFFECT OF PHILPOTT'S SANSFLECTUM CRINOLINES.
E. PHILPOTT,
Family Draper and Jupon Manufacturer, Wholesale and Retail,
37 PICCADILLY, W.

explaining "whereas a handsome figure may be found amongst the common folk, a fine hand or slender foot scarcely ever comes from that class. Thus from the sight of the hand alone, or a glimpse of a well-turned ankle, it is possible to judge to what class she belongs." Thus were established contrary philosophies of feminine elegance and beauty that held sway until well into the twentieth century.

By the middle of the second half of the eighteenth century the steadily increasing availability of consumer goods—a result of the Industrial Revolution—enabled many ordinary people to dress and adorn themselves attractively. To cater to this new market a number of specialist magazines began to appear, advising readers about the new fashions and adornments for both males and females. The styles worn by the upper classes did, however, remain at the head of the pecking order, as did the opulence of the aristocrats who frequented the European courts.

During the early 1780s the number of fashion magazines available increased dramatically, and the hand-colored engraved illustrations were designed by many leading artists. Paris was the dominant outlet, and the work of artists such as Le Clerc, Duhamel, Watteau, and Desrais was featured in the costliest of the publications; copies of their work were also included in the pirated German, Austrian, Dutch, Spanish, English, and Italian editions. Also published in Paris was a series of magazines containing hand-colored illustrations of styles from other parts of the world. For the first time members of the European middle class were able to admire the great variety of beauty and adornments to be found all over the world, thus opening the door, if only so slightly, for future change. But the French Revolution of 1789 put an end to thoughts of experimentation for a time, as well as to the extravagances of courtly life at Versailles.

By the end of the eighteenth century, simplicity reigned: female dress was reduced from panniered constructions 1.5 meters wide or more to simple robes of fine Indian muslin—the complete dress and accessories often weighing less than 200 grams—which were draped across the naked body in the Grecian style. The fashionable male costume became an adaptation of the style originally worn by the proletariat: satin knee breeches, jewelled garters, silk hose, embroidered waistcoats, wigs, fine leather shoes and gloves, elaborate and costly toiletry, and all other frippery were quickly discarded lest the wearer be perceived an enemy of the people. The original intention of the new styles was to help create an egalitarian society, free from the ostentation and privilege that characterized the now dispossessed aristocracy.

From 1792 Pierre de la Mésangère included charming illustrations of the new Grecian styles in his *Le Journal des dames et des modes,* which triumphantly proclaimed the birth of a new era free of the tyranny of the court of Louis XVI and his sycophants. To promote acceptance of the new style, for men and women, *Le Journal des dames et des modes* and several similar magazines, including the English *Lady's Monthly Museum* and *La Belle Assemblée,* quoted from Homer, Plato, and Persaeus, who, they declared, would have been delighted by what had been dubbed the "naked fashion." They also described in detail the draping of diaphanous muslin, what jewelry or other adornments should be worn, who made the best slip-on shoes, which style of coiffure to adopt, what form of underclothing, if any, should be worn, what style of cosmetics to use, and general information about body care. At least one magazine gallantly tackled the subject of trimming and decorating the pubic hair. Even today this is a subject ignored by fashion magazines, and most art and costume historians dismiss it, and the "naked fashion" itself, as indecent and indecorous, saying it was "one of the most lascivious styles ever worn by civilized people."

In the 1790s, the French gloried in the new near-naked fashions. At last the nubile daughters of the bourgeoisie and lower classes could vie in manner of dress and physical beauty with the wives and daughters of the remaining wealthier classes, to display their charms in the hope of improving their social position. This freedom did not last long, though: Napoleon Bonaparte's First Empire reintroduced all the etceteras of sartorial splendor, which developed by Brobdingnagian proportions as the new century unfolded, creating many outstandingly hideous styles by the 1860s, particularly in France. As Octave Uzanne commented in *Fashion*

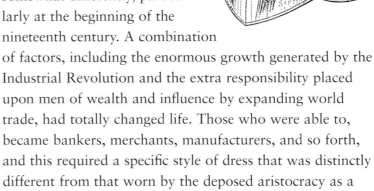

in Paris (1898), "With the second Empire we reach the most hideous period in female dress that has ever vexed the artistic eye." I believe that the same comment could also be applied to the fashions worn in England and much of the United States.

In general, menswear fared somewhat differently, particularly at the beginning of the nineteenth century. A combination of factors, including the enormous growth generated by the Industrial Revolution and the extra responsibility placed upon men of wealth and influence by expanding world trade, had totally changed life. Those who were able to, became bankers, merchants, manufacturers, and so forth, and this required a specific style of dress that was distinctly different from that worn by the deposed aristocracy as a form of collective identity. They chose an adaptation of an army uniform that had already made its mark on male fashion—a fashion adopted by several leading Savile Row tailors in central London from the uniform worn by Napoleon during his more successful military campaigns, for several leading members of British society, including the Duke of Wellington, as a form of riding gear. Flügel claimed that this change from the ornate and sumptuous aristocratic mode of satin knee breeches, embroidered waistcoats, silk stockings, and high heeled shoes amounted to the male abandoning his claim to be considered beautiful; henceforth his only aim was to be useful, the recognizable bread winner and provider, correctly and appropriately attired, rather than beautiful, elegant, or modish.

By 1810 while still living under the continuing threat of war and possible revolution, most wealthy men dressed as discreetly as possible, almost anonymously, adopting either the commercial ideal, which during the first decades of the nineteenth century had been transformed from its military beginnings into a dark, three-piece business suit—which, apart from shortening the jacket and the introduction of pinstriped trousers, was to remain virtually unchanged until very recent times—or the more expensive but still very discreet version that featured tightly fitting buckskin trousers, cutaway jacket, and the fine linen advocated by George "Beau" Brummell.

Brummell's philosophy hinged around his belief that a man should never be noticed for what he wore. He should never be seen to be ostentatious, and whatever he wore he must always look at ease and never give a hint of any newness about his clothing—he always had his newest suits broken in by his valet. He believed that a gentleman should distinguish himself from the less well born by small details—such a style is still available in modified form among the more prestigious tailors of London's Savile Row. Then, as now,

the ploy depends on the small details being so discreet as not to be noticed by the average man, or so expensive to carry out correctly that the average man would not deem it worthwhile. Either way, the details should be of sufficient interest to be observed by other gentlemen, and by ladies of society upon whom the wearer generally depends to maintain his social position. Beau Brummell also became famous for his obsession with cravats and his refusal to wear jewelry other than a diminutive cravat pin, a modest signet ring, and a prosaic watch chain—this, he believed, was as far as a gentleman should go in terms of decoration. He also decreed that a man should always be scrupulously clean—he often showered three or more times day and always with a complete change of under linen and clothing. Pearl Binder explained the Beau Brummell phenomenon in *The Peacock's Tail* (1958): "Beau Brummell was a modern man. Hollywood is where he really belongs. Nobody knew the news value of his affectations better than he did, and the legend he was so skilled in creating has lasted successfully into our own times."

And as far as male beauty is concerned Hollywood is where it finally reemerged, in the early 1920s in the form of an obscure Italian actor named Rudolph Valentino who, like Brummell was an acknowledged bisexual and an occasional cross-dresser. In fact being bisexual and indulging in cross-dressing, especially for parties became quite fashionable in the early nineteenth century. This can

also be seen today, particularly in the entertainment world, where "coming out of the closet" often means flaunting sexual differences in extreme styles.

For women, and for a few gay or bisexual men, the early-to-mid-nineteenth-century feast of styles, depicted by artists such as David, François Gérard, Ingres, Goya, Antonio Canova, and Delacroix, meant that every coquetry and aid known were being used in the daily quest for a beauty ranging from near nakedness to one more ornate than ever before. Ringlets came and went. Frills were introduced, banished, and then reintroduced. Multitudinous layers of lace were used. Corsets got tighter, skirts larger, and sleeves fuller and much more ornate. Each new style was captured and frozen in time by the growing number of artists—Winterhalter, Rossetti and the Pre-Raphaelites, and then Renoir, Degas, Toulouse-Lautrec, and the other Impressionists and Post Impressionists, the American James McNeill Whistler, Paul Gauguin, and other individualists who were opening up new vistas of the possible. There was also a growing interest in the more unusual styles of illustrations in the vein of Thomas Rowlandson, whose work had been republished in the new medium of colored lithography (they had been originally published as expensive hand-colored engravings). One of the new illustrators was Peter Fendi, an artist of the Imperial Habsburg Court

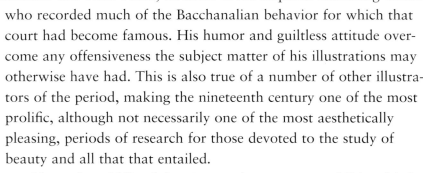

who recorded much of the Bacchanalian behavior for which that court had become famous. His humor and guiltless attitude overcome any offensiveness the subject matter of his illustrations may otherwise have had. This is also true of a number of other illustrators of the period, making the nineteenth century one of the most prolific, although not necessarily one of the most aesthetically pleasing, periods of research for those devoted to the study of beauty and all that that entailed.

About the middle of the nineteenth century, an additional influence on contemporary perceptions of human beauty came to the fore, which evolved from the expansion in production of children's books for the growing middle class. Prior to the 1830s, children's books had been relatively expensive, their illustrations were somewhat idiosyncratic, and the market was limited. But as the middle classes became more affluent, and as interest in education grew, the

market for books expanded rapidly. In addition, the increasing use of the new steam-driven printing presses and mechanical methods of color printing allowed prices to fall to a level that made books readily accessible to a large number of children, whose visual vocabularies were beginning to be fed by imagery created by the likes of Walter Crane, Kate Greenaway, EVB (Eleanor Vere Boyle), Juluis Happner, Richard Doyle and Gustave Doré.

This market was given a tremendous boost in the 1860s and 1870s when many western countries finally introduced various forms of compulsory education, which was to have a dramatic effect on publishing of all kinds—an effect that was to increase in importance as the century progressed. We are all aware of the effect that the growth of the mass media and in particular the introduction of television has had on our visual vocabularies, as well as the influence that film stars such as Brigitte Bardot and James Dean, and pop and rock stars such as the Beatles, Cyndi Lauper, and Madonna have had on our dress styles and moral attitudes. The same sort of influence was being felt in the mid-to-late nineteenth century by the increasing distribution of the printed page and accompanying visual images, particularly those aimed at the young whose visual vocabularies were beginning to be fed by an array of new imagery—an imagery that was soon to have a profound effect on both the ideas and ideals of the decorative and fine arts once this younger generation had become adults. It is of interest to note in this regard that several Post Impressionist painters, including Paul Gauguin, readily accepted the influence that the illustrations of the likes of Kate Greenaway and Walter Crane had upon their paintings—an effect noted in *The Sources of Modern Painting* published by The Institute of Contemporary Art of the Museum of Fine Arts in 1939, which clearly shows the aesthetic similarity between several of Gauguin's paintings of late 1880s and the work of Kate Greenaway that

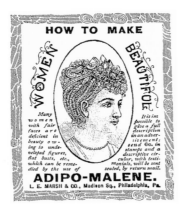

had been published in such children's books as *Little Ann and Other Poems* a few years earlier. These illustrations were also to influence the revolutionary early-twentieth-century designer Paul Poiret and the influential artists and designers George Barbier and Paul Iribe, who became instrumental in creating a new style of feminine dress and beauty during the early years of the Art Deco period. (I have dealt with this subject in *The Golden Age of Style: Art Deco Fashion Illustration*, 1976, and *The Fine Art of Fashion: An Illustrated History*, 1989.)

Another form of artistry also emerged during the same period in the form of photography, which during the latter part of the century gave rise to a number of truly beautiful and influential images. So, too, did the importation and exhibition of Japanese and other oriental works of aesthetic sensibility—originally referred to as *Orientalism*, although by the beginning of the twentieth century it had become totally dedicated to *Japonisme*. This latter influence was acknowledged in the Institute of Contemporary Art's 1939 publication and also in the Japonisme exhibition held at the Cleveland Museum of Art in 1975, in which paintings by Whistler, Pissarro, and van Gogh were shown alongside their inspirations—*ukiyo-e* prints by Hiroshige, Toyokuni, Utamaro, Hokusai, and others of the *Edo* period. Japonisme dramatically affected Western concepts of human beauty and adornment, as well as the fine arts, as indeed did the aesthetic styles of other cultures, such as those of Africa, Egypt, Oceania, and Mexico.

As for Japan itself, which had been forcibly opened up in 1854 by the American Matthew Perry and his gunboats, after two hundred years of self-imposed isolation, Western ideas were beginning to take root and soon began to affect many traditional aesthetic notions, including notions of human beauty. In other countries such as Australia, New Zealand, South Africa, and the United States, traditional cultural values were also changing. The traditionally accepted Western notions of human beauty, which had long been closely entwined with established religious beliefs, notions of social propriety and elitist modes of adornment, were becoming irrelevant to the late-nineteenth-century middle classes and their offspring, who, together with great numbers of working class people from all over Europe, were rapidly colonizing vast areas of the world that were climatically and socially quite different from Europe.

In order to survive in what were often wild and rough environments, women needed to be robust and open-minded—a stark contrast with the delicacy and comfort so characteristic of their predecessors' courtly, urbane existence. "Frontier women" needed to be adventurous, young in attitude, and less constrained in their social behavior. A change in diet and an emphasis on outdoor life also began to affect the physical and mental development of such women. The traditions of courtly or romantic love had little place in their lives: their physical needs were purely practical and they had little use for traditional styles of feminine coquetry.

Many of these women, by dint of hard work and an adventurous, risk-taking way of life, soon became wealthy. They began to travel to Europe to fulfill their fantasies of dressing in the alluring styles that they heard about or read in books and magazines. Due to a number of factors—a change of diet and lifestyle, a remixing of genes, etc.—these wealthy women were often taller and bigger boned than their British and European cousins, and because of their often humble background they generally lacked the small rib-cages and waists that were created by having to wear a tightly laced corset during early childhood, and the delicate hands and feet by which feminine beauty had traditionally been judged. And, although initially they dressed and adorned themselves in the current styles, they soon began to demand fashions that would enhance what they considered their more attractive features and would underplay their less attractive ones. These changing perceptions had begun to emerge as early as the 1850s, when individuals such as the eponymous Amelia Bloomer attempted to introduce an American notion of a "rational mode of dress," the effects of which were to display the wearer's legs and ankles in Turkish-style trousers under a shortened skirt. Naturally, this only took the observer's interest away from the wear-

er's traditional feminine display areas—her facial features, hair, and upper torso, and instead displayed the legs—a heinous sin in many European minds, for female legs reminded them of their sexual and hence animal origins. This style of dress was angrily attacked by most upper class European women as freakish and "unfeminine" and thus didn't last for long.

This American tendency to display the female legs, when it was the European fashion to hide the legs under a long and elaborate style of dress, became even more noticeable in the 1870s, after a number of newly established American fashion magazines such as *Harpers Bazar* (the second "a" in *Bazaar* was not added until the late 1920s) and *The Demorests Monthly* had drawn attention

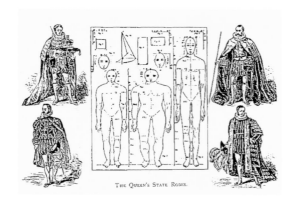

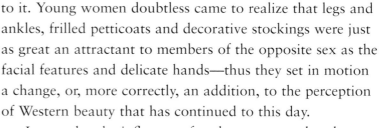

THE QUEEN'S STATE ROBES.

to it. Young women doubtless came to realize that legs and ankles, frilled petticoats and decorative stockings were just as great an attractant to members of the opposite sex as the facial features and delicate hands—thus they set in motion a change, or, more correctly, an addition, to the perception of Western beauty that has continued to this day.

It was also the influence of such women, and perhaps even more the influence of their children, that was responsible for the eventual acceptance of cosmetics, along with the change in emphasis from purely facial beauty to overall physical beauty, and to a large extent for the acceptance of adorning that physical beauty in decorative styles of lingerie. Due to inhibiting European laws, and all sorts of social condemnation enacted to prevent such a dramatic change, it has taken over a hundred years to gain social and cultural acceptance for these types of beautification. And it was probably the wealthy American daughters who engendered the American obsession with youth as an essential element of feminine beauty—it was necessary during this time of national geographic expansion for wives to be as young and healthy as possible in order to survive the rigors of the wild.

Changes in lifestyle and the distribution of wealth and political power throughout Europe had helped to make these new ways more acceptable to most people, although many of those in authority avidly fought such changes. Before the Industrial Revolution, for instance, those of inherited wealth and privilege had sought to distinguish themselves from the working class and the *nouveau riches* not only by their mode of dress and adornments but also by the paleness of their skin. During the nineteenth century, however, vast numbers of weather-beaten, sun-tanned farm workers had left the fields to work in the factories of the cities, so that by the end of the nineteenth century to have pale skin was no longer perceived as an exclusive sign of noble birth or inherited wealth. Thus arose the fashion for participating in outdoor sports and even naked sunbathing—a trend that became increasingly important during the next hundred or so years. Also of importance was the trend for world travel: from the 1860s travelers of both sexes often journeyed huge distances, first by train and later in the new steel-hulled steamships. The consequence was that increasing numbers of influential people were able to see for themselves the marvelous range of sartorial and beauty possibilities the world had to offer.

Travel books were also becoming popular, and many displayed the more unusual modes of dress and body adornments of remote cultures, while books on various aspects of human psychology were beginning to create interest in our own cultural ways, such as Richard von Krafft-Ebing's *Psychopathia Sexualis* (1886) and *Psychologie Comparée de L'Homme et de la Femme* (1898) by Madame Céline Renooz, who astutely observed "In the actual life of a young girl today, there is a moment when by a secret atavism, she feels the pride of her sex, the intuition of her moral superiority, and cannot understand why she must hide its cause. At that moment, wavering between the laws of Nature and Social conventions, she scarcely knows if nakedness should, or should not affright her. A sort of confused atavistic memory recalls to her a period before clothing was known, and reveals to her as a paradisiacal ideal the customs of that human epoch"—a belief put into action by the young American dancer Loie Fuller, and a little later by another American dancer and teacher, Isadora Duncan, who made fashionable that which had been celebrated by many can-can and music hall dancers on both sides of the Atlantic since the mid-1850s—i.e. glorifying and thus further championing the cause for the natural feminine beauty ideal. They felt themselves free to be able to publicly display the charm of their natural bodies, including their pubic hair, if they so wished, which despite our so-called "individual freedom" is still much frowned upon by those in authority.

It is not generally realized that much of the appeal of the early can-can dancers, such as the famous French dancer Nini, was not because of their facial beauty or dancing expertise, but was because they wore open-legged underpants (or *drawers*) under their frilly petticoats, or in some cases, no underpants at all, as was the common custom at the time, with Nini (or *Nini-les-belle-cuisse* as she was known at the time) happily displaying this custom by finishing her act standing upside down on her hands. Loie Fuller and Isadora Duncan also discarded their underclothing whilst dancing, including the then *de-rigueur* laced-up whalebone corset, and glorified in the scandle of wearing little more than a single layer of diaphanous material when performing. Perversely, however they also glorified in the scandle of wearing the new forms of decorative lingerie and other fashionable innovations for more normal social occasions, thus helping to set in motion a pattern of change which was destined to transform our twentieth century perception of femine beauty.

The new photo-mechanical printing techniques that were being introduced to the Western world made unusual imagery and illustrations of new fashionable products more readily available to a far larger public than ever before. The sewing machine and methods of mass production were

making the new styles cheaper. The number of couture houses had increased dramatically since the 1860s, when Charles Worth introduced the concept of seasonal fashion shows to cater to the needs of his *nouveau riche* and overseas clientele—these seasonally changing collections were also to contribute to the changing concepts of fashionable dress and feminine beauty, even for the most elite members of society. Additionally, in the design of items for everyday use, the various British arts and crafts movements, under the influence of William Morris, Walter Crane, Christopher Dresser, and others, were helping to change people's concepts of what was desirable in manufactured products.

By the end of the century, millions of people were emigrating from Europe and the British Isles to the United States, Australia, South Africa, and New Zealand, in search of a fortune or simply a more comfortable way of life. Missionaries everywhere appear to have continued their xenophobic crusade of destroying indigenous cultures and unique forms of body decoration and modes of adornment. Vast quantities of merchandise were flooding into Europe from the East, which sparked enthusiasm for the new oriental-inspired *Art Nouveau* style of design. Electric light had been introduced in many cities. Road transportation was beginning to improve, with the motor car slowly taking over from the horse and buggy. Outdoor sport and physical exercise were growing in popularity. Education was on the increase. The birth rate was up and cities everywhere were expanding. Experiments were under way for flying machines, record players, wireless transmission, and for projecting moving pictures onto a large screen (the Kinetoscope arcades had already proved the viability of this kind of mass entertainment). Nude photography had become big business and everywhere there was political unrest. Life would never be the same again.

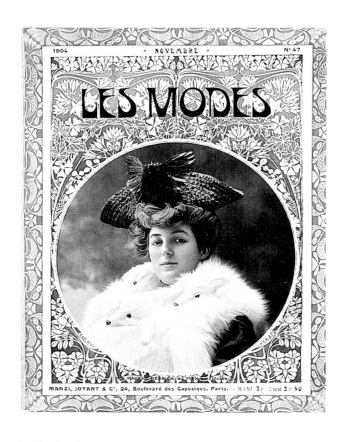

THE REASONS FOR CHANGE

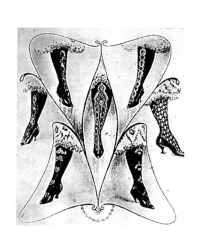

At the end of the 1890s, a number of events took place in Europe and North America that would profoundly affect the way people were to see themselves and others in the twentieth century, and particularly the way they perceived human beauty.

The first of these events took place in the Koster & Bial's Music Hall in New York City, in mid-April 1896: The *New York Times* reported that an Edison "moving picture" had been publicly displayed for the first time, featuring two burlesque performers doing an umbrella dance. A much improved concert hall version of Edison's "phonograph" had also been featured at about the same time. In Paris the experimental Lumière and Méliès moving pictures were also being shown to great acclaim, and Méliès was soon researching ways of hand-coloring his films, frame by frame, and projecting them with synchronized sound recorded on flat discs—the first "talkies".

Experiments were also underway for perfecting color photography, which was being used for the production of color slides for projection onto a screen and for viewing in three dimensions through a handheld

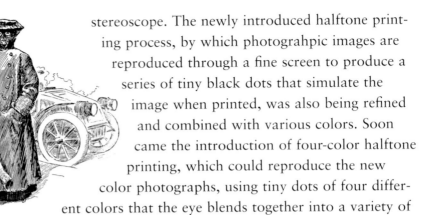

stereoscope. The newly introduced halftone printing process, by which photograhpic images are reproduced through a fine screen to produce a series of tiny black dots that simulate the image when printed, was also being refined and combined with various colors. Soon came the introduction of four-color halftone printing, which could reproduce the new color photographs, using tiny dots of four different colors that the eye blends together into a variety of hues when looking at the printed image. This method of color printing is still in use today.

Eighteen-ninety-six was also the year in which Marconi first demonstrated his invention for sending sounds over long distances by what became known as wireless transmission. A very significant advance over the wired telephone system, Marconi's method was initially employed for intercity and intercontinental telegraphy, but it soon came into use for radio broadcasting. In the following ten years, a number of other momentous events also took place. The first Zeppelin airship was flown in Germany in 1898, and just five years later the Wright brothers successfully launched their first airplane. The Secessionists held their first meeting in 1897 in Vienna, and in 1899 the first International Women's Congress was held in London: the consequent development and promotion of the suffragette movement, a new female aesthetic, and a new morality was to have dramatic political repercussions. And in the following year the *Exposition Universelle* opened in Paris.

This great international exhibition had been arranged as a celebration of the beginning of a new century, to demonstrate to the industrial world French preeminence in all matters pertaining to the decorative arts and the world of fashion and feminine beauty. It opened to great critical acclaim and with worldwide publicity, and almost fifty million visitors passed through the turnstiles between April and September. One of the most successful international exhibitions ever held, its influence was pro-

found. In addition to the display of French artifacts, there were exhibitions of Japanese *ukiyo-e* prints, African sculptures, Impressionist paintings, oriental ceramics, furniture in the *Jugendstil, Sezessionsstile, Baudwurmstil, Stile floreale,* and the *Art Nouveau* style, and fine examples of the English Arts and Crafts movement. Works from the Glasgow School, under the direction of Charles Rennie Mackintosh, and other new styles of design and aesthetic expression were also being shown at smaller independent exhibitions dotted around the center of Paris and in the other great cities of Europe.

The *Exposition* had been built in the very center of Paris, the main entrance facing Alexandre Eiffel's great steel tower, originally constructed as the centerpiece for the earlier 1889 *Exposition,* which had heralded the beginning of the *Belle Epoque* and the closely associated ornate *fin de siècle* style of design. The new exhibition covered a huge area from the specially constructed Pont Alexandre III to the Pont d'Iena. The pavilions and galleries, linked by esplanades, displayed the work of some 75,000 exhibitors, as well as that of many internationally acclaimed artists such as Watteau, Corot, Renoir, Gainsborough, Degas, Whistler, Turner, and Delacroix, and many others of American, African, Asian, Oceanic, and Middle Eastern origin. The prestigious *British Art Journal*—not renowned for its love of the French decorative arts—declared that the new designs in the French *Art Nouveau* style "had reached a new high-water mark of originality and excellence" and added, "Art-loving people from throughout the world found in the Paris Exhibition a collection of works such as has rarely, if ever, been brought together in the history of the human race."

While in Paris many of the tens of thousands of visitors from abroad visited the famous *ateliers* of Gallé, Lalique, Grasset, de Feure, Gaillard, and Majorelle Freres, the small exhibitions of works by Henry van de Velde, Alphonse Mucha, the American Louis Comfort Tiffany, and the *Maison de l'Art Nouveau Bing.* This maison was the originator of the *Art Nouveau* design style, which with its distinctive use of free-flowing curves, irregular and often asymmetrical shapes and clear pastel colors, had supplanted the ornateness of Victorian design and the cloying *fin de*

siècle style with its jumble of over-ornate detailing and guady color.

Many also visited the grands couturiers—Cheruit, Doucet, Doeuillet, Callot Soeurs, Laferrieres, Redfern, Worth, and Paquin. Here they could choose simple or ornate peignoirs, at-home dresses or more elaborate dresses for morning visits. Outfits suitable for luncheon, afternoon walks, and receiving visitors. There were dresses for a visit to a theatre, restaurant, or cabaret, the races, holidays at the seaside or in the mountains, weddings, christenings, and funerals. There were also more sumptuous modes for special occasions: official ceremonies, family gatherings, motoring excursions, sermons and lectures, exhibitions, receptions, first nights, dinner parties, concerts, the opera, or grand balls. Since nothing could be left to chance, the *haut monde* also visited milliners, furriers, jewellers, shoemakers, the corsettier, and exclusive shops that specialized in gloves and leather accessories, ruffled petticoats, lingerie, and the finest and most ornate silk stockings and decorative garters.

Many of the international visitors entertained themselves in the evenings at the Moulin Rouge and other theatrical events for which Paris had become famous, among them performances by Loie Fuller, the Gibson Girls (the invention of the American fashion illustrator Charles Dana Gibson, who had used his heiress wife Camille Clifford as his original inspiration), and even Zulu warriors. In these spectacles semi-nude male and female dancers performed acts that combined enough erotic symbolism—including rape, masochism, sadism, and bestiality—to give even the most jaded member of the audience some form of satisfaction. Many also visited the specialty houses of Montmartre, where the madams offered every conceivable variety of sexual delight for their male and female customers. Not since the days before the fall of the Roman Empire had such a variety of carnal pleasures been so openly offered to the general public.

This was also the era of the *demi-mondaines*—or *grande horizontals* as they were often called—who were considered the elite of this most ancient of professions. They had risen to prominence in the court of Napoleon III and the Empress Eugénie, although it could be claimed that they were the direct descendants of the courtesans of the mid-eighteenth century who had been so delightfully painted by Boucher and Fragonard. The *demi-mondaines* exerted their influence not over the Court of Versailles but over industrial barons, international bankers, and millionaires, who openly competed for their favors. The most famous of these *demi-mondaines*—Cora Pearl, La Belle Otero, and Mlle. Lantêlme—aroused great interest among the general public, who avidly followed their amours and copied their fashionable styles. They engendered the same interest and admiration afforded many film stars during Hollywood's Golden Age and television soap operas of the 1980s. The famous couture houses often dressed these "stars" at little or no cost, in hopes that the couturiers established clientele, who envied these professional beauties and were always wanting to be *à la mode,* would pur-

chase similar styles. All of this started the laborious process of broadening our Western ideas and ideals and loosening our ancestors' uptight Victorian morality—allowing the average person at least a small glimpse of the possible.

At the beginning of 1901 the first of the large-format glossy magazines featuring color photographs was published in Paris for worldwide distribution: *Les Modes.* The magazine featured the latest fashionable styles: for the first time international readers

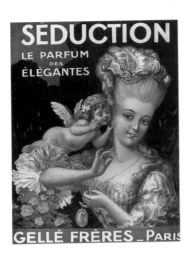

were able to see and covet, in their own homes, the changing array of fashionable furnishings, clothing, adornments, accessories, and beauty aids that was available. For the previous two hundred and fifty or so years such styles had been promoted by magazines featuring hand-colored engraved copies of artists' illustrations. In the process, the illustrators and engravers often elaborated, making their images much more ornate than the real thing. As a consequence, nineteenth-century fashions became reflections of the illustrators' and engravers' desire to embellish, and they openly competed with one another to see whose work was most appealing for its own sake, not for the sake of the fashions themselves. As the famous nineteenth-century art critic John Ruskin commented on the fashionable engravers' skill, "The object of the engraver is, or ought to be, to endow the surface of the engraved metal plate with lovely lines, forming an interesting pattern and including a variety of spaces delicious to the eye," which unfortunately was often taken to extremes for the glory of the engravers' skill rather than that of the fashion being illustrated.

With the publication of *Les Modes* these illustrative skills became outdated. More and more magazines were captivated by the photographic images of the Reutlinger, Nadar, Boyer, Felix, and Talbot studios, and then by the Seebergers, Steichen, and Baron de Meyer, who with their technique of soft focus and back lighting not only changed how people perceived themselves and others, but also changed them physically and mentally. This opened the way for a revolution in human beauty—a revolution that, by introducing new, identifiable icons, more accurately reflected the ideas, ideals, and "dreams" of the new century.

In this context it is important to understand the use of the term "dreams." Our perception of human beauty changes not only because artists', designers', and photographers' ideas and techniques change but also because society itself changes, and along with this people's own hopes, aspirations, ambitions, and "dreams" change. Such

changes are in fact the most visually conspicuous of the mechanisms by which we all hope to alter ourselves and our way of life. We seem to believe instinctively that by creating a new kind of environment, by wearing different clothes, and by accepting a new icon that we can all relate to, and do our best to imitate or desire, we will become different people, closer to the ideal we have formulated for ourselves in our dreams. Each attempted transformation seems to be at least partly successful—social commentators and many art historians have noted with interest how our bodies actually seem to change in response to the changing times, which of course embody our newest "dreams." This desire to transmutate from one set of dreams to another, using our clothing, adornments, style of hairdressing, cosmetics, etc., as an aid, could well be the reason why so many paintings of the great beauties of the past, though nude, often seem almost to be wearing the essential essence of the latest fashions. So complete was the desire for the "look" of the newest style that the painters willingly accentuated the symbols of the prevailing mode —the cut and shape of the newest fashions, and how they shaped the body and changed various physical characteristics so that the subject's body seemed to emulate the fashionable style of the day. In many ways, these paintings are the visual manifestaion of what people call *Zeitgeist* (spirit of the time or thought and feeling of the period). The *Zeitgeist* is also noticeable in many other aspects of the arts, of course, as indeed is our cultural attitude toward

Geisteswissenschaft (spiritual and intuitive knowledge), *Naturwissenschaft* (natural or scientific knowledge) and *Gesamtkunstwerk* (a sort of all-inclusive form of total art work), which I will refer to later.

The camera and its magic images had already been instrumental in creating a new aesthetic vision through the work of the Impressionist and Post-Impressionist painters. Artists such as Toulouse-Lautrec, Seurat, Cezanne, Manet, and Renoir are known to have used the new photographic images in their work,

just as many painters of the mid-eighteenth century had enlisted the aid of the *camera obscura* and the silhouette frame to help them in their more formalized works. Many Impressionist and Post-Impressionist painters also worked from there own collections of Japanese *ukiyo-e* prints of the Edo period, reinterpreting the prints into the European idiom, juxtaposing European features and symbols with Japanese ideas of space, color, and form. Between 1900 and 1920 other artists experimented with ancient works: Derain owned and worked from fine examples of early Fayum burial paintings; Klee worked from Hellenic and Roman mosaics; Matisse, Picasso, and others based some of their work on early Greek originals; Rouault made use of early-Christian textile designs and examples of medieval stained glass windows; Klimt combined the influences of Japanese kimono stenciling with Byzantine mosaic murals; Braque was influenced by examples of medieval and Renaissance paintings and by Coptic woven patterns; other members of the Fauvist movement drew their inspiration from similar aesthetic influences. Later still, following the lead set by Gauguin, members of a variety of art movements—Modigliani, Ernest, Moore, for example— often relied directly on a variety of other sources, such as their collections of African and New Guinean carvings and other so-called "primitive" works to create their own interpretations of mixed cultural beauty, interestingly and succinctly demonstrated by the landmark exhibition, *Primitivism in 20th-Century Art,* held at New York's Museum of Modern Art in 1984.

The beginning of this mixed cultural change, which was to have such a profound effect on Western concepts of human beauty had already begun to take shape in the first few years of the new century. Mixed bathing for instance was allowed at some holiday resorts. Bathing costumes as well as fashionable styles of clothing were beginning to get scantier and nude sunbathing had become fashionable in

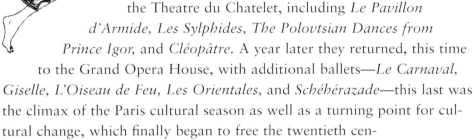

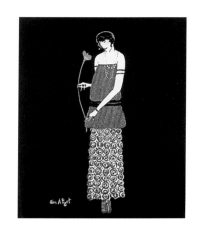

some European countries as had the reading of risqué novels. And in 1909, the Russian impresario Sergei Diaghilev arrived in Paris with his newly formed company, the *Ballets Russes*, comprising dancers, choreographers, musicians, and designers from the imperial dance companies of St. Petersburg and Moscow, among them dancers Anna Pavlova, Ida Rubinstein, Vaslav Nijinsky, Michel Fokine, Tamara Karsavina, and Léonide Massine and designers Alexandre Benois, Léon Bakst, and Korovine. During their first season they performed a selection of new ballets at the Theatre du Chatelet, including *Le Pavillon d'Armide, Les Sylphides, The Polovtsian Dances from Prince Igor,* and *Cléopâtre.* A year later they returned, this time to the Grand Opera House, with additional ballets—*Le Carnaval, Giselle, L'Oiseau de Feu, Les Orientales,* and *Schéhérazade*—this last was the climax of the Paris cultural season as well as a turning point for cultural change, which finally began to free the twentieth century from the weight of the outdated middle-class ethics that had lingered from the previous century.

Schéhérazade, with its sumptuous decor, brilliant Persian-inspired costumes, sensual dancing, and display of nudity, was based on a story of lust and intrigue, and it acted as a catalyst in popularizing the new mood of the time among the *haut monde*. Although the production was condemned as barbaric, vulgar, and licentious, a great many artists and intellectuals saw in this vulgarity and barbarism a means of freeing themselves from an inhibited past. The depth of social repression made this cultural rebellion all the more electrifying as the Western world was swept along in the euphoria of change. Many of the more sedate members of society were horrified to see "respectable" women paint their faces, in the mode of the *demi-mondaines* and Diaghilev's dancers, and throw off

their corsets and layers of plain linen petticoats so that they too could wear the new tantalizing lingerie and figure-revealing dresses. Even more horrifying was the fact that many of these women were demanding the right to vote, to drive a car, to smoke and drink in public, to dance the forbidden tango, to participate in active sports wearing apparel that revealed their legs, and even to don a skimpy bathing costume and mix with unmarried men on the beach.

Many other aspects of Western life were changing, too. The film industry had grown rapidly and by 1912 had a regular weekly audience of many millions. The films seemed to have the power to change people's ideas, ideals, and dreams overnight, especially in relation to their clothes, choice of adornment, and styles of beauty. Cars were becoming larger, faster, more reliable, and more numerous. Airplanes could fly great distances, linking major cities in a matter of hours. Ships were becoming larger and more comfortable, enabling more people to travel abroad, and trains were able to transport people and large quantities of saleable merchandise over the vastness of Europe, Russia, India, parts of Africa, Canada, and much of the United States. The electric light was now in common use, while the sewing machine, with its improved electric motor, enabled the new simpler fashions to be mass-produced for the growing population. This was a great boon, particularly in the United States, where the population was increasing by over a million immigrants each year, and people naturally wanted to dress in the style of their new country.

Toward the end of 1910, several new fashionable styles of design had begun to emerge that would soon outdate the flowing curves and pastel hues of the *Art Nouveau* style—a style originally based on the ideals of aesthetic functionalism voiced by Rousseau in the mid-eighteenth century, but which had become lost under the weight of applied decoration. One of these new styles was established in Vienna, under the direction of the *Wiener Werkstätte*. Its protagonists—Gustav Klimt, Adolf Loos, and Josef Hoffmann, among others—aimed to evoke the spirit of the Secessionists, combined with the *Gesamtkunstwerk* philosophy, to create a theory of design as a form of total artwork, somewhat in the style of the earlier British Aesthetic, and Arts and Crafts Movement. The French

protagonists of the new style, which is now referred to under the general title of Art Deco, also drew on the theories of Adam Smith, Henry Home, Christopher Dresser, and William Morris, who had proposed that "utility is one of the principal sources of beauty." This proposition had inspired both the earlier British and Austrian design movements, as well as the theories of the American Thorstein Veblen, who had written so scathingly of

conspicuous consumption, pecuniary beauty, and the obscenity of waste by the wealthy elite during the latter half of the nineteenth century in his *Theory of the Leisure Class* (1899).

The unique style of this pre-1914 form of Art Deco was promoted by a number of colorfully illustrated limited edition magazines and by folders of design ideas that both reflected and influenced the changes then taking place. The illustrations were not straightforward line-by-line representations of actual designs; instead, each illustration was an interpretation of a design, an attempt to capture the spirit of the Art Deco style rather than merely the surface detailing. The illustrators also added their own idiosyncratic touches, drawing on the myriad images from all over the world that could be seen in the museums, galleries, and bookshops of Paris.

The very best of the new Art Deco illustrations were the work of such artists as Bakst, van Dongen, Picasso, Iribe, Barbier, Erté, Lepape, Leon Carré, and Martin. They were printed by the expensive *pochoir* method of hand-coloring over an engraving, lithograph, or woodcut background. By means of very accurately incised stencils, the skilled *pochoirist* could reproduce the exact color, texture, and nuance of the artist's original painting, whether fifty or five hundred copies were being made. Each *pochoir* illustration, with its pigment adroitly applied during thirty or more different coloring processes, was an artistic revelation, not only delighting the *haut monde* but also helping to revitalize the art of book illustration, which since the turn of the century had been

suffered from an obsession with cost-efficient photomechanical printing techniques.

The *pochoir* printing technique was not new—it had been used in Europe and North America for several centuries to decorate walls and furniture, to color tarot cards, and to print broadsheets. What was new was the skill of the *pochoir* stencil maker—Jean Saudé was perhaps the most famous—who blended the ancient Japanese art of fabric stenciling with new cutting and coloring techniques originally developed for printing the luxurious *Art Nouveau* design folders of Grasset, E. A. Seguy, M. P. Verneuil, and Alphonse Mucha. (Many examples of *pochoir* prints and the aesthetics of the period itself are included in my book *The Brilliance of Art Deco*, revised edition, 1996.)

However, the outbreak of World War I put an end to all further experimentation in the Art Deco style. The next four years and three months of conflict, deprivation, and carnage changed almost every aspect of the Western way of life for all levels of society—the way people thought, the way they looked, the way they lived, and their vision of the future. The change was especially profound for the younger generation. It was they who were most involved in the mechanics of war, and it would be they who, after the fighting was over and the peace treaty signed, were going to create a new world, one worth living in, and one worthy of their "dreams."

By the beginning of the 1920s, young women, liberated from work on farms or in hospitals or munitions factories, or from driving ambulances at the front, were painting their faces, raising their skirts, and cutting their hair so as to look glamorous, like their favorite movie stars. The young men who were left, freed at last from the bloody conflict that had claimed so many of their lives, seemed to kick up their heels. Together these young men and women began to dance to the new rhythms of jazz.

Attitudes toward sex and morality had already changed: It would have been foolish to expect that women, having filled men's jobs and often shared much of their danger, should be denied the right to change their lives as they wished. And, although to some degree this desire for change was mollified by the granting of the vote in some countries,

most younger women were much more interested in alleviating their social, sexual, and economic disadvantages. This, coupled with the fact that in both Europe and the United States there was a marked shortage of eligible young men, greatly affected women's dress styles as well as their moral and social behavior.

The young woman of the 1920s quickly learned that the more attractive she made herself, the better were her chances of promotion, the right marriage, or finding a paramour. And she learned from films and magazines that being attractive was something that could be worked at and upon which money and skill could be used. A young woman had no excuse for collapsing in despair because she lacked a good figure or a well-shaped face. Proper diet and exercise, she was told, would correct one, proper cosmetics and hair styling, the other.

The sunny, ordered world of sentimental romance novels was also being swept away, in its path marched a new morality preached by Cecil B. DeMille in sociosexual epics such as *Forbidden Fruit* and by Erich von Stroheim in *Foolish Wives*. In addition, photographs of glamorous, near-naked starlets at casting sessions were regularly published; almost weekly there were sex scandals and reports of licentiousness in the Hollywood "dream factory"; and provocative forms of lingerie were introduced, along with semitransparent dance dresses,

shorter skirts, and topless and even nude bathing on the Riviera. It was also voguish to read risqué novels, to talk more openly about sexual matters, and there was beginning to be an increased availability of various forms of birth control.

The new, overt sexual beauty was continually promoted through advertisements and specially written syndicated articles. Millions of readers were told that the newest cosmetic products "would do wonders for the skin," "reveal their own hidden beauty," and make them "interestingly different" and "avidly sought." This sexual,

glamorized beauty was further promoted by scantily clad movie stars, such as Joan Crawford in *Our Dancing Daughters*, Betty Blythe in *The Queen of Sheba*, Hope Hampton in *Does It Pay?*, Myrna Loy in *Why Girls Go Back Home*, Nazimova in *Salome*, Fay Wray in *The First Kiss*, Colleen Moore in *Flaming Youth*, Clara Bow in *The Plastic Age*, and Gloria Swanson in von Stroheim's *Queen Kelly*.

Actors such as Douglas Fairbanks, John Gilbert, Ronald Coleman, and the young Gary Cooper and Clark Gable were also helping to change the stereotyped dress styles and facial appearances of the men of the period. The great Rudolph Valentino added an exotic look that fired young women's loins with desire. Valentino's death in 1926, at the very height of his career, created a gap in male modes of beauty that has never really been filled. Before his death, however, young women saw in him a new kind of sex symbol, entrancing and titillating, and they wanted their boyfriends to emulate him. Young men on both sides of the Atlantic began to plaster their hair with pomade to obtain the glistening, sleek appearance that Valentino projected in his films. This was an era of escapism, and the movie theaters—or picture palaces, as they were called—swiftly developed as the most accessible and affordable temples of dreamland and escapism. There was an almost insatiable lust for glamor and romanticized adventure, and Valentino was the epitome of these fantasies as both villain and savior. When he died the world wept. A frenzied mob of nearly a quarter of a million fans lined ten city blocks in New York for the funeral procession. A legend was dead, but he would not be forgotten, as the regular placing of flowers on his grave for the next fifty years bore witness.

In general, however, most men of the 1920s were not expected to be exotic,

beautiful, or even handsome so long as they offered a safe and comfortable nest. In normal circumstances, when there is an ample supply of single males, most young women appear to admire a man's social superiority, which he demonstrates by body signals and his choice of dress, rather than what might be referred to as beauty. The advantage of social superiority is that it is a promise of the ability to support a family in comfort, even affluence, and because of this, many women see (subconsciously or not) social superiority as having aphrodisiac qualities.

In the realm of feminine beauty we accept that sexual desire in its most obvious visual form contributes to our notion of beauty—this is further reinforced by displays of wealth in the form of jewelry, embellishment of physical beauty by cosmetics, and attractive styles of dress. Why cannot we admit that a similar combination of factors are needed for what we call masculine beauty, beyond the shape of a man's buttocks, his crotch bulge and his more muscular, broader shoulders? Is it because such an admission of the need for beautification would dent the male ego? Surely all cultural intertwining in the realm of human beauty is beyond question, regardless of the egos involved. Acceptance of male beauty as a combination of factors certainly occurs in areas such as the highlands of New Guinea, where a man's beauty is acknowledged as being judged on the basis of his adorned entirety and the social messages that such modes convey. Similar forms of adornment also take place in the animal world: the males of some species of deer, for instance, adorn their antlers with moss and grasses to give a more impressive look to their silhouette and to convey the message that they are superior males and have possession of the best areas of forest or grazing land. And there are male birds that display an assortment of colorful items around the entrance to their nest, or in their display area, to attract females. The better their display, the more mates they attract. This is just one of Nature's many ploys, but one with which we can surely identify. In the mid-1920s,

though, no such theoretical musings influenced a young woman's choice of a mate. She made her choice from the best available and, in general, all she asked was that both she and her mate be well housed and appropriately attired at all times. This was the era in which, if you lived in a city or large town, to be incorrectly dressed according to the unwritten laws of society suggested a lack of sophistication, if not gentility, thus destroying one of the most important offerings a man could make his mate—elevated social position. This was why there was such a wide range of garments available at men's tailors and specialist shops during this period, particularly in the larger urban centers like Paris, London, or New York. Young women were advised that, regardless of any personal charm or handsomeness, the man in their lives should always be dressed as well as his finances would allow: "if he dresses less well he is unpardonable negligent. And if he is negligent at twenty-five he would be an uncontrollable sloven by the age of thirty."

The variety of fashionable entertainment, including films, cabarets, the *Folies Bergeres*, the *Ziegfeld Follies*, and the revues at the *Casino de Paris*, as well as the exotic images contained in numerous publications began to fuel the desire for different ethnic forms of physical beauty, as symbolized by the success of the American entertainer Josephine Baker. From the mid-1920s to the end of the 1930s she was famous not only for her sensuous dancing and singing, but also for the coloring of her skin, her lithe form, and her vibrant sexual beauty.

The notion that peoples from other parts of the world, or from different racial groups, are, in certain respects, more beautiful, or at least alluring and exotic, has a long history and has contributed significantly to the development of Western aesthetics, particular during the 1920s and 1930s and again in the mid-to-late 1980s. In the 1920s and 1930s

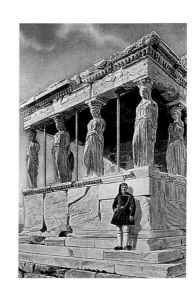

what is now referred to as "modern primitivism" was dramatically influencing the avant garde artists, who had left their home countries to work in the creative ferment of Paris. As an aesthetic influence, primitivism is now regarded as of major importance in the development of modern forms of aesthetic expression, and one that has certainly changed our current notions of human beauty with some very interesting recent developments.

For most people, however, beauty, glamor, and sexual yearning were much more personal, and they dreamt of being swept away by Valentino, or later by Charles Boyer, to experience an exotic, or even erotic, night of passion, or of being able to marry someone who in their imagination resembled Merle Oberon, Dolores Del Rio, Pola Negri, Anna May Wong, Alla Nazimova, Greta Garbo, or Hedy Lamarr. The average person's imagination was also fuelled by such books as *Peoples of All Nations* and *Women of the World* and the more specialized photographic epics like the German *Der dunkle Erdteil: Afrika*, which featured an assortment of colorful beauties of both sexes resplendent in their feathers and paint, and not fearful of showing their natural figure shapes or sexual differences. It was books such as this, and others by the great illustrators of the period, such as François-Louis Schmied, Georges Lepape, Charles Martin, and George Barbier, and the erotic images of Jean Dulac, that aroused my

interest in the ways that the varying cultural groups of the world create their own distinctive modes of beauty and sex appeal. I realized that the methods used in our Western society—such as cosmetic surgery, which the advertisements of the time were claiming could change a plain Amy Bloggs into a ravishing beauty, and which in the 1930s had been successfully employed to improve Johnny Weissmuller's profile, remodel George Raft's ears, and add inches to the bustline of numerous Hollywood actresses, and the use of electrolysis, which had changed Rita Hayworth's hairline—were only marginally different from the practices of head binding or scarring used in other societies.

During the bleak years of the 1930s Depression and World War II, it was still mainly the Hollywood star system that continued to supply glamorous idols for people to admire and envy. Hollywood also supplied audiences with a neverending array of attire, jewelry, furs, and accessories with which to embellish their dreams, with designers such as Adrian, Walter Plunket, Travis Banton, Howard Green, Bernard Newman, Charles Le Maire, and the Australian Orry-Kelly rivaling even the great Paris couturiers.

The journalists whose job it was to provide a steady stream of beauty articles and

snippets of Hollywood gossip for publication in such prestigious magazines as *Vogue, Harper's Bazaar*, and *Le Jardin des Modes* as well as the popular press, realized that it took an array of specialists—photographers, lighting experts, hairdressers, costumiers, makeup artists, and retouchers—to produce a "glamor photo" for use in a magazine or newspaper. The average reader, however, oblivious of this, would always want to emulate their idols in some easy-to-copy way, so journalists often concentrated their efforts on a single feature or collection of features that had helped to make certain stars famous. The plucked eyebrows of Dietrich are an example, as was Crawford's mouth, Harlow's platinum hair, Colman's moustache, Gable's smile, Garbo's flawless skin and, a little later, Betty Grable's legs and Jane Russell's breasts. The journalists also wrote of "beauty tricks" and "dress secrets" and promoted the use of "add-ons" such as false fingernails, fake eyelashes, stick-on nipples, and derrière padding. They described "makeovers," explaining how any young woman, short or tall, thin or fat, blonde or brunette, broad-shouldered,

small-breasted, pear-shaped, with kinky, curly, or straight hair, blue, brown or green eyes, could be transformed through the skilled use of cosmetics, hair coloring, styling, and a special selection of clothing, into a beautiful, desirable, and highly successful individual, who would be avidly sought by members of the opposite sex, as well as being the envy of her peers.

The majority of these articles relied on the skilful use of newly developed techniques

of fashion photography. Successful photographers of the caliber of Baron Adolphe de Meyer, Edward Steichen, and Man Ray had invented their own ways of creating very influential images, and had been instrumental in changing the direction of fashion and beauty promotion from the rather stereotyped format used in many earlier magazines. By 1925 they had created a genre of imagery that not only promoted but also influenced the changes that were taking place in the world of fashion and adornment, creating images of human beauty that continually fuelled the dreams of readers and viewers.

Their success was due primarily to the believability of the images reproduced by the newly improved mechanical methods of printing. With the skills they had acquired during their years of experimentation, and their complete mastery of the mechanics of the camera, lighting, and retouching, de Meyer, Steichen, and others had developed individual ways of stylizing the face and figure of photographic models or movie actresses. By emphasizing just one aspect or feature, and with the adroit use of lighting and precise editing techniques, they were able to create a totally unreal yet completely believable image that had the power to persuade as never before.

A number of commentators have recognized this power of persuasion,

TATTOO

and have referred to the camera as being a "mechanical engine used both to create and then to impose particular styles of beauty and glamor." The use of the word "impose," rather than "promote," is noteworthy: it is commonly believed that once a new style of beauty, glamor, or fashion becomes widely reported it tends to be selected by its devotees, but in reality it now appears from recent research that such selection is imposed by weight of such publicity, and by peer group pressure. In this respect, glamor is a form of imposed beauty substitute that relies on artifice and reproducibility to create an idealized look that is exaggerated by the photographic image. In general, such idealized looks are based around one or more distinctive features that, when skillfully promoted, fulfill spectators' expectations of beauty—the eyes and eyebrows in one image, hair or lips in the next, then a display of firm breasts or shapely ankles. The mode of beauty is localized and reproducible but, more importantly, it can be purchased. The bleach used for Jean Harlow's platinum hair, the lipstick used by Joan Crawford, Garbo's face creams and powder, and Dietrich's eyebrow liner—millions of Western women scurried to their local drugstores for these products in the expectation that they too would become as glamorous as their idols.

This reproducibility of glamor was, and still is, dependent upon our acceptance of concepts of machine-made beautification, its purchasability, and our willingness to conform to the current standards. It is in this area of willingness to conform that the idea of imposition rather than selection can be more clearly seen: all forms of conformity, even conformity with change, are, I believe, imposed on individuals by the sheer weight of publicity and public opinion. Una Stannard takes up this argument in *The Mask of Beauty* (1972) when discussing the growing acceptance of female nudity in the West, which she says did not signify women's sexual liberation, only their willingness to conform to the culturally accepted standards of the day. *In Ways of Seeing* (1972) John Berger discusses a similar relationship between glamor and conformity, which he says is achieved by the promotion experts first building up a scenario of envy, making the spectator envious of how the photographic model looks when wearing the glamor products being advertised. Spectators are meant to imagine themselves transformed by these products into objects of envy for others. It is the envy of others that is being purchased, not the product itself. The promotion executives are selling ideas of envy and dreams of future happiness—happiness as judged from the outside by others. This envy and dreaming creates a form of conformity, and it is this conformity that has become such an important factor in the marketing of glamor and fashion, satisfying our need for change, variety, and novelty but at the same time allowing our need to conform to be fully expressed. In other words, what we have in our culture is an orchestrated system of fashionable changes, changes that help fuel our industrial way of life and give handsome profits to the manufacturers and publicity agents. It should be noted that the actual cost of many of these beauty and

glamour products is made-up in large part by the cost of their marketing publicity, and not the actual cost of the raw materials and their manufacture.

The conflict between our inventive nature, our interest in novelty, our inner need for recognizable symbols of conformity, and our industrial way of life is continually being fuelled by the mass media. The vogue for thinness is just one of many recent examples, created and then perpetuated by a campaign aimed at selling a wide variety of products and publications, regardless of any real benefit to the purchaser. In the fantasy world created by this media hype, being slim was identified with love, wealth, success, happiness, sexuality, and fulfillment. Those of us who live in the real world are well aware that being slim is only one of a wide range of figure options that have been regarded as beautiful over the centuries. Slimness is, however, an obsession with us, one that clearly distinguishes us from those who lived in the mid-to-late nineteenth century. It reminds us of the shift from the enviable and well-fed *demi-mondaines* to the hyperactive Hollywood stars of the 1920s, 1930s, and 1940s who so greatly influenced our current way of life and notions of beauty. Slimness symbolizes the change from monied experience and overindulgence to a less refined, more obvious and more easily copied, although not always more easily achieved, notion of beauty. Nevertheless, it has become a sign of Western egalitarianism and freedom (although in truth it is not truly egalitarian as it has its own built-in notions of privilege and affluence—having the leisure to excercise and the income to eat healthfully or purchase surgical body-sculpting—which add considerably to its overall allure). Slimness is also a good example of what Elizabeth B. Hurlock meant when she wrote in 1929 that ridicule and scorn were the sanctions that force people to follow such fashions and the dissenters are powerless before them. Anyone today who is a little overweight can certainly relate to such sanctions.

Hollywood stars are living proof of the popular American belief in equality of opportunity and an equal right to make the best of oneself,

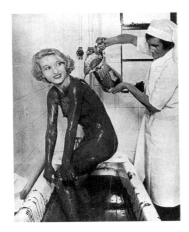

although I must add that the odds were very heavily weighted against an aspirants eventual success, especially in the areas of show-biz. But in regard to feminine beauty, many commentators have rightly observed, including Margaret Mead in *Male and Female* (1949), that in this century in America almost every woman has been able to aspire to both beauty and fashion: "The belief that any woman can succeed in making herself beautiful and charming gives every American girl, even the poorest and least schooled, the most graceless and lonely, the hope that she may get to the ball and win Prince Charming"—or meet a Hollywood film director.

Other commentators believe that this freedom allowed or persuaded many American women to look like prostitutes, postulating that the young American urban female is an open-minded exhibitionist who looks like a cheap hooker. The reason for this they say is that she has been reared in a society where it is acceptable for all females from 5 years to 75 years old to wear makeup, high-heeled shoes, to show lots of leg and cleavage, and to be unashamed of flaunting her body. Thus given the right circumstance most American women are willing to strip off their clothing if there is some advantage in doing so: and although many English and European women are willing to follow suit when the moment is right, their more pronounced cultural hesitancy often creates a barrier and an unease, an unease which I perceive as having distinct biological and cultural overtones. The English author and broadcaster Malcolm Muggeridge commented in the mid-1970s, "How American women mortify the flesh in order to make it appetising. Their beauty is a vast industry, their enduring allure a discipline which many find excessive beyond endurance," while the Tasmanian-born anthropologist Robert Brain commented to me in 1980, that "the beauty culture in the United States is all pervasive and has virtually replaced all forms of for-malised religion"—as indeed had happened in the Court of Versailles in the late eighteenth century— a phenomena noted by Margaret Mead when she said "this is something that often happens in affluent societies as one way of using leisure." With

this use of leisure time, particularly in the more fashionable areas of the United States, becoming all-consuming, with vast amounts of money being spent on all the beauty aids available including the current art of body customization (cosmetic surgery) with the quest for the accepted symbols of feminine beauty becoming an essential part of the economy.

But returning to my earlier observation that Hollywood stars projected the American ideal and belief in equal opportunity, there are European precedents. During the post Revolutionary period in France Mme. Récamier showed just how far an attractive woman could go in an egalitarian society if she was not afraid of flaunting her most precious asset—her natural beauty. The young courtesans of the court of Versailles, so beautifully depicted by Watteau, Boucher, and Fragonard, also bear witness to this fact, as do the great *demi-mondaines* of the late nineteenth century. Hollywood's Goldwyn Girls and Busby Berkeley's chorus line followed this tradition. These free-spirited, scantily clad young dancers, were willing to kick their legs up high and were not ashamed to show just as much of their bodies as did Madame Récamier, and along with other actors, actresses, and dancers, created a revolution in modes of beauty and adornment and in our subsequent modes of perception.

The influence of these Hollywood stars and their directors was just as great as that of the automobile, which in its day aroused more anger and condemnation than any other innovation: It allowed freedom from social control and stultifying moral ethics and was thus seen as an invitation to fornication and licentiousness. But then, we must remember that these critics of the motor car and film actresses had also condemned the introduction of jazz music, sports on Sundays, radio and television, the tango and the Charleston, air travel, Diaghilev and the *Ballets Russes,* and a number of other events and advances that have greatly affected our lives and that we now take for granted, including nudity and risqué modes of beauty.

Throughout the 1920s and into the 1930s and 1940s such films as *The Women, The Outlaw, Moon Over Miami, The Gang's All*

Here, and *Bathing Beauty* were feeding their audiences' expectations and dreams with a cornucopia of novelties, which, although often trivial in themselves, nevertheless symbolized freedom, power, beauty, luxury, adventure—all those values loosely associated with the word "modern." These films, together with the magazines and newspapers of the period, created many of our most enduring beauty symbols. Slimness was one, our modern concepts of glamor another, and our current acceptance of nudity yet another: Many stars of the late 1920s and early 1930s had been more than willing to reveal their more intimate physical charms for magazine publication. Numerous stories were also published about their hectic sex lives, which readers were told had become an essential part of their beauty routine, that helped maintain their vibrant looks. Their various diets were also widely reported, and several journalists noted that, in their eagerness to stay slim, some stars regularly purged their bodies of toxins by the use of enemas, or drank their own urine so as to recycle valuable chemical substances and minerals. And to help make the most of their particular physical assets, many of the Hollywood stars developed "tricks" to help emphasize their distinctive sex appeal. Jean Harlow, for instance, used to rub her breasts and nipples with ice before a photo session so that her breasts would become taut and her nipples erect, and applied a special oil on parts of her body to make the fabric cling, while the French actress Claudette Colbert applied a shiny lacquer to her lips and teeth for close-up shots and administered irritating eye drops to make her eyes glisten.

During this period many magazine and newspaper articles were also devoted to the growing fashion for outdoor sports—riding, tennis, golf, skiing, swimming, polo, archery, shooting. These sports required not only special garments, but also an array of cosmetics, lotions, and creams, particularly if this healthy outdoor approach to beauty was also to include topless, or even nude sunbathing, which was very fashionable for those with wealth enough to afford a Mediterranean holiday or a South Seas cruise. It was also surprisingly popular with many young urban dwellers who owned a car, and were able to drive into the country on a sunny weekend for a picnic, an hour or two of sunbathing, and a little illicit sex. This was, of course, why the motor car was so condemned, but if he was lucky enough to own one it did seem to add considerably to a man's sex appeal and hence his perceived beauty, as indeed is still the case today, particularly if the car also shows an added opulence as displayed for instance by a Mercedes sports coupé or a Porsche.

The beauty articles in the media were often based on new products introduced by Max Factor, Helena Rubinstein, or one of their competitors, which often promoted an outdoor "tanned" look in complete contrast to the pale indoor style that had been so fashionable and so lethal. For over two thousand years, until well into the nineteenth century, men and women who could afford to enhance their beauty had used white ceruse composed of lead oxide, hydroxide, and carbonate—deadly cumulative poisons that are progressively absorbed and stored in the body—to achieve the much-admired pale complexion that denoted privilege and good breeding. In earlier times, before the Industrial Revolution, the peasants and common folk spent most of their time working in the fields and thus could not aspire to a pale delicate complexion; their skin was well tanned. To differentiate themselves from the working class, those who could, stayed out of the sun and whitened and softened their skin as much as possible with many substances, some of which were highly dangerous, even lethal.

In addition to white ceruse which was spread liberally onto their faces, necks, shoulders, and upper torsos, the privileged also used other poisonous substances, such as fucus, a red lip salve made from mercuric sulfide. Kohl eyeshadow was composed mainly of lead and antimony sulfide. Quicklime was used to remove any sign of facial hair, and belladonna to make the eyes sparkle and the pupils dilate—a drug that not only encouraged the blinding disease, glaucoma, but also robbed the eye of its natural reflex protection against damaging bright light.

The new range of safer cosmetics, despite the obvious improvements over those used in the past, nevertheless brought forth howls of condemnation from the moralists about the "sins of cosmetics," and the sexual connotations of being "a painted lady." The new wave of travel and holiday-style films that featured exotic locations and new

modes of casual dress were also attacked by these moralists, who seemed to continually search for something new to condemn. Their rebukes, denunciations, and tirades seemed to produce a satisfaction akin to that which most normal people obtain from satisfying their own sexual instincts. As Dr. Cunnington so perceptively observed about such forms of moral indignation, "it may be regarded as a rarefied and subtle form of sex satisfaction whereby a warm glow of moral disapproval can be extracted from quite commonplace spectacles that will even rival the heat of passion itself"—a form of voyeuristic frisson, which I will refer to later, and which, together with other forms of voyeurism is a particularly western obsession due, I believe, to the very rigid social moral controls exerted over our normal and natural sensual and sexual inclinations.

The complainers, however, oblivious of their own psychological motivation, continued their tirades throughout the remaining years of the 1930s, through the war years, and into the 1950s. They condemned swing music, beboppers, and the songs of Frank Sinatra, and they railed at the styles of beauty displayed by Dorothy Lamour, Betty Grable, Rita Hayworth, Hedy Lamarr, Veronica Lake, Jane Russell, and Lana Turner, at the pin-ups featured in *Esquire, Men Only,* and similar magazines, at Christian Dior's "New Look" fashions of 1947 and the H, Y, and A lines that followed, and at any other changes that drew attention to some previously neglected part of the female anatomy. It was similar for new male modes of dress, such as longer hair, narrower ties, or similar changes in silhouette.

In the mid 1950s, their voices reached a crescendo, and the force of their declamations catapulted a young singer to the center of public scrutiny. His name was Elvis Presley—the rest is legend.

CURRENT CODED SIGNALS

The 1950s started rather inauspiciously. In most of Europe and North America the first winter was an unpleasant one, and the effects of wartime rationing were still apparent—heating, food, clothing, and many everyday items were in short supply, and there was little choice in the shops. In many of the larger European cities only token attempts had been made to clear away the devastation of war, and everywhere there were hundreds of thousands of refugees. The Cold War was well underway and there were numerous uprisings in the Middle and Far East.

Nevertheless, this was the beginning of a new decade that promised to be better than the last, and optimism was in the air. Demobilization of the armed forces was almost complete, although this had often been replaced by a system of conscription. Intercity trains were now running regular service, and international airline service to exotic locations had been reintroduced. In London, construction was underway for the 1951 *Festival of Britain*, which had been planned to launch the *Left Bank Exhibition* of art and manufactured products—the latter primarily aimed at the export markets of the world. In the United States, a new genre of consumer items was being

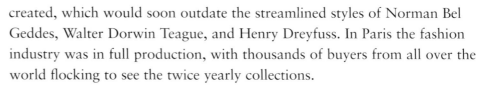

created, which would soon outdate the streamlined styles of Norman Bel Geddes, Walter Dorwin Teague, and Henry Dreyfuss. In Paris the fashion industry was in full production, with thousands of buyers from all over the world flocking to see the twice yearly collections.

In many parts of the world, television service had been reintroduced—transmission had begun as early as 1936 in some countries, but had been interrupted by wartime restrictions. Now the audience was millions strong, and television began to have an effect not only on consumer sales but also on box-office receipts: some cities showed a drop-off as much as 40 percent in the number of filmgoers. This was soon to have dramatic repercussions in Hollywood where, because of a lack of competition during the war years, entertainment ideas had remained static since the end of the 1930s and many of the aging stars, directors, and producers had not been replaced. Most of the new talent was seeking out opportunities in television, and for a time it looked as if Hollywood was heading for total bankruptcy.

During most of the Depression and the war, Hollywood films had had an unchallenged market, and most of the producers and directors had willingly made concessions to various lobby groups, such as the self-appointed American League of Decency, toning down their films in matters of bodily display and sex, although not in violence. The audiences of 1950, however, had had enough of violence and killing, and they were no longer willing to accept the imposition of an outdated moral code on an entertainment for which they were paying, particularly when they could see more livelier forms of entertainment on their television screens, on the stage, or in one of the new-style magazines, in which titillation was often more important than "literature."

The young Marlon Brando had already made an impact on the postwar generation, in a T-shirt and drills, in the Broadway production of *A Streetcar Named Desire*. He was soon to make an even bigger impact in studded black leather in the 1953 film *The Wild One*, which was quickly followed by *On the Waterfront*. Jane Russell had also stirred up quite a controversy in Howard Hughes' *The Outlaw*, which had originally been banned in 1943 because of

the display made of her more obvious physical attributes. She also featured in the delightful 1953 film *Gentlemen Prefer Blondes*, along with the new sex symbol Marilyn Monroe, and of course the 1955 film *Rebel Without a Cause*, starring James Dean. Films such as these were a huge success throughout the western world, as were those being made in England, France, and Italy. I can remember working at the Denham and Pinewood Studios just outside London, and looking in admiration at the beautiful young stars and starlets I was working with. I was only a bit-part player and so did not get to know them very well, but I did note that the success of the young Joan Collins, Jean Simmons, Petula Clark, and the slightly older Jean Kent and Valerie Hobson had more to do with their physical looks than with their acting ability—Joan Collins, of course, soon built up her reputation for her sexual prowess and willingness to flaunt her more obvious physical attributes, while Valerie Hobson became more famous for the sexual prowess of her husband, the British Cabinet Minister John Profumo, whose involvement in the early 1960s with several young women of ill repute caused a major crisis in the British Government.

The British have always been obsessed with the sexual potency of their MPs (Members of Parliament) and of royalty—a leading member of the royals had also been involved with Profumo and the young showgirls Christine Keeler and Mandy Rice-Davies, together with a third showgirl who, because of her very close association with the number one royal male remained out of the headlines. I knew all three, having made many dresses for them, paid for by Lord Astor, son of the free-thinking American heiress Nancy Clifford. This British obsession with sex is, I believe, a manifestation of a sexually repressive society, a society that, partly prompted by the Profumo scandal and other similar events, was soon to break free from the shackles of the past in what became known as the "swinging London era," which gave birth to so many new modes of human beautification.

During the decade following the end of World War II, many changes were taking place that were also destined to change the western perception of human beauty. Photographs of topless South Sea island girls in provocative poses were beginning to be featured in many travelogue-type television programs and in magazines, and experimental visual tricks were beginning to be used in order to overcome the outdated ban on publishing all sorts of nude images. A range of "illegal" nudist-style publications from Scandinavia was being widely distributed, as were similar local "naturalist" publications, and in 1953 Hugh Hefner published his first *Playboy* magazine with the new sex goddess Marilyn Monroe on the cover and a full-

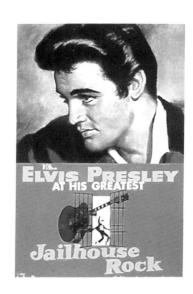

color nude of her inside wearing little more than Chanel No. 5—the flip-side of a photograph by Tom Kelly that had been used by Champion Calendars in 1951, and that became one of the great postwar images of feminine beauty, and which still fires many artists with creative enthusiasm. This and much more was having its effect on how the postwar generation perceived human beauty, human sexuality, and human morality. Although many clerics complained, their influence had already begun to wane.

Christian Dior's New Look, launched in 1947, had dramatically changed the symbolism of western women's dress. Dior reintroduced the use of tightly laced corsets and padding to focus attention on the wearer's breasts, waist, hips, and ankles, and the popular press loved every little detail, although several western governments, including the British, had initially tried to ban its introduction on the grounds of the expense and waste of fabric involved. In America, many women had also denounced the introduction of Dior's New Look as the longer skirts covered up what they considered their most attractive feminine feature, their legs, and many picketed the shops and stores selling this un-American style. The popular press on both sides of the Atlantic had, however, grown weary of wartime restrictions, and the years of writing "make-do-and-mend" articles, and they cooed approvingly at each of Dior's and his rivals' collections. They advised their readers to purchase the new ankle-strapped, high-heeled shoes, smooth nylon stockings, frilly petticoats, shapely corsets, panty-girdles that uplifted and separated the *derrière,* and the *décolleté* bra, which maximized the cleavage; and those who persisted in wearing the old styles were marked first for pity then ridicule.

Men's fashions were also changing. "Zoot suits" had come and gone, as had the double-breasted lounge suit and the casual college styles of the "beboppers." By the early- to mid-1950s, the embryo styles of what later became known as Teddy Boys, Mods, Rockers, and Skinheads were beginning to make their appearance in city centers and large colleges, as a little later did the styles introduced by Marlon Brando, Elvis Presley, and James Dean—i.e. T-shirts, black leather, and Levis that, over the years, has become associated with youthful casual dress.

In general, young women encouraged their boyfriends to wear these more adventurous styles, but they still tended to marry those who, by their choice of traditional attire, projected wealth, social standing, and financial security. Many of these young women were, however, beginning to change, too, under the influence of a new group of film actresses—Leslie Caron, Audrey Hepburn, Brigitte Bardot, Sophia Loren, Gina Lollobrigida, and of course Marilyn Monroe, and a revamped Elizabeth Taylor—whose films were making an impact on the outdated dress codes and moral attitudes of the more conservative Hollywood producers. Fashion photography was also changing under the impact of a new group of photographers such as Hiro, Henry Clarke, William Klein, and Richard Avedon.

In the mid- to late-1950s, I was a post-graduate design student at London's Royal College of Art, having failed to make my mark in the highly competitive film industry, and I witnessed the changes going on around me. Young female students, like the starlets I had been working with, made the most of their nubile bodies by wearing styles that openly displayed their young feminine charms: short, tight skirts that emphasized the shape of the *derrière* and displayed the legs and knees to advantage, or short, flared skirts that, although they concealed the actual shape of the wearer's hips, nevertheless added considerably to their perceived femininity. They also wore tight, wide patent leather belts to emphasize their narrow waists, and tight sweaters to display their breasts. This was before the official launching of the miniskirt and, since tights and pantyhose had not yet become widely available, the young women invariably wore stockings with garters and brief frilly underpants, so that when they sat down, or climbed a flight of stairs, a fleeting glimpse of stocking tops and thigh might be visible. At the end of semester dances, they were even more daring, often wearing little more than nipple rouge, or two tassels and a patch of sequins, and it was in such a costume at the Chelsea Arts Ball that I first met the young avant-garde designer Mary Quant, who was destined to have such an effect on the "swinging London" era and what came after.

The young male students on the other hand, having served their compulsory two years of conscription in the armed services, discarded the enforced mode of the authoritarian armed services and donned thick crepe-soled suede shoes, long, square-cut jackets, often with contrasting velvet collar and cuffs, narrow stovepipe trousers, a decorative, sometimes frilled shirt, and a narrow tie. Their hair was much longer than their fathers—probably a reaction against the armed forces' regulation crewcut. Both young men and young women were perceived by their

peers as beautiful by virtue of what they wore. The styles were symbols of youthful independence and a changing society. To be seen not wearing these new styles marked the individual as "out of the scene," regressive, unattractive, and boring.

At the beginning of the 1960s the first of the "baby boomers" were beginning to have a noticeable effect on clothing and perceptions of beauty. They had been born during the first few postwar years and had created quite a hiccup in the age statistics of the Western world. As more and more of this generation grew up to become teenage workers or students, so their economic power increased. It is estimated that by 1965 nearly 50 percent of all spending on clothing, beauty products, pop records, and other consumer items in the Western world was done by this age group. In Britain, many had decided to leave school at the age of fifteen or sixteen, and by the time they were eighteen they were earning enough money to spend regularly on new modes of attire and entertainments, thus creating a distinct need for styles that differed from those of their parents' generation. And there were now plenty of young entrepreneurs willing to satisfy their needs.

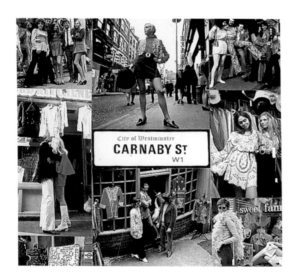

The actual financial mechanics of this new generation's affluence, and the power that flowed from it, were the brainchild of the slightly older age group of *The Wild One* and *Rebel Without a Cause* era. Some of these entrepreneurs conceived the notion that the baby boom generation, given the right range of consumer choices, would both create and fuel its own economic boom. It was this slightly older generation that initially controlled the marketing of the new aesthetic and was responsible for the early success of stars such as James Dean, Elvis Presley, and Brigitte Bardot, Little Richard, the Beatles, fashion model Jean Shrimpton, and the designer Mary Quant. This age group was also responsible for wresting the mass communication industry from those twice their age, although the remaining members of the older media club quickly jumped onto the bandwagon once it had started rolling.

The new bosses had been brought up in a time of educational and social upheaval during the war and then the early, stumbling years of the postwar era. Parents whose youth had been curtailed by the Depression, and who had then been deprived of a normal married life during World

War II, brought up their young to a vision of a better—or
at least a different—world. They did not want the same
deprivation to be visited upon their children, although they
perhaps naively expected that their offspring would respect
some of their sacrifices, and possibly their moral outlook.
Once the changes were underway, though, many of these
parents were unable to adjust to, or understand, the new
symbolism. In their confusion, they tried to stop what
amounted to a cultural revolution, which they had engineered. Thus was created a schism, which became known
as the "generation gap," out of which grew a new morality
and a new form of masculine and feminine beauty.

A new, younger generation of image-maker also emerged whose job it
was to create images that would reflect the changes taking place, and that
would be even more sensational than the images of yesterday. These image-
makers soon found themselves caught up in a spiral of artificially stimulat-
ed sensationalism, and by the end of the 1960s fashion and beauty image-
making had evolved into a dazzling display. If a particular fashion or style
was not as startling as the art director wanted, then the journalist and the
photographer would find ways of creating an image so that the reader
would be persuaded into thinking that it was. I was often involved in such
creative sessions as a designer-stylist. I can remember, for instance, helping
a fashion journalist and a photographer to totally reshape a rather sack-like
dress worn by an up-and-coming pop singer for a weekend color magazine.
With the aid of pins, scotch tape, and clips, we made the garment fit the
pop star like a second skin, while orange and green filters and blue lights
changed the color and design of the fabric, adding psychedelic interest to
what in reality was a dreary printed cotton sack.

The following week the fashion journalist, the photographer and I set to work
on a feature for a glossy magazine, where
the look in the model's eyes was far more
important that what she was wearing. I
recall all the "sweet talking" and verbal
seduction that went on between the
photographer and the model to achieve the
effect required. The photographer would
start the session by casually flattering and
flirting with the model, telling her he had

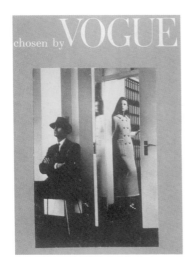

seen the most marvelous photos of her. Then he would tell her she had fantastic eyes, a seductive mouth, a sensational figure, a stunning neck, a really fabulous behind. Only when she was aroused did he begin the actual photographic session. He told her she looked a million dollars, a dream come true; she was the model he had been looking for all his life. He said he was as horny as hell for her. He wanted to take her now and he didn't care who was watching. He asked her to pout a little, to wiggle her hips, jut out her jaw, and curve her back slightly. All the while he was taking her photo, hoping to catch that certain glint that the journalist wanted for the story.

The photographer continued to sweet talk. He suggested the model open her legs slightly, to expose the soft inner flesh of her thighs. She responded and raised her skirt slightly to make sure the front wrap would open a little to reveal more of her sensuous body. The animal magic between photographer and model was reaching a climax. She was projecting all the signals of sexual excitement. He was using the camera like a phallus—he had had it specially modified so that when he held it it became a part of his body, in the same way that many pop stars use a microphone or guitar. The resulting photographs embodied all the sexual elements to excite any observer, who would instinctively look at the girl, not at what she is wearing.

The readers of the magazine feature loved the photograph, and if they could afford it they would purchase the garment the model was wearing, and the beauty products she had used, because they wished to look as sensually exciting and feel as sexually attractive as she did. Every move, every pose and gesture, was provocatively created for sexual and sensual response. The model and photographer were able to call upon the symbols of envy, admiration, desire, and, more importantly, buyer identification. The photograph created an illusion of the obtainable that would color the observer's buying habits, aspirations and dreams.

Having worked on numerous similar sessions with models such as Jean Shrimpton, Twiggy, and Veruschka, and photographers such as John French, Henry Clarke, David Bailey, and Helmut Newton, promoting my own designs as well as those from Carnaby Street and Kings Road, I have come to the conclusion that it was the creative journalists, the skilled photographers, the intuitive models, and the talented stylists who were responsible for inventing and popularizing most of the more adventurous dress styles and modes of beauty of the "swinging London" era, possibly more so than the new young dress designers.

At the end of the 1960s the entire industrial world was once again on the threshold of tremendous change. The underlying dynamics were technological revolution, expansion of education, a growing desire to explore the unknown, an expanding middle class, the replacement of an established political structure and ideology with a structure based on the power of new money and new discoveries, the desire to travel throughout the solar system—or at the very least to reach the moon—and the introduction of satellite television and the invention of the microchip.

The end of the 1960s also saw the introduction into worldwide service of the first of the jumbo jets—the Boeing 747—which heralded the age of world travel for all. Soon, fuelled by the images they had seen on television travelogues, average people from the great morass of Western urban settlements were traveling to India, the Pacific islands, southern Africa, Brazil, and Mexico for their holidays. Naturally enough, they began buying a variety of clothing and adornments at their destinations, and they observed the exotic styles of local beauty. Gradually, the styles of dress, jewelry, and even some of the indigenous modes of beauty that had originated in such cities as Cairo, Jaipur, Bangkok and Rio became

fashionable in Europe and North America. Local tradesmen in these far-flung cities began to adapt their merchandise to appeal more to the increasing numbers of Western tourists, and they also began to copy many of the Western styles for local sale. Influences began to mix. Aesthetic ideas that had originated in Mexico were being copied in Los Angeles and then transported to Delhi by a visiting tourist. They were then copied or adapted by a local tradesman and sold to a visitor from London or New York. Thus, within a short time an international style of "ethnic-based" design began to evolve, featuring juxtaposed patterns, colors, and details that had origins everywhere and nowhere.

In addition, the casual travel styles of many of the Western tourists began to influence the peoples of the nonindustrialized world, who often bartered their traditional adornments for such items as jeans, T-shirts, and sneakers. These casual Western styles had become popular on American college campuses in the late 1950s and early 1960s, introduced mainly by students from the Midwest, who, although wealthy by world standards, had not fallen under the East Coast and large city spell of opulent dressing. Many had grown up on farms and in small country towns where there was little separation of the sexes in their formative years, and they had all learned to ride a horse—a necessity as well as one of the pleasures of the Midwest lifestyle. Wearing practical leg coverings such as the Levi Strauss 501s—later to become more widely referred to simply as "Levis" or as "jeans"—was a necessity. With their popularization by Elvis Presley and James Dean, jeans quickly became a symbol of American college life, and ultimately a symbol of the enviable American lifestyle, which young people all over the world wanted to emulate. The influence of this culture was spread not only by tourists, but also by television, as people everywhere began to tune into American-produced programs.

In the Western world, this new mode of mass communication had also begun to feature programs about many traditional forms of beauty among non-Western peoples. Japanese, Eurasian, African, and African-American models became popular in many of the top fashion houses, where their exotic coloring and dramatic features enhanced the bold colors and patterns of the new ethnic-inspired fabrics. In Paris a range of stick-on tribal scars made from skin-colored latex were launched along with a variety of dark-skinned cosmetics and Afro-style wigs. Black rock and pop stars also became popular and soon a new pride in ethnic origins began to emerge, illustrated by the words of James Brown when at an all-black rock concert declared, "We are black. Our noses are broad. Our lips are thick. Our hair is matted. We are beautiful," and then repeated several times "Black is beautiful, black is truly beautiful"—which gave birth to the "Black is beautiful" catch phrase.

Many television travelogues began to focus on the variety of cultural beauty among widely differing ethnic groups. I recall, for instance, seeing a program about the once-a-year ritual of the nomadic Wodaabe of the Niger, where the young unmarried men gather together for a week-long *Geerewol* celebration. They spend hours painting their faces, arranging their hair and headdresses and donning finery to make themselves as beautiful as possible, using every device available to them. They then line up in long rows for inspection by the single women and women who, although married, wish to exchange their mate; the selection process is celebrated by an unusual jumping style of dance called the *Yaake,* in which the young men display their athletic ability and physical stamina—important for a successful sexual liaison—as well as their beauty and charisma. Other programs in the same series featured groups, such as the Yoruba of Benin and others elsewhere in West Africa, in which both the men and women practice a very complex form of tattooing combined with scarification called *kolo* that gives an interesting and attractive textured look—a distinctive mode of body art much celebrated in these areas. Programs such as these were quite different from anything I had ever seen or imagined; they were crucial in determining the direction of my future career.

Some time later there was another series of documentaries on indigenous peoples, one devoted to the then recently discovered Zoe people of the Amazon jungle who adorn their mouths not with lip plugs like their neighbors but with a more complex phallic-shaped lip shaft, which is about six inches long and up to two inches thick, that is worn in a slot made through the lower lip so that it hangs down over the chin, and nothing else except a foreskin tie. There was also another program on the beautification techniques used by the young Maasai and Samburu warriors of Kenya and another about the modes of body art used by such cultural groups as the isolated Mondari tribe of the Sudan and the Tiv, who live in the Benue Valley of Nigeria.

These tribal peoples and many like them believe in scarring their bodies for aesthetic reasons, but it also acts as a survival technique, which may

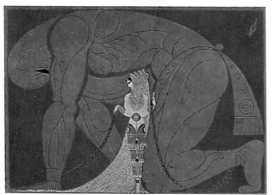

well be the reason why they survived while many other tribal peoples perished. Regular cutting of the body over a long period builds up the immune system so that on completion the scar patterns contain the specific information that the individual can withstand pain and will be able to survive most accidents or indigenous diseases. When a person reaches puberty his or her skin is incised in such a way that the resultant scars resemble shadows—remember that these groups live in an equatorial region where the light source is not as angled as it is in more temperate regions. Thus prominent cheekbones are made to appear more prominent by cutting the skin just above them. A nose can be made to appear longer, shorter, or broader by the placement of other cuts. A really handsome set of scars, incorporating the face, chest, shoulders, back, and legs—together with teeth chipping or splaying, body painting, oiling, and other local forms of enhancement—gives each cultural group a very distinctive sculptural appearance. An unusual one by Western standards, perhaps, but one that the Tiv and the Mondari insist gives them great beauty, symbolizing tribal identification and pride in their varying traditional ways.

In some of these northern African groups, as in some other societies in the world, there is also an added bonus to having these scars: A really beautifully scarred warrior is often given the honor of siring extra children; some husbands, in their quest to have beautiful offspring, which traditionally brings great honor to himself, his family, and the village, encourage their wives to mate with the handsomest warriors at specific festive times, and, of course, the handsomest warrior was also the warrior with the handsomest scars.

Many other tribal groups go to extraordinary lengths to perfect their ideas of an aesthetic style of body decoration, as Victoria Ebin pointed out in *The Body Decorated* (1979) when talking of the Nuba warriors. "The decorated body is valued as an aesthetic object and the designs which he

applies are only a means to that end," Ebin observes that decorative motifs can even be used to remedy physical faults: "Eyes which are too small can be widened by circles of white clay," and "the natural contours of the face can be emphasised by dramatic lines drawn diagonally from the crown of the head towards the centre," thus appearing to reshape the very silhouette of the individual. Concern about the look of their bodies is paramount to their existence, and they have special words for every visible muscle and indentation, and also for the sheen and texture of the skin, which should be burnished to a deep brown or black color to signify health and well-being. And if a warrior has been even slightly injured, or his skin has been abraded, he will not decorate or call attention to himself in any way, and will remove himself for the time being from normal social interaction—the emphasis is always on perfection coupled with health and vigor which, in turn, helps to maintain the "look" of the health and beauty of all the tribe, as well as that of the individual.

Another documentary showed the cast metal Kalacha phallic ornaments, measuring four to five inches in length, worn on the forehead by Boram elders of Southern Ethiopia, just north of the Kenya border, during various rites of passage ceremonies. But it is among the South Sea islanders and the highlanders of New Guinea that phallic ornaments are most common and also that the art of male body decoration and beautification are probably more developed and more exotic than anywhere else in the

world—it is their main method of artistic expression and thus one to which they devote a great deal of time. My first glimpse of these flamboyant images was in the pages of *National Geographic* in the early 1950s. I was mesmerized by the magnificently deco-

rated people and the exotic birds of paradise, set in an extraordinary geography that resembled the creation of a Hollywood set designer rather than reality. I had to go there and I arranged my career accordingly.

When I visited the Huli tribe of the Southern Highlands province in 1985, I found that they were still wearing traditional lozenge-shaped wigs made from human hair, often impregnated with powdered ochre pigment and fringed with dried everlasting flowers, which I had seen in the earlier *National Geographic* photographs. The wigs, which curve upward for the young members of the tribe and downward for the older, more respected men, are a symbol of sexual maturity and are generally decorated with iridescent-blue fan-shaped feathers obtained from the superb bird of paradise, a tuft of cassowary feathers, and a band of speckled blue, yellow, and black snakeskin called a *legpge*, if the wearer is able to afford such luxuries. The Huli males by tradition also wear a crescent-shaped chest ornament cut from mother-of-pearl shell called a *kina*; a *yari mabu* made from sections of cassowary quills slotted together; cowrie-shell or dog-tooth necklaces; additional body ornaments to decorate their nose, ears, arms, and waist; and a *nogo ere dambale*—a short woven apron impregnated with ochre clay and fringed with pigs' tails, with a bunch of fresh leaves inserted under the apron strap at the back as a form of rear covering commonly referred to as "arse grass."

In another area of Papua New Guinea that I visited, the Western Highlands province, the local Kauil tribesmen were quite different from their Huli cousins when painted and adorned. They used a lot of black and red coloring for their face and upper torso, and their headdresses were very tall and decorated with the tail feathers of the sickle-bill bird of paradise. They also used carved cassowary leg-bone hair decorations and wore an *omak*, which is a ladder-like chest decoration made from strips of local wild pit-pit cane. The *omak* denotes how much the wearer has given away during the important ceremonial exchanges that are still an integral part of highland life. Jungle-string arm-bands are a further indication of the wearer's importance, as are ceremonial stone axes, and some of the older men still wear boar's tusk or quill nose and ear ornaments, along with the highly valued *kina* chest ornament.

In the Asaro River region, I saw for myself how the men cover their bodies with gray clay and wear clay helmet-like masks that are decorated with boars' tusks and dogs' teeth. In other areas I saw special headbands made from small *nassarius* shells backed with bark cloth, worn with a shimmering blue occipital plume from the adult male King of Saxony bird of paradise, which frame the wearer's face. The face is blackened with ground charcoal mixed with pig fat, while the body gleams with freshly applied vegetable oils made to very specific traditional recipes. In yet other areas red and black Pesquet's parrot feathers interlaced with green lorikeet feathers are used to offset the brilliance of Princess Stephanie bird of paradise or other rare plumage, which denotes the wearer's origin—each village or cultural group by tradition uses only those feathers that occur naturally within its territory.

During the twenty years from 1970 to 1990 a great many programs about tribal forms of body adornment and beauty have been broadcast, via satellite, resulting in worldwide interest in traditional styles of expression. This has spawned a huge number of magazine articles and books dealing with the customs and adornments of various cultural groups. This, in turn, has resulted in tourists visiting these often isolated communities. In their eagerness for souvenirs, they purchase traditional heirlooms, such as rare nose and lip ornaments, necklaces, bracelets, earrings, hair and toe adornments of all sorts, clasps, beaded aprons, and scarring knives, many of which have been handed down for generations and are not replaceable. Museums have also been actively collecting such items—it has been said there are now more examples of original ethnic modes of attire and adornment in the West than there are in their countries of origin. And in the non-Western countries there is a growing desire to wear anything and everything that is Western, as a symbol of association with an envied lifestyle

and as a means of exciting peer group envy.

One television program dealt with the tradition of the Oriental harem, ruled over by a sultan and his eunuchs, which proved to be totally different from that which I had imagined hitherto, and having subsequently been a guest in a small harem just outside of Cairo, I now understand better how such institutions work. Drawing on historic accounts the program showed how many of the more famous harems were palaces of

sensual pleasure, not so much for the sultan or his friends as is generally thought, but for the women themselves and to some extent the eunuchs as well. And for whatever reason, most of the female "inmates" and "wives" rarely if ever attained regular visits to the sultan's bed chamber.

What was of main interest to me about such harems was the sensual beauty and voluptuous pleasure that the women enjoyed among themselves, and the great lengths they went to obtain the soft sensual skin for which many became famous, but which unfortunately is not widely appreciated in the Western world today. Undoubtedly there were strong homoerotic/lesbian overtones in such establishments upon which Lady Mary Montagu had earlier commented in her famous diaries written while traveling in Eastern Europe and the Middle East in the early eighteenth century. She also observed that "there were many amongst them as exactly proportioned as even any goddess was drawn by the pencil of Guido or Titian— their skin shiningly white, only adorned by their beautiful hair divided into many tresses, hanging on their shoulders, braided either with pearl or ribbon, perfectly representing the figures of the Graces...to see so many fine women naked whilst their slaves—generally pretty girls of seventeen or eighteen—were employed in braiding their hair in several pretty fancies...." This scene is beautifully captured by the French painter Jean-Auguste-Dominique Ingres in *The Turkish Bath* (1832); throughout his career, Ingres gloried in depicting such women, who were somewhat plumper than is now generally admired.

The ancient art of henna decoration of hands, feet, and face was also explored in these programs. A technique still widely practiced throughout the Middle East, Henna decoration is as an essential part of the preparations for a wedding and is used at other festive times. On the special Henna Night, which occurs on the evening before a wedding, the women of the bride's family, after spending the day in the traditional *hamam* bathing and grooming, would spend the night decorating the bride's hands, feet, and face with henna—a warm gray-green, paste-like dye made from special munched up leaves, which is applied to the skin in traditional patterns. The patterning then must be wrapped in cloth bandages and allowed to cool overnight before being washed clean the following morning to expose the dyed orange motifs—a truly wonderful decorative mode of adornment, which with care lasts for many weeks.

In addition, many television programs were now beginning to reach the more inaccessible areas of the world, featuring not only the traditional modes of beautification, but also such glitzy Western-based events as Mr.

Universe, Miss America, Miss World, Miss Universe, Miss Teen, and now Ms. Androgyny, in which the physical attributes of the participants are compared and judged. This encouraged many non-Western aspirants to participate in such events, with some having great success. Many young Western women saw this open competition as a cultural threat and they responded by willingly displaying more of their physical attributes than they had hitherto.

Through the effects of television and music videos, "sexier" modes of dress in the 1980s became more widely available. Many fetish styles featured in a number of the more avant-garde music videos were used for inspiration when designing party and club styles, more adventurous forms of body decoration also become popular, culminating in the risqué styles worn by the pop idol Madonna at some of her gigs and in publicity shots of the early 1990s—styles that were only slightly less revealing than those worn by Traci Lords and Cicciolina (Ilona Staller, an anglo-Italian stripper turned Member of Parliament) in their X-rated movies. In fact, in the early 1990s, X-rated movies had become so popular and influential that they were used as inspiration for many new modes of dress and

for ways of beautifying the body when going to a party, concert, or club. Such influence, particularly among the young, has been a general trend since the days of Elvis Presley, Little Richard, the Shangri Las, the ex-Go-Go dance group the Ronettes, the Sex Pistols, and the Rolling Stones. The stiletto heels, plastic go-go boots, and skin-tight cha-cha pants worn by the Ronettes and other members of the early sixties girl groups caused an uproar at the time, and, in retrospect, one can see that from a social point of view they were only marginally less outrageous than the styles worn by Madonna—both had crossed the line of acceptability, which I believe is to their merit. Other styles that also crossed this line, and thus helped to move our beautifying modes into new areas of experimentation, include the Beatles' and Elvis's hairstyles, Mick Jagger's flaunting of his ambiguous sexuality, the punk mode of Sid Vicious, the outrageously dressed Freddie Mercury, and now forgotten male singers like William "Bootsy" Collins, Ian Anderson and

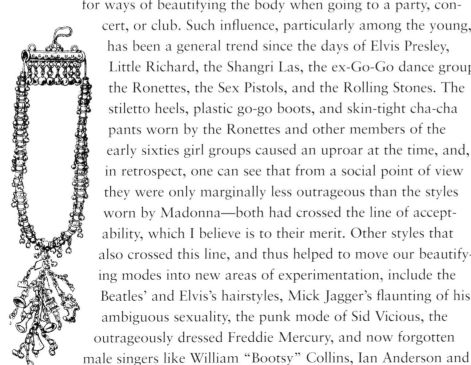

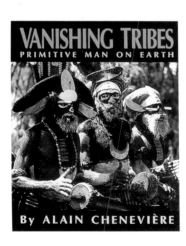

Roy Wood, who created an outrage by sporting a larger-than-life crotch bulge—a distinctive feature that greatly added to their allure and mystery and gave an extra potency to their silhouette—but one which few ordinary males had the courage to adopt for their own personal enhancement. At the time there was much talk about the return of the codpiece and a return to the era of male pride in his mode of dress—the "era of the peacock"—but nothing came of this in general society.

Like the curve of a young woman's breasts, which are often improved by a little padding, the male crotch bulge is of aesthetic and psychological importance and therefore is an area that would lend itself to improvement, but apart from a few advertisements for "decorative codpieces" and other "outstanding aids," and special health foods that were supposed to "greatly increase the size of the male jewels," little progress was made, with most male rock-n-roll singers of the late 1960s simply improving their silhouette with the aid of a rolled-up sock. But even this practice was attacked as immoral as it was in complete contrast to the flattened male genitalia of their fathers' era, achieved by wearing constricting underpants, or a special flattening jockstrap. Other advertisements of the same era were, however, aimed at increasing a singer's androgynous or hermaphroditic appeal, a trend started by Marc Bolan and continued after his death by David Bowie, who turned androgynous bisexuality into a very remunerative marketing ploy with the influence of his on-stage costuming being profound—a male mode of decorative dress which, by being sexually neutral, was nonthreatening to the predominantly teenage audience. In many respects, though, it was the Beatles who gave the sexually nonthreatening "androgynous trend" its biggest boost. They continually hinted at the breakdown of traditional masculine codes of behavior and admitted the feminine side of their nature into their songs, styles of dress, and personal behavior. John Lennon, the most masculine member of the group, took androgyny to its logical conclusion to become a "male housewife." The Beatles showed the Western world that the time was right for young heterosexual males to display and even glory in their more feminine qualities—a notion that has been widely accepted for thousands of years among other cultures.

Of course bisexuality and androgyny, together with the gay scene and transvestites was not new to the Western world in the late 1960s, but the

decriminalization of homosexuality at that time opened up a whole new range of possibilities for those who wished to dress and beautify themselves a little differently from the norm, and to express another aspect of their psyche rather than accepting the enforced stereotyping of our gender-oriented dress code which, by implication publically indicates the type of genitalia of the wearer. For many years such a choice was forbidden by law, even to those who had no homosexual or androgynous inclinations, but who wished to discard the enforced masculine modes of dress. I had done this but not without running foul of the law on several occasions and spending many hours in a prison cell on suspicion of homosexual behavior. I had even attempted to submit a portfolio of designs for a Royal College of Art design project of a new breed of "young men about town," based on the eighteenth-century theme of dandies, but in 1957 I was a little ahead of my time. I did, however, get a write-up in several international newspapers, and I did meet the then fashion editor of *Vogue*, who introduced me to my first employer, the London couturier Michael of Lachasse, and later Digby Morton and Norman Hartnell, for whom I also worked. But couture was not my *métier* and I soon left to start my own line of young ready-to-wear designs, including some menswear, and I have continued to work on freelance menswear designs ever since, as well as some freelance female designs of an experimental nature.

As a designer I have been able to chart the changing attitudes of the press, manufacturers, store buyers, and the general public toward avant-garde menswear and party wear, particularly those inspired by fetish activities, or those that display previously concealed areas of the female anatomy, together with other forms of female body decoration—nude body painting, body jewelry, bondage wear, and the like. Fortunately, the laws and social attitudes that were used to curtail the making and wearing of such styles have now been relaxed, as indeed have the laws relating to female nudity and some forms of so-called pornography, a subject I still find difficult to understand. I can recall, for instance, while in Paris in 1957 on a RCA traveling scholarship, purchasing a whole array of the most wonderful eighteenth-, nineteenth-, and early twentieth-century design books and reference materials relating to fashion and modes of

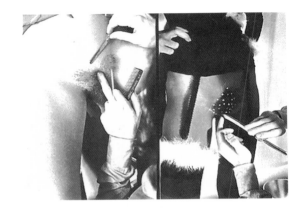

body decoration, some of which were described by the customs official on my return to England as "pornographic." They were confiscated and burned despite my protests that similar eighteenth- and nineteenth-century erotica was housed in the British Museum's Reading Room. "Well then, young fella, I will have to notify the police and we will have those burnt as well," came the reply. I didn't take the matter further, as I remembered the advice given to me by Quintin Crisp. He was a life model at my first art school in East London and vividly detailed the persecution he had received from the police because of his usual dandified dress, blue-rinsed hair, and painted fingernails, and his preference for not wearing his jockstrap when posing—a punishable "pornographic crime" in 1953 for which he could have spent many months in prison. He had advised us not to challenge the police or those in authority over sexually sensitive matters, as they would always win.

A fellow student, Eric Hepburn, would make the most wonderful drawings of Quintin and his co-female model, "Big Bertha," detailing their pubic hair and anatomical features, which he sold to a Bond Street art dealer, who resold them (after a little chemical work and aging), as recently discovered Renaissance masterpieces, a skill that he was to further develop— many of his drawings are now held by leading art galleries and museums as bona fide works of old masters. Photographs, however, of the same pubic hair and anatomical features were, and in some cases still are, regarded as pornographic, or so I later found out when I gave a series of lectures on the subject, displaying them and photographs of tribal differences and modes of genital and pubic hair decorations to design students at a Sydney art college in 1983. I was accused of obscenity and a purveyor of pornography and was suspended from my position as Principal Lecturer of the Design School. The police also became involved, but luckily with the help of the anticensorship lobby and journalistic friends I was able to show that the times and views of such matters had changed since the late 1960s and that the new pop singers like Madonna and Michael Jackson had outdated the views of zealots and college authorities. However, pornography as such was not the purpose of this digression, which was intended to show the illogicity of this type of censorship and that, given the chance, the zealots would prevent us from seeing and enjoying many of the freedoms of dress and body display we now have.

Attitudes toward male dress, although not male beauty and nudity, which in the popular Western imagination are still too closely associated with continuing taboos about transvestism and homosexuality, have been changing since the mid-1960s, although not as quickly as I would like, and the media now promote a much wider range of options. "Beauty," "aesthetics," and "sensitivity" are the vogue words for menswear, and designers have declared that for the 1990s and into the next century, "anything goes." For instance, at the 1990 Paris menswear collections, a spokesman for the organizers declared,

> Men should no longer be afraid of colours, of cosmetics, of perfume, or of self-expression. It is now possible for men to state their independence other than by wearing red socks or a green tie. Individuality is no longer a dirty word to the fashion *literati*, nor is it a sign of being a deviant. Fashionable clothing for men will be the boom industry of the decade.

The same sentiments about menswear were expressed in 1970, in one instance under the banner headline "Male Plumage: He-Men Return to Elegance." It happened again at the beginning of the 1980s, yet, as an expression of male pride and male beauty, for the public at large, however,

menswear seems to have changed very slowly indeed, possibly because of the association such innovative styles have with the growth of the homosexual population as it emerges from the closet.

Unfortunately, as a culture we do seem to have a phobia about homosexuality and transvestites, which greatly reduces the possibility of male forms of aesthetic experimentation , and our notions of male beauty, shaped by our religious and social beliefs, fail to acknowledge this side of our psyche. These beliefs also prevent us from

acknowledging that many famous men admired in the past embraced their natural androgynous, bisexual, and homosexual tendencies—a subject I will return to in the final chapter, *Embellishing the Psyche*. As I was adding the final lines to this manuscript, I read that most menswear designers still believe that the traditional dark suit, plain-colored shirt, and classic tie would remain "king of the male wardrobe" into the next millennium, with the influential Japanese designer-*cum*-philosopher Yohji Yamamoto declaring that "any drastic change in the suit would have to be preceded by major upheavals in the world as we know it"—in fact, as dramatic an upheaval as happened at the end of the eighteenth century, with the effects of the Industrial Revolution, the American War of Independence, the French Revolution, and the wars against Napoleon, which all contributed to the dramatic change that took place in the then traditional mode of male dress.

Other commentators on the current form of male dress observed that, according to a 1994 Chamber of Commerce report, traditional suit sales were up, possibly, the report said, as a "backlash against the predilection for casual styles,"—as James Laver (art historian and author) observed on this subject during an earlier phase of male experimentation in the mid-1950s, "Our choice of clothing is not arbitrary, but is dictated to us by the deepest unconscious desires of the opposite sex." This is still true today and for whatever reason, women today still seem to like the men in their lives to wear a traditional dark-colored suit with a plain shirt and tie. Some changes are taking place, however, as can be noted in the arena of political dressing. In mid-1995, British Prime Minister John Major, in a front-page article in *The (London) Times* told members of the ruling Conservative party to abandon their pin-striped shirts and dark-colored suits and to start wearing jeans and casual sweaters. He also advised them to ruffle their hair and buy a pair of loafers. They were told to pluck their bushy eyebrows and shave off their moustaches and beards, while female members of parliament were told not to wear any sort of trendy leather gear in public, and to always make sure they were always correctly attired and made-up with suitable cosmetics.

Politicians, try as they might, are rarely able to influence public taste in matters of dress with John Major's advice being no exception—the ruling Conservative party lost the next election. Sometimes, however, the most

surprising changes do occur, but usually without political help, such as the fashion for older, successful women to have younger men as live-in lovers—"toy boys," a few of whom live a lifestyle of luxury akin to that of the *demi-mondaines*. These women insist that their lovers dress in an adventurous trendy style that is aimed at complementing, but never overpowering, the styles they choose to wear themselves. And it is these young men, and others like them who have access to money and the time to enjoy it, who may lead the way into a more enlightened age of male dress and male beauty.

Another aspect of our changing modes of clothing and lifestyles that affects our notions and perceptions of human beauty is our recent Western addiction to what can best be described as a form of "ritualized voyeurism." My attention was first drawn to this phenomenon in the mid-1960s, by numerous magazine articles and by the publication of Desmond Morris's *The Naked Ape* (1967). It appears that while sexual contact may keep a married pair together it does not necessarily eliminate interest in outside sexual activities, particularly when the average couple are able to enjoy more free time than has ever been possible before. But where outside sexual liaisons would conflict too strongly with the pair bond, some less harmful substitute has to be found. In the Western world, this substitute appears to have presented itself in the form of "ritualized voyeurism," using the term in its broadest sense.

In a very strict sense, voyeurism means obtaining sexual excitement from watching others copulate, but it can include any non-participatory interest in any sexual activity, including admiring various aspects of intimate beauty as well as the art of flirting. Almost the entire population of the Western world now regularly indulges in this ritualistic activity. They watch it, read about it, listen to it, and talk about it. The vast bulk of all television, radio, cinema, theater, and fiction-writing is concerned with satisfying its insatiable demands. This was the appeal of so many fashion photographers during the 1960s. It is also why soap operas became so successful in the 1970s and 1980s, and why the X-rated video market has grown so rapidly from its humble beginnings to a multi-billion-dollar

industry. We were, it would seem, once again attempting to reclaim our natural birthright of being able to see, admire, and enjoy our unique forms of human beauty, as well as enjoying our natural pleasure centers.

Another manifestation of our attempt to reclaim our birthright, and one that has a more direct bearing on current styles of beauty and modes of social behavior is the growth of *Playboy*-style magazines such as *Mayfair, Club International, Penthouse,* and *Playgirl,* which, together with *Cosmopolitan, Forum, Hustler,* and specialist rubber, S&M, and bondage magazines all deliver tempting and enviable images, sexual information, humor, readers' thoughts, fantasies, and questions, and so on, month by month—thus broadening our erotic horizons and making us realize that there is far more to the aesthetic appeal of the human body than a pretty face or muscular shoulders.

During this period, with the aid of a variety of methods of birth control, young people became more sexually active than had previously been the norm, so that today many adults of both sexes are able to view sexuality in a less inhibiting way. It is now normal to view sexuality as an important factor in people's identity, and more is expected of sex and sexual relationships than in the past. This is why when the inhibiting laws relating to such matters were changed, there was such an explosion in sex books and magazines and the home video market. X-rated movies, for instance, now account for nearly 50 percent of video rentals in some urban areas, and many supermarkets now promote the sale of previously illegal publications—all of which has given us the opportunity to discover the difference between mere nakedness and naked beauty.

Interestingly, during this time of sexual liberation, there was also a marked increase in the sale of leather and rubber bondage wear, underwear as outerwear, and of more decorative forms of lingerie—it seems that we had become addicted to var-

ious forms of fetish clothing and intimate adornment. Unadorned nakedness was never so arousing. One of the promotional staff at Fredericks' of
Hollywood told me that in the past only a small percentage of American
women liked to dress sexily, but that with the proliferation of *Playboy*-style
magazines in the 1970s and 1980s business had boomed. She went on to
say words to this effect:

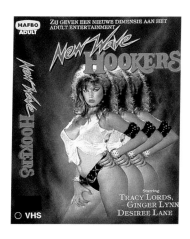

> Nowadays, it's a broad spectrum of women who like to dress in a sensual
> way, no matter what their size and no matter what their particular figure
> type. They now know that there is something out there available to make
> them feel and look good. Some women might feel sexy in something very
> brief and very revealing as in a *Playboy* magazine, whereas others might
> feel more sexy in a flowing peignoir. It all depends on the woman and her
> current relationships. Nowadays a woman also thinks a lot more about
> lingerie and what it can do for her body. About what she is going to wear
> under something in order to make her feel extra good inside—so good
> that it makes her body vibrate and glow. That is what is now so impor-
> tant. Because if she can find a style of lingerie that gives that special feeling
> that makes her body project a certain allure, then she feels that she's
> almost irresistible, and that certainly boosts her confidence and hence her
> projected beauty.

The notion about the beautifying quality of fine lingerie was also prevalent among the sales staff and customers of the specialist shops of London,
Paris, Zurich, and Milan when I visited them recently—a belief that echoes
back to the 1920s when Florenz Ziegfeld, aware of the stimulating effects
of lingerie, used to insist that the young chorus girls featured in his Follies
should not be totally naked as in many other reviews, but should wear
loosely-cut lace-trimmed silk cami-knickers or the like, which would
improve their looks in two ways, first by making them feel special, not just
naked bodies to be lusted over, and second because such lingerie would
stroke the insides of their thighs when they moved, so that their faces and
bodies would project a state of sexual arousal and appear particularly
vibrant, appealing, and even more beautiful to the audience, who undoubtedly would respond to the chorus girls' subliminal body language.

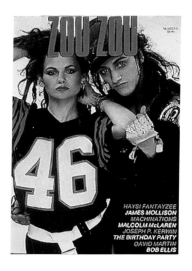

Havelock Ellis also detailed much the same form of sexual body language experienced by many women of his acquaintance while writing his
Studies in the 1890s. He said these women had confided that they often
received a degree of sexual pleasure from the rhythmic movement created
within the labia and presumably the clitoris while dancing in a tightly laced

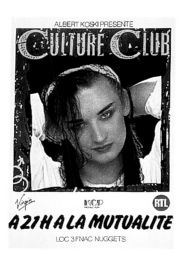

corset and high-heeled shoes. Although this stimulation didn't always lead to an orgasm, several confessed "it makes one feel quite ready for it!" Undoubtedly such a woman radiated a sexual "glow" at these times, which would have greatly enhanced her feminine appeal and possibly beauty. It would appear that this may also be the unique appeal of several brands of designer jeans, which have been specially cut to be worn very tight, with several letters being published in specialist magazines in recent years from young women who claim that they get considerable pleasure from the front seam of their jeans gently rubbing their mons veneris which often keeps them in a constant state of sexual arousal and gives them a most attractive "glow." I have also been told by a number of young women that this is one of the "rewards" of having a stud piercing through the clitorial hood. I have also been told by several models during the course of my design work that certain styles of high-heeled shoes also create a form of sexual stimulation presumably by tilting the pelvis forward, which puts pressure on the labia creating the same form of pleasure as confided to Ellis. I must confess that such physical experience would certainly add to the sales appeal of such items and could well be the reason why so many young women in high-heeled shoes and tight-fitting jeans project such a healthy feminine vibrancy and "beauty"—a vibrancy and beauty that most men find irresistible and that undoubtedly adds considerably to these young women's own perception of their attractiveness.

The feedback from looking sexually vibrant, transmitted by the passing male population, helps to reinforce this feeling of attractiveness, and this is further aided by the automatic change that occurs in the female's gait at such times, which in turn increases the observer's ardor and hence the female's perceived beauty. Actresses, dancers, and models are prepared to artificially stimulate the same flow of these sexual chemicals in order to project this appealing sexual "glow." Several Hollywood personalities have spoken of aspiring actresses, and even well-established ones, using a technique of intimate stroking, masturbation, and sometimes copulation before or during the filming of romantic close-ups in order to project on film an irresistible look of sexually enhanced beauty, and while working with numerous fashion photographers, I have seen and helped models do much the same. This form of sexual allure is also the main appeal and purpose of glamorizing cosmetics, which simulate the look of sexual arousal—this is why they are seen as "beautifiers" and why glamor products are such a boom industry. It seems almost all women want to look sexually appealing.

Technology-based forms of beautification have also been widely used by both men and women in recent years to make them more attractive, both to themselves and to members of the opposite sex—or to members of the same sex if that happens to be their preference. Many men, for instance, have been remodeled by cosmetic surgery, or what is now referred to as body customization, in order to create within them a feeling of self-respect and confidence. Their faces have been made over—removing an unsightly mole, reshaping the nose, tightening the skin around the eyes and neck, clipping back the ears, and modifying the chin. Their teeth have been capped, and contact lenses have been fitted. Their shoulders have been remodeled, their waistlines reduced, and their hips and buttocks reshaped. Many have had their more intimate features enlarged with silicone injections, an erection device fitted if necessary, and some have had their foreskin replaced and an erotic stud, ring or bar fitted. Once made over, these men are advised to exercise regularly to keep in shape—word has gone around that at job interviews, trim men who give an impression of vitality are the ones who are chosen.

Many women also resort to the cosmetic surgeon's scalpel in their search for the good life. They have facelifts and nose jobs. Hairlines are redefined, waistlines reduced, hips and thighs reshaped. They want totally new breasts—more cleavage, better shape, increased fullness, higher placement, more projection, new nipples. When they go topless they want to look as pleasing as a centerfold model, with just a hint of individuality; to wit, Cher's tattoos or Naomi Campbell's navel piercing.

New Wave eclectic "street fashions" have also been growing in importance during the last two decades as a manifestation of the growing desire for some kind of individuality or as a kind of tribal identification. The young designers of these New Wave street fashions are trying to create a new way of thinking about human adornment and human beauty within

what they perceive as a very conformist society—a tribal kind of individuality currently a mixture of "ravers," "grunge," "funky sleaze," "hip-hop," "technos," "cyberpunks," "skaters," and "New Age primitivism." This new approach has been particularly successful in larger urban areas such as London where earlier tribal modes sported by Teddy Boys, mods, rockers, and skinheads originated, and in Tokyo, New York, and Berlin. The devotees of this new form of

tribal individualism have invented a "dress etiquette" aimed at keeping out intruders, a variation on the traditional beautification game, in which a newly evolved set of signs and symbols is used to exclude all those who do not know the rules.

In the past, most styles of beautification and dress have been aimed at making the wearer appear younger, more virile, sexier, more learned, even taller, wealthier, more athletic, trustworthy, reliable, or whatever, all of which had become an accepted and well understood code of symbolism within our cultural framework. The new rules, however, are deliberately inward looking and are thus only understood by the wearer's tribal mates; the tribe is saying, "We have our own coded vision of ourselves and we like our form of symbolism better than yours." But, of course, it is all a matter of perception, as in reality no particular mode of perception is any better or more aesthetic than any other.

It should also be understood that although we may well come to admire the clothing styles or forms of glamorization and beauty of members of the opposite sex, they no longer necessarily wear such styles and beautify themselves for this particular reason. The rules have, in fact, changed. Today many women choose their style of dress, cosmetics and hairstyles as a means of career advancement or social one-upmanship. Whereas this is generally true of many younger women's modes of adornment, most men still seem to be willing to dress in a style conducive to the ideals of their female partners—a notion noted by Flügel, who said that women were particularly conscious of any disapproval or ridicule that other men or women may tend to effuse on to any unusual or avant-garde form of dress of their male partner—"They feel especially, perhaps, the implied taint that the reformer is lacking in virility and to that extent dislike associating themselves with him." Instinctively knowing this, most males still invariably acquiesce to their partners' wishes and forgo any form of experimentation; some dare not even wear a colored necktie or patterned socks unless they are ones purchased or sanctioned by the current partner.

As most fashion manufacturers now perceive that women dress much more to please their own vanity, to adorn their psyche and to compete with other women, they have geared their marketing strategies accordingly, and are producing a range of merchandise that will best capitalize on this new phenomenon, which, however, does little to diminish male ardor. As Flügel has also astutely observed "Man is so irresistibly attracted to woman that he will love her in the most outrageous and hideous contraptions—not, however, because of them, but in spite of them." Thus, it is that male comments and likes concerning female styles of dress and beauty are now almost irrelevant, as women will, by and large, do as they wish. But in truth, as Gina Luria has so correctly pointed out in her book *Everywoman* (1976), coauthored with Virginia Tiger, "No woman ever really dresses for a man—men like their women undressed. For men, the naked female animal has fur and smell and secretion and flush enough." And she goes on to say that a woman never feels herself more beautiful than after getting out of bed with a lover: "her nakedness dresses her beautifully then." Her clothing in fact is usually used to wrest power and prestige from other women—women's dress and adornment is therefore a mode manipulated for social advancement and personal prestige.

Within the current framework, a new, young group of college-trained designers have been instrumental in introducing a range of "tribal" fashions into our popular culture, working within the orb of the young Paris couturier Jean Paul Gaultier. The social value of these tribal styles, as with all fringe fashions, is that they help to break the constricting monopoly of large multinational conglomerates, whose styles and ideas are franchised around the world, and whose only real interest in the fashion business is to make vast profits. These young designers, helped by mass-production conformity, have challenged the notion that fashion aesthetics are governed by commercial laws and profit margins, and they have begun to produce a smorgasbord of alternatives that have been unexpectedly successful, forcing the multinationals to follow suit and thus produce many more exciting designs. This has created a situation whereby many journalists, eager to impress their magazine bosses, have suggested that the time has come for us all to dispose of our bulging wardrobes of outdated clothes to make way for the new, New, NEWEST styles: "We should all *burn* our jeans and T-shirts; *trash* our dresses and suits; *nuke* our coats and jackets; *torch* our shoes and sneakers; *incinerate* our accessories and costume jewelry; and throw out whatever else remains. *Be brave,*" they say, "*don't waver.* Great new styles are on the way that are more in keeping with the times." The inspiration ironically did not come from the multinationals, as should have been the case if those in charge had had a grain of commercial good sense, but from sources both local and idiosyncratic. This is a true *Zeitgeist,* which may yet save fashion and beauty from the heavy hand of unfeeling autocrats, who are only in the fashion and beauty business for the

easy money. They don't understand when to take a chance, and the time is right—if I'm any judge—for them to take a plunge into the fetish fashion scene. Kinky boots, corsets, second-skin garments made of latex, PVC, leather, and rubber, S&M uniforms, underwear as outerwear, tattooing, and body piercing—today everything from a fetishist's dream appears on the fashion runways of Paris, London, Tokyo, and New York. This trend toward various forms of fetishism in clothing and beauty styles has been growing in importance during the past decade—a trend detailed by fashion historian Valerie Steele in her books *Fashion and Eroticism* (1985) and *Fetish Fashion: Sex and Power* (1996). Steele convincingly argues that the influence of many specialized fetish clothing styles have begun to enter mainstream fashion and therefore are part of our beautifying vocabulary. It is true that some theorists regard such fetish fashions as exploitative and misogynist, but Steele sees them as a "positive Amazonian statement" and points out that for the past thirty years or so the iconography of sexual fetishism has been increasingly assimilated into popular culture—from Emma Peel's black leather fetish costume worn in the 1960s television series *The Avengers* to Michelle Pfeiffer's catsuit worn in *Batman Returns* (1992). As she observes, the concept of fetishism itself has "recently assumed a growing importance in critical thinking about the cultural constriction of sexuality." Many readers may protest that fetishism is a perversion and that the pervert is always somebody else and shouldn't be featured in a book such as this. But our own fantasies betray our hypocrisy and our ambivalence about the erotic and the forbidden, the "normal" and the "perverse." As Steele observed, "Perhaps we are now seeing played out in fashion our ambivalence about what seems to be a disappearing boundary between the 'normal' and the 'perverse,' " and this "disappearing boundary" certainly affects our notions of human beauty and the way we will dress and adorn ourselves in the future. Not that I believe we will all accept these styles as they are now. Rather they will be absorbed into mainstream consciousness and reemerge as a remix of fetish, ethnic, and theatrical influences, which I am sure—once we have adjusted our psyche to fit the new ideals, or adjusted these new styles to fit our psyche—we will accept, imitate, and enjoy before they too are replaced by yet other styles influenced by other factors, which, like their predecessors of the 1950s, 1960s, 1970s, and 1980s, will be a reflection of our ever changing dreams, hopes, and aspirations—and worthy of taking their place with the fashion and beauty icons of ages past.

EMBELLISHING
THE PSYCHE

Creative expressions seldom flourish in complete isolation—their essential energy often rests on fortuitous and unpredictable influences. This is particularly true of the art of human beautification and adornment, a manifestation of our constant quest for a sexually desirable and socially

accepted body. Many people today regard their particular style of adornment and decoration as symbols of their tribe or cultural group; and whether we in our insular high-tech world fully understand this or not, these symbols are nevertheless still the basis of our notions of human beauty, and with them we embellish our psyche.

Of course, there are many people who believe that they adorn themselves in the ways that they do simply because as a member of an established society they have

no choice but to follow the established conventions, and so identify themselves according to their place in that society. They also believe that their particular form of adornment evolved over time and is therefore the most appropriate style, or that its purpose is not for sexual attraction or

enhancing personal appeal but simply the way it is because of its appropriateness. Many of these people also find it difficult to recognize the aesthetic appeal of any other form of body art and adornment, and often regard them as inappropriate, unnatural, or even barbaric.

Experience tells us, though, that we have a certain latitude in our choice of styles of body marking, adornment, and decoration and that, over time, some styles will become unfashionable and others will emerge to take their place. Generally, however, such changes are not dramatic, even if they generate controversy, since they are all within the bounds of a traditionally clothed and adorned society. But if we look back over the past thousand or so years, at the multitude of styles of our forebears, it may be difficult to comprehend that each one of these was for a time accepted as being socially correct—the only way to adorn and mark one's body according to society's code. Our forebears would surely find our current fashions just as difficult to understand.

Like all other forms of human aesthetic expression, efforts to make us beautiful are entirely subjective, based on a combination of inherited notions and personal experiences. However, as a culture, members of the industrialized world are addicted to change and novelty, within certain social constraints, so we orchestrate these changes into what we call fashions, whereby new forms of adornment and body marking that feature previously neglected areas of our physical selves, can be displayed, admired, and adorned and if necessary, we excuse this personal display on the grounds that it is "the fashion." Such changes, however, carry a dual message, the second component being a reminder to those in authority that there are certain aspects of life that are beyond their control. This is one of the reasons why such changes still elicit condemnation from those in authority, and why, in the Middle Ages and even into the seventeenth century, attempts were made to control or suppress change by numerous laws and edicts. Even later, attempts were made to use the law to control the lengths of dresses and the amount of body exposure, and to prohibit the use of cos-

metics, perfumes, and other beauty aids. For example, in England in 1770 a bill was introduced into the Parliament that decreed,

> All women, of whatever rank, profession or degree, whether virgin, maid or widow, that shall from and after such Act, impose upon, seduce and betray into matrimony, any of his Majesty's subjects by the use of scents, cosmetic washes, artificial teeth, false hair, rouge, iron stays, hoops, high-heeled shoes, and bolstered hips, shall incur the penalty now in force against witchcraft.

In more recent years, similar laws have also been enacted in many other countries, and even today in many totalitarian regimes, ordinary people are obliged to conform by law to the establishment's standards of behavior and adornment—so that they are clearly marked with the logo of that society. When such regimes lose control, however, people clamor for the fashions of other societies as we witnessed during the fall of communism in Eastern Europe with jeans, T-shirts, and sneakers, previously among the most profitable black market items, are now widely available throughout these ex-communist countries.

Such dramatic changes are a visible manifestation of a changing society, a symbol of a change of management, so to speak. They can also indicate a change in the balance of power from one generation to the next, as happened in our own society in the early 1920s and again in the early 1960s. The designer's role at such times of change is to challenge the public's mind and moral attitudes, and to explore and define the new boundaries of social constraint—crossing and recrossing these boundaries in order to extend our vision of the possible and the acceptable. And, no matter how unappealing such experimental styles may be to some, once the new boundaries have been established the styles will quickly become beautiful in the eyes of the new regime's devotees and those that follow. The deposed styles, however, often retain a nostalgic beauty in the eyes of older and disenfranchised members of society.

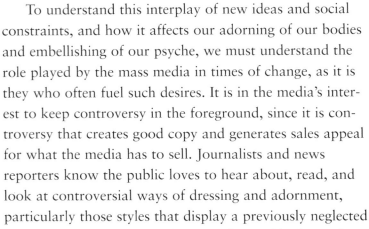

To understand this interplay of new ideas and social constraints, and how it affects our adorning of our bodies and embellishing of our psyche, we must understand the role played by the mass media in times of change, as it is they who often fuel such desires. It is in the media's interest to keep controversy in the foreground, since it is controversy that creates good copy and generates sales appeal for what the media has to sell. Journalists and news reporters know the public loves to hear about, read, and look at controversial ways of dressing and adornment, particularly those styles that display a previously neglected erogenous zone or involve another previously risqué form of body marking. They know that controversy will sell more copy or gain more viewers and therefore make more money for their employers and raise their own value—the bulk of the media's income comes from advertisers, who pay in proportion to the number of viewers audited or publications sold.

Since the end of World War II many changes have taken place in the world that have had a direct influence on the world's notions of human beauty. In Asia and the Far East, for instance, many cultures have begun to change from their traditional ways as they reap the rewards of technological advance—changes that have irrevocably altered their notions of beauty and acceptable adornment, and news of these changes has been spread around the world. These changes have undoubtedly begun to affect the ideas of the West, as the industrial world as a whole has begun to adjust itself and its products to reflect the changing attitudes of these new poten-

tial rich markets, reflecting their dreams, wishes, and desires. I suspect these ideas will ultimately change our own views and notions to a greater extent than most of us now realize. The unexpected success of the new group of non-Western designers and stylists, such as Issey Miyake, Yohji Yamamoto, Carolina Herrera, Rifat Ozbek, Kenzo, and Rei Kawakubo, to name but a few, are already beginning to reflect this change. Their success would have been unimaginable only twenty-five years ago, a success that was achieved with a great deal of help from the media. They were, after all, very different from the

established designers, and their seasonal collections made good news stories.

Since the mid-1950s the influence of television has grown in importance, bringing as it does a whole range of visual images, from Mardi Gras to lithe athletes performing gymnastic feats, into our homes. Our children have grown up knowing such visual differences are possible. Other influences include air travel, music videos, mass market and specialist magazines, sports, and, of course, advertisements in newspapers and magazines as well as those seen and heard on radio and television. All of them have had an effect and all of them carry the message of buy, Buy, BUY. The exhilaration of spending money, coupled with the envy of others that we delight in sensing when we are wearing something new, seem to have become the main motivation for our adornments, rather than the adornments' aesthetic appeal. This appetite for the new and the different has been fed by a neverending array of novelties that, although often trite or banal, nevertheless give us a sense of luxury, power, beauty, adventure, and the all important freedom of choice, and it has been to the media's benefit to encourage and fuel such insatiable appetites. It is, however, as if our entire reason for living has become one of spending money. As one leading American journalist wrote in mid-1996, "I LOVE shopping. I ADORE shopping. I WORSHIP the god of shopping. To me it's the ultimate thrill and far better than sex," and she goes on to say that the thrill of buying a new dress is far better than any orgasm—an obviously culturally learned transference that has been engineered by our consumer society to become an essential part of our way of life and that will undoubtedly affect our future notions of human beauty and modes of adornment. The specialists are already at work to ensure this—in the future we will all be seduced by new techniques in shopping psychology and manipulated by the latest sophisticated methods designed to part us from our money.

The new strategy for selling is aimed at making us discontent with the way we are and the way we look. It promises us that if only we would buy the latest fashions, the latest accessories, the latest cosmetics, or get a nose-job, colored contacts, our teeth recapped, we would look more beautiful and desirable, and our lives would become more exciting. Every psychological and physiological trigger will be pulled to persuade each of

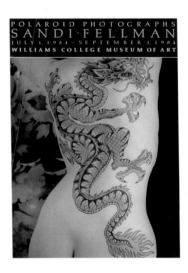

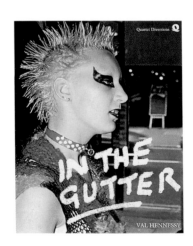

us to spend more money than we are now spending, thus forcing us to work harder to earn more. The new shops are now being designed to put us into a buying mood and to activate us so that we will willingly buy what they have to offer, with little thought being given to whether we really need this new merchandise or whether it will make us better, happier, or more fulfilled.

Advertising campaigns have and will continue to use every device known to gain sales, even crossing over the line of social restraint that could land them with criminal charges. As a spokesmen for CK (Calvin Klein) Jeans recently said in defense of what some critics called "blatant use of teenage pornography" in ads aimed at the multi-million dollar jeans market, "All we are trying to convey is the idea that glamor is an inner quality that can be found in regular people. Not something exclusive to models and movie stars." The problem was that, although all the girls used were over 16 years old, they were half undressed, and to the untutored eye, they looked much younger than their actual age. It was the looking younger that appears to have been the "crime," but as we all know, we live in an age in which youthfulness is at a premium and most women aim to look younger than their years—it's part of today's beauty culture.

It seems this notion comes from the time of the great expansion when it was accepted that brides be as young as possible in order to survive the rigors of outback life—some were as young as thirteen, the same age chosen by Shakespeare for his Juliet. Today, marriage laws and statutory rape laws forbid this, but is it really a crime and is it a crime for an older girl to look so young? Are teenage girls out of the beauty ballgame? Are they to be excluded from all future fashion ads? Are they no longer to be seen as attractive, glamorous, or even beautiful, and are we being forbidden to have another Juliet? And who is to be the arbiter of what is called feminine beauty and what is called child pornography?

For several weeks the debate raged in the American press about the Klein ads, about the evils of today's society, about the effects of rap music, about the decay of the social structure, cyberporn, bestiality, and violence in the current crop of movies and on

television. Accountability was urged by politicians before there was a social meltdown. Nobody seemed able to look at the controversy rationally or objectively. The decay of moral standards and of the social moral fiber was on their minds. The brouhaha over the ads worked in Calvin Klein's favor, just as many advertising agencies said it would. Calvin Klein jeans, and all other items with the CK logo, registered a big leap in sales, particularly to the young. As Alan Millstein, editor of the *Fashion Network Report* wryly put it, "It's more than he paid for and more than he could have prayed for." With its success, created more by the controversy than the quality of the ads themselves, we can look forward to many more such ads and controversies—but here I must add that there is a rumor that the controversy was fueled by a creative journalist to get extra mileage out of the story, a practice much used in fashion reporting and one which I remember so well from my own excursions into fashion journalism. With this in mind we can look forward to many more ads that step over the line of social acceptance to intentionally outrage and provoke—shocking millions in order to impress a few but, at the same time, opening up new vistas of the possible and broadening our current narrow notions of such topics as teenage beauty. Ads after all are just another visual stimulus from which we gain inspiration, while controversial stories help us to think, and sometimes they do help us to change our minds.

In their search for something new and hopefully controversial to write about many magazine journalists are now turning to the past, writing

risqué articles about the unusual practices and other secrets, plus inventing some, of the love goddesses and beauty icons of yesteryear—Jean Harlow, Garbo, Marilyn Monroe, Betty Grable, and the like, and others like Betty Page, who became famous in the 1950s and 1960s for her excursions into bondage and fetish wear, and whose photographic books are now being republished.

Magazine articles on the bygone era of the "beefcake boys" or "super studs," as

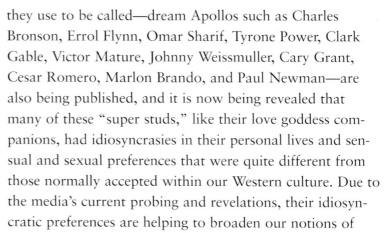

they use to be called—dream Apollos such as Charles Bronson, Errol Flynn, Omar Sharif, Tyrone Power, Clark Gable, Victor Mature, Johnny Weissmuller, Cary Grant, Cesar Romero, Marlon Brando, and Paul Newman—are also being published, and it is now being revealed that many of these "super studs," like their love goddess companions, had idiosyncrasies in their personal lives and sensual and sexual preferences that were quite different from those normally accepted within our Western culture. Due to the media's current probing and revelations, their idiosyncratic preferences are helping to broaden our notions of masculinity from that of the stereotyped macho image, which for far too long has been perpetuated by La La Land press agents.

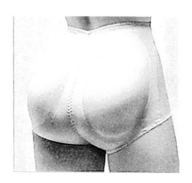

Many of the current crop of younger female icons have also readily confessed to a wide range of sensual and sexual options in their constant quest for beauty and media coverage. This too has helped to broaden our horizons of acceptability and prompted much personal experimentation, which is now reflected in individual ways of body packaging and beautification. Many of the leading stars of the entertainment world, both male and female, have also agreed to change their physical selves in the full glare

of publicity—being regularly done over by the cosmetic surgeon's scalpel in order to keep in shape and to further boost their publicity ratings.

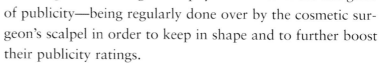

In their constant battle to keep fit and look attractive, some of our current icons, on the advice of their dieticians and gurus, drink their own urine and use a urine concentrate to cleanse their skin and as a skin tonic. It's also used as an eyewash, for curing dandruff, and to heal cuts, sores, or abrasions. It also bleaches the body hair and keeps it soft and sparse. Some regularly purge their bodies by the use of enemas, enforced vomiting, and so forth; others prefer techniques ranging from mud-baths, massage, working out with weights, or regular aerobic sessions. Still others prefer an assortment of unusual diets, some of which contain strange ingredients, like dried ground pigeon droppings, yak sperm, or extract of goat fetus—although as an historian I know far more unusual ingredients were used by the world's great beauties in the past for both dieting and as forms of cosmetics, including menstrual blood and

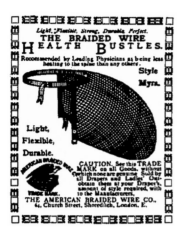

semen and vaginal fluids. These practices still exist, with some young Asian women, for instance, using their first day's menstrual blood to beautify their face and skin, while young South Sea Islanders, both male and female, traditionally use their combined lovemaking secretions for the same purpose. All this and much much more are regularly used in Beverly Hills and elsewhere to keep our film stars, pop singers, and other performers healthy and looking beautiful, according to our current notions. (Of course as a researcher, I have tried these various beautifying methods, as has my current partner, Velvet-Moon, and we can both vouch for their effectiveness.)

In the 1990s, the supermodels of the fashion runways and magazines, with their trim, polished, steel-like bodies and finely honed features, seem to have taken over the role of glamor queens from the Hollywood stars—it is now they who shape our aspirations and psyche. In numerous articles we learn that the new beauty icons, such as Naomi Campbell, Cindy Crawford, Claudia Schiffer, and the slightly older Elle Macpherson grew up under the influence of television, with Naomi in particular, like so many of her generation, being greatly influenced by pop-stars, including the androgynous Boy George who was so popular in her formative years. In one article quoting from "*CATwalk: Inside the worlds of the SUPER MODELS*" by Sandra Morris (1996), the journalist wrote that "the new breed of supermodel celebrities had eclipsed pop stars and movie stars as today's modern beauty icons." Another journalist, paraphrasing the writings of Camille Paglia, the American feminist, wrote, "The nineties cult of super

models is a revival of the great system of Hollywood stars, which I totally applaud. I've never regarded Hollywood glamour as superficial—it is an art form," and goes on to say that "Super models have made the transition into what films used to provide— that of glamour." On the subject of being beautiful and using all human inventiveness to add to that beauty, this journalist said, in effect, "that it is all a form of aesthetic expression: a form of art work for the mass-

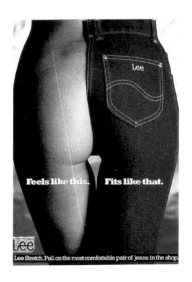

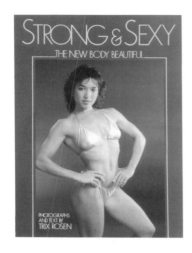

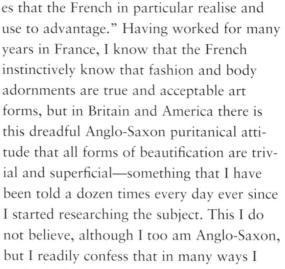

es that the French in particular realise and use to advantage." Having worked for many years in France, I know that the French instinctively know that fashion and body adornments are true and acceptable art forms, but in Britain and America there is this dreadful Anglo-Saxon puritanical attitude that all forms of beautification are trivial and superficial—something that I have been told a dozen times every day ever since I started researching the subject. This I do not believe, although I too am Anglo-Saxon, but I readily confess that in many ways I wish I had been born French or Italian and preferably female.

Supermodels are not professional actresses and very few are able to cross over into the realm of acting: Their appeal is entirely visual and not on a continual basis as in acting, but on a momentary basis, just when the camera clicks. Even the runway performances are only an extended version of this special talent—it's not acting, it's attitude, and for this they are paid much more than most actresses. They are, however, well aware that their professional career as a beauty icon is limited and hence they try to forge an extended career—they are far too narcissistic to settle for early retirement or marriage, except, of course, to a rock, pop, or film star. Of those I regularly worked with while running my own fashion business in the 1960s, I remember in particular Jean Shrimpton who, once she lost her looks after just six years in the headlines and after love affairs with numerous celebrities, had a very hard time before she found any sort of happiness and eventually settled into running a small hotel in the West Country of southern England. Twiggy—Leslie Hornby—who I introduced to Ken Russell and with whom she made a pleasant but unremarkable film, *The Boy Friend,* in 1971, had to settle for being a cabaret performer for a time before becoming a merchandising consultant at Marks & Spencer, while Veruschka—Vera Lehndorff—after appearing in a number of films, including

Antonioni's *Blow-Up* in 1967, wisely teamed up with the artist Holger Trulzsch and built a new career in body art. Their book *Veruschka: Transfigurations* (1986) became a bestseller and greatly helped the cause of body aesthetics. Others, like many of the 1930s and 1940s Hollywood stars, took to drink or drugs or committed suicide once their "looks" had started to fade.

To be beautiful, really beautiful, is very demanding and very difficult. Many of today models are simply so attractive that they project a look of inaccessibility for us mere mortals and therefore we assume that they are entirely self-sufficient and are above needing any help. As Hal Lifson, executive producer of Hanna Barbera Productions told Lesley-Ann Jones, author of *Naomi: The Rise and Rise of the Girl from Nowhere* (1993), "They are chiselled to perfection, they are always working on their looks. They are not just beautiful women, they are awesome. This tends to make them completely unap-proachable as people." A comment that seems to be borne out by the recent glut of books and magazine articles on the subject, which have also told in great detail the plight of many famous and lesser known ex-models and other unfortunate hopefuls. It may be true, as the Polynesians and many other cultural groups believe, "that beauty is the gift of the gods and should be honored as such," but in the industrialized world, where high honor just doesn't seem to be enough, beauty does seem to take its toll on human life—a fact exemplified in 1996 by the suicide of Margaux Hemingway—the "face" of the 1980s.

Ambitious mothers, however, are not deterred from starting their young offspring in the very competitive field of modeling,

often at the tender age of six months, some even younger. By the age when most normal children are first attending kindergarten, these experienced "troupers" are wearing high-heeled shoes, skin-tight, form-revealing bathing suits, bouffant hair styles, expensive jewelry, and a full range of facial cosmetics, as they compete with other toddlers for the "Beauty Crown" of this or that East or West Coast resort. On reaching maturity a sufficient number of these competitors have become so professional at exploiting their looks and physical assets, with many column inches praising their success and beauty crowns to prove their ability, they quickly become icons of envy for those who follow in their footsteps. They also continue to influence the media, who are always hungry for news stories, and thus a schism is formed between reality and their fantasy world of being rich and famous, with the public being oblivious of the fact that many of those they aspire to imitate are total failures as people—their appeal is the "Dynasty style" of outside gloss. The inner person has little merit. This is unfortunately also true of many of our other beauty icons from the fashion world, films, television and the pop 'n' rock scene.

Androgyny is another subject that has greatly interested the media in recent years, and one which has prompted many articles about its current origins and influences; from Marc Bolan and the Beatles to Boy George and David Bowie. It is a subject that has opened up a whole range of possibilities for those who wish to dress and beautify themselves a little differently from the norm, and who want to express another aspect of their psyche, rather than accepting the enforced stereotyping of our gender-oriented dress code. For many years such choice was forbidden by the church and the law, although its close cousin, dandyism—also regarded by many as a very effeminate, or unmasculine mode of dress, hated by the zealots—was from time to time fashionable among wealthy and well-connected young men about town. During the seventeenth and eighteenth centuries, for instance, young dandies who had the time and money to devote to their chosen way of dressing their psyche as they wished, spent many hours each day at their toiletry, painting and powdering, arching their eyebrows, dressing their hair, and scenting their linen. They used ground pumice-stone to prevent

their hands from becoming rough, and they slept with them in the finest chicken skin gloves to keep them small, soft, and white—the hands being a very important means of distinguishing members of the leisured rich from the *nouveau riche*. By experience and breeding they were also able to wear their face patches, high-heeled shoes, curled and colored wigs, face powder, rouge and lipstick, eye shadow, fur muffs, and exotic fans with more *panache*—a man not brought up to such modes often finds it very difficult not to show some kind of unease when so adorned and beautified, and it certainly doesn't sit well with his psyche.

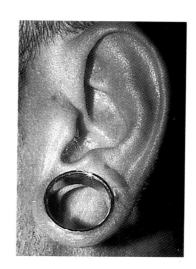

Dandyism in the mid-eighteenth century became very extravagant, fashionable young men spending vast fortunes on the latest novelties, such as embellishing their new shapelier, long-tailed, velvet jackets with gold and jewel-encrusted embroidery; jewelled shoe buckles, jewelled buttons, extravagantly decorated lace-trimmed gloves, and laced-up steel and whalebone corsets. They also wore embroidered waistcoats, the finest linen trimmed with rouleau edgings, tassels, and much braiding—a fashion that reached its most extreme form with the members of the Macaronis—a young men's club founded in London in 1772 for those who had completed a minimum of a year-long cultural tour to Italy, Greece, and France to see the ancient monuments and soak up the continental culture.

During the early- to-mid-nineteenth century, dandyism, or foppery, as it was then called, began to combine in the public mind with homosexuality, cross-dressing, transvestitism, and forms of androgynous behavior. Prompted by the clergy, people began to regard it as deviant, lustful, and licentious, and it was outlawed in most Western countries—punishable by imprisonment. It was completely forgotten that in ancient Greece androgynous and even homosexual behavior had been glorified, particularly during the great festivals, and that, for example, the first Governor of New York

GUICHE NAVEL PRINCE ALBERT NIPPLE HAFADA

BODY PIERCINGS
BY DOUG MALLOY

AMPALLANG DYDOE FORESKIN CLITORIS LABIA APADRAVYA FRENUM

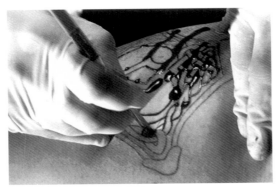

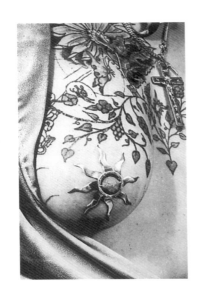

had been well known for his incursions into the world of femininity—Lord Cornbury possessed a remarkable resemblance to Queen Anne and was very fond of appearing in facsimiles of her clothing.

To cater to this side of the male psyche, and at the same time to allay the clerics' horror of having to come to terms with both their own and their congregations' androgynous and bisexual tendencies—which whether we like to admit it or not, seems to have been encoded into our DNA—our forebears had originally institutionalized a system whereby selected males were notionally "licensed" by society to undertake certain female characterizations. This acting out of others' fantasies was noted in early accounts of village and courtly life, and by the Middle Ages numerous theatrical companies were specializing in training young men in the art of female impersonation.

These female impersonators were taken into training as young boys and instructed in the art of feminine makeup, gestures and mannerisms, apparel, and voice control. Several noted performers, like their famous castrato cousins in the world of music, were castrated so as to retain their youthful looks and more feminine voice. Their life was highly regimented and they pursued their profession with zeal, progressing from simple walk-on parts to more difficult female roles. Shakespeare wrote many of his biting female characterizations around the skills of these male "actresses": Nathaniel Field is believed to have played the first Ophelia around 1601 and in 1607 Robert Goughe [or Goffe] played the first Cleopatra. From 1660, however, with more liberal attitudes prevailing after years of religious, political and social unrest, the young, more feminine dandies began to usurp this social role from the professionals, and its theatrical manifestation began to wane.

But controversial novelty did not disappear from the theater. While the dandies were parading their skills in country life and at fashionable soirees, actresses were beginning to adopt male modes of attire: "Exposing those parts of the female form which nature teaches all civilised peoples should be concealed from public view," with some actresses' legs reportedly being "revealed in a close-fitting male habit, which gave the audience a view of the exact turn of the shape of the feminine form, as complete as if seen without any covering on at all," and which was described as being "more degrading than nakedness itself." But when dancers disposed of such covering to display their legs there were furter outbursts of condemnation.

The clerics in their wisdom were able to add to the allure of such styles by their denunciations—as Robert Burton had so aptly pointed out in

1621, "women are of such a disposition they will mostly covet that which others have attempted to deny them." Gradually, however, during the intervening years, the continual experimentation of females wearing male modes of dress by the fashionable elite and theatrical performers eventually broke down the religious and social resistance against women wearing male dress styles to a point where a woman today can wear any item of male dress, including his Y-front underpants, without fear of being arrested and, hence, most masculine modes have lost their inherent erotic appeal and many women are beginning to look elsewhere for styles to embellish their psyche. Men, however, are still not the equal of women in this matter, and even today they do not fully enjoy the same socially accepted privileges in matters of cross-dressing and experimentation, although this does appear to be changing for those who want to flout such conventions.

As in earlier times, most males today still appear to prefer to delegate this androgynous side of their psyche to the professionals—female impersonators, pop singers, theatrical and film performers, and a few members of the social elite. There has also been a marked increase in the number of annual Mardi Gras and carnivals in various countries of the world, at which it has become almost commonplace for otherwise perfectly ordinary men to wear very ornate styles of feminine or fetish attire. Some of these are screened around the world via television and documented in numerous books and magazines for us all to see and to be influenced by. In recent years, television has also screened a variety of programs about places in the world where male cross-dressers are believed to have special religious or sacred powers, and there are numerous films in which notable male actors have appeared as women or in feminine and fetish modes.

The change in social attitudes toward androgynous behavior and cross-dressing was greatly assisted by the decriminalization of homosexuality in most Western countries in the late 1960s. The resulting dress styles became the medium for displaying all the portents and symbols that had been conveyed by the earlier dandyism. After decriminalization, a number of gay groups entered the pop music scene, giving rise to "glam-rock," a form of glitzy institutionalized vaudeville camp. Heterosexual groups "in drag," various heavy metal bands in variations of S&M and bondage gear, groups such as Kiss and Queen, and many pop stars, by

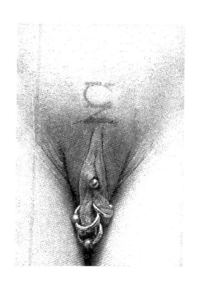

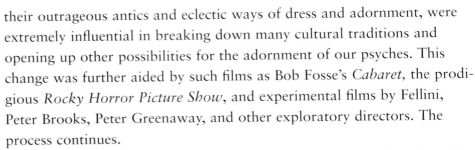

their outrageous antics and eclectic ways of dress and adornment, were extremely influential in breaking down many cultural traditions and opening up other possibilities for the adornment of our psyches. This change was further aided by such films as Bob Fosse's *Cabaret*, the prodigious *Rocky Horror Picture Show*, and experimental films by Fellini, Peter Brooks, Peter Greenaway, and other exploratory directors. The process continues.

The younger generation are now generally more openminded about the new and the different and how to adapt it to their advantage, thus giving them the opportunity of dressing, adorning, and beautifying their bodies as well as their psyche and sexuality, as they choose. They have grown up in an atmosphere of continuous change, and their appetites for new styles of imagery have been fed from a cornucopia of ideas presented by the media. For some their mode of body packaging has become a glittering kaleidoscope used to flaunt their sexuality. Today, "anything, but anything, goes," black leather, studs and chains, rubber wear, the use of body painting, tattooing, and stick-on keloid scars, and even branding and body piercing have appeared in the repertoire of these young people, as has the wearing of lingerie as outerwear.

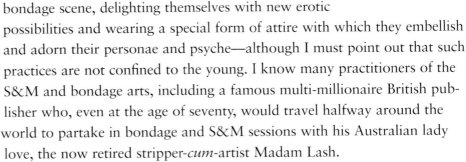

Many young people are also into the S&M and bondage scene, delighting themselves with new erotic possibilities and wearing a special form of attire with which they embellish and adorn their personae and psyche—although I must point out that such practices are not confined to the young. I know many practitioners of the S&M and bondage arts, including a famous multi-millionaire British publisher who, even at the age of seventy, would travel halfway around the world to partake in bondage and S&M sessions with his Australian lady love, the now retired stripper-*cum*-artist Madam Lash.

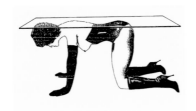

Another relatively recent innovation in the realm of choice is that of body building, which has become a widely accepted form of body modification akin to many tribal practices and which has an effect on the mind and the psyche as well as the body. With the aid of hormone treatment, exercise machines, cosmetic surgery, silicone implants, the use of steroids, liposculpture, and rigorous diets, the newly reshaped body has begun to redefine body aesthetics for both sexes. Taken to extremes it can create men of huge proportions—Arnold Schwarzenegger is a much admired example—while in the case of female body building the remark of a journalist who attended one of the first major competitions of women body builders in the late 1970s is pertinent: "A woman today who chooses to remake her body by exercise may be developing a more efficient living machine, but she is also redefining the boundaries of femininity. One man's Helen of Troy is another man's sideshow hermaphrodite," and is in reality, the flip-side of androgyny.

Other forms of body modification have also gained in popularity in recent years. The practice of traditional aesthetic forms of tattooing, which is often used by individuals to express their inner feelings or psyche, has a growing number of Western devotees who, over a period of years, have been transforming their entire skin area into a single designed unit, in the way that some Oceanic peoples have done for many centuries. Others are having their genitals, breasts, backs, and thighs tattooed in modern interpretations of this ancient art form—based, for instance, upon the Trobriand Islanders' custom of beautifying the labia and surrounding area of the pubic region and thighs at puberty as a sign of sexual maturity, independence, and tribal beauty. As one of the new Western devotees recently said in an article on the subject:

> My tattoos are an affirmation of my cultural independence. You have
> them carried out on your body in the full knowledge that this is your body
> to have and enjoy while you're here. You have fun with it—nobody else
> can control what you do with it unless you let them. It is one of the few
> remaining freedoms we have. I was tattooed as an act of personal choice
> and as a demonstration of my social independence.

At a tattooist convention held in California in 1994, a number of other devotees confirmed this individualist attitude, and one that I also found was strongly echoed in the beliefs of many others who had been branded or had their bodies pierced. Like tattooing, the exact origins of body piercing is not known, but there is evidence to show that it was widely practiced during Egyptian, Greek, Minoan, and Roman times. The Aztecs and various African cultures have also depicted various forms of body piercing in their sculptures, and even today in many of the more remote areas of the world, a wide variety of nose, lip, nipple, genital, navel, and ear ornaments that require the body to be pierced are used as traditional ways of beautification.

In the *Kama Sutra*, the ancient classic Hindu treatise on love and social conduct, lovers are advised to perfume every part of their bodies,

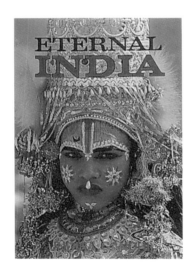

to wear a wide variety of jewelry and other allurements, and to practice all the other arts of beautification and enhancement so as to keep their partners happy and contented. One such device, the *apadravya*—a stud-ended bar placed vertically through the center of the head of the penis—is highly recommended as it has the power "to excite one's lover into the realms of ecstasy." Others recommended are the *palang* or *ampallang* placed horizontally, and the *dydoe* placed through the ring of the crown of the glans—with these studs and bars being made from bone, ivory, gold, or silver. In addition, rings or studs and bars can be placed through the foreskin and scrotum. In the traditional areas where such adornments are still widely worn, these devices are perceived as adding greatly to a man's beauty, and they often tattoo themselves in special ways to indicate the type of piercing with which they are adorned. Among the Iban of Sarawak and Kalimantan they indicate they have a *palang (ampallang)* piercing by displaying a *Buak Trong* tattoo on their shoulders and back—their throat tattoo is an added attractant, indicating they have killed an enemy warrior and therefore have special inherent powers. And generally the women in these areas deny marriage to a man not so adorned, some preferring a man who has a double *palang* or other device fitted, and they frequently specify the size and the shape of the studs, bars, or rings to be worn, in much the same way as many Western women today specify their own special foibles and delights in such matters.

Women's genital regions are also receiving a more enlightened mode of beautification within the realms of what is now referred to as a new form of tribal primitivism, including the revival of decorated pubic hair, and their own selection of personalized designer jewelry with which to decorate their labia or clitoral hood. In the sixteenth through eighteenth centuries there was a fashion for such intimate styles among the nobility of Europe, with ribbons, plaits, semiprecious jewels, and pearl droplets creating a trea-sure chest for the delight of those involved in unexpected encounters. There are numerous detailed accounts of these free-thinking women, who made no secret of the assumption that if their newest lover was to be allowed to enjoy the pleasures associated with such forms of refinement, then they had to add to this form of embellishment by a gift of a baroque pearl droplet or similar costly bauble. Many modern day women are also beginning to dec-orate their pubic hair, and to have their nipples, navels, eyebrows, tongue, lips, and nose pierced. They are also having their hips and thighs reshaped and tattooed, and other areas remodeled in order to conform to today's canons of beauty.

In fact, from the puberty rites of orthodontia, to slimming diets, fitness classes and aerobics, silicone breast implants, penile enlargement, nose jobs, manicure and pedicure, the wearing of colored contact lenses, electrolysis and laser treatments, regular purges, exfoliation and liposuction, visits to the hairdresser, to the cosmetic surgeon who can sculpt your *derrière* into a facsimile of Naomi Campbell's, or give you Christy Turlington's lips, and all the other devoted specialists' attempts to deliver the perfect face and figure, it can be clearly seen that we in the West are far from "normal" in our approach to beauty. And while bound lotus feet, stretched necks, and duck-bill lips may not be to our personal liking we must be very careful to remove those decorative bones from our own nose before passing judgment on our neighbor's. All peoples, including those of our own tribe, should have the freedom to adorn and decorate themselves according to their own wishes, even if we feel they should know better, whatever "better" may mean.

The introduction of these new ideas and approaches underlines the notion that although beauty is a matter of aesthetics, aesthetics are not immutable. They are simply a matter of cultural agreement arrived at by our forebears—a phenomenon based on inherited ideals—with these ideals being nothing more than an acceptance of previously ordained standards. These standards are never permanent however, as they have always been gradually changed as our culture itself changes. Human aesthetics, which of course includes all forms of beauty, including that of our own tribe, is therefore no more than conventional acceptance of an ever-changing norm and it is up to us to change it according to our wishes.

With the increasing number of Western tribal groups that are breaking away from the homogeneous whole—"bikers," "cyberpunks," "surfers," followers of various rock groups, the "urban ferals," "skinhead revivalists," addicts of particular designer clothes, those who like to display their allegiance to/ownership of a Porsche or Harley Davidson, S&M and "bondage freaks," the devotées of the work of Allen Jones and his contemporaries, those whose preferences is the *La Cage aux Folles* or *Les Girls* scene, the "modern primitives," etc., and more traditional tribes like the preppies and the debutantes—it would seem that we are experiencing a backlash against commercialism. It would appear that more and more members of the younger generation, like some of their older compatriots, are seeking out symbols of belonging to smaller communities, rather than the huge industrialized conglomerate into which they feel they have been forced to live. In fact, there is much the same kind of fragmentation of society as happened in the early 1960s, which spawned the beatniks, flower

children, the beautiful people, the jet setters, the mods and rockers, etc. Today in many large cities small ethnic groups are also joining together to celebrate their cultural differences by wearing traditional styles of dress—and it is often by these distinctive styles that they perceive members of the opposite sex as being beautiful according to their ancient customs. Ironically, in the nonindustrial world the younger generation are discarding the traditional symbols of their own tribes as they take on the insignia and regalia of our Western ways in order to more closely associate themselves and particularly their psyche with our privileged lifestyle. And they are also attempting to adapt themselves to our Western styles of beauty.

Such changes have been fuelled by the encroachment of what is referred to as the global village. In almost every country I have traveled through in recent years I have seen changes that reflect the influence of Western industrialization. These changes are in evidence even in the most remote villages, where the main source of outside influence is a communal television set. Every evening the villagers watch the same programs and commercials as we do, which naturally enough affects their psyche, as well as how they wish to adorn and beautify their bodies. The somewhat ironic nature of this became evident when I was researching a little-known head-hunting tribe in central New Guinea near the Irian Jaya border. After several days trekking with a Japanese photographer and his assistant through dense jungle and mountainous terrain, we were invited to join the villagers for a sort of television dinner. Being on top of a mountain range, the village was able to receive a number of stations beamed in to service the more populated lowlands and Cape York peninsula of northern Australia. Flicking from one channel to the other we watched segments from *Sale of the Century, Tom and Jerry, LA Law,* and a re-run of the 1980 South African film *The Gods Must Be Crazy*—a very apt title in the circumstances.

In the film, the male lead is a Kalahari San bushman named N'Xau; typical of his race, he is small and slender by European standards. The female lead is a young blonde of Anglo-Dutch descent. When N'Xau first sees his co-star he becomes a voyeur for a few minutes while he watches her change her lace blouse; he talks to himself about this apparition. Having never seen a white woman before, he thinks her the ugliest person he has ever seen—as pale as something that has just crawled out from under a rotting log; her blonde hair is quite gruesome, long and stringy and nearly white as if she were very old. She was big, too (by bushman standards): He would have to dig the whole day to find enough food to feed her. And although it was a hot day she was covering her body with

something quite hideous that resembled a cobweb.

Although this sequence was obviously scripted into the film as an amusing diversion, it nevertheless clearly illustrates the great divergence of opinions that exist about human beauty. The Japanese photographer, his Czech assistant, the villagers, and I were all viewing the film from our own different perspectives, and all our perceptions were different from those of the San bushman or the South Africans for whom the film was originally made. The highlanders believe that only men can be beautiful anyway, and they wondered why so much fuss was being made about the white South African woman. Since that experience, I have been unable to view young female Caucasians in quite the same way.

Alongside the tribal life of Papua New Guinea there are Chinese takeaways, instant coffee, *Pepsi Cola* and *Coke*, English-style bacon-and-egg breakfasts, American hamburgers, French croissants, and multinational cigarettes. Many highlanders now drive to their traditional *sing-sings* in imported cars, changing into their feather-bedecked costumes and colorful makeup on arrival and leaving their everyday jeans and T-shirts in the car. In some areas the more successful businessmen, whose tribal valley contains gold or some other valuable resource, fly to their appointments by helicopter, wearing elegant suits but proudly retaining their nose decorations. And at important tribal gatherings, there are sky divers and Muppet-style puppet shows alongside stalls selling traditional dog-tooth necklaces, *kina* shell chest medallions, boars' tusk nose ornaments, and decorative penis gourds. In many areas of the country, beauty is a male prerogative and such beauty resides in a "Big Man's" beard, his strong masculine features, his hair or wig, the bird of paradise feathers he wears, his nasal decoration, and his tribal makeup. But it is in symbolism that the real beauty of a truly Big Man resides. The *omak* of the Kauil, for example, is the nearest equivalent they have to the robes of office of a hereditary autocrat. Unlike such robes, however, the *omak* is merely a simple adornment made from local jungle string and a number of identical horizontal strips of wild *pit-pit* cane; the greater the number of strips,

the greater the wearer's tribal wealth and the greater his perceived beauty.

From a Western standpoint, there are several points of interest here. First, in many areas of Papua New Guinea, particularly in the highlands, beauty is a male prerogative, with a Big Man being the top notcher by virtue of the length of his *omak* or some other similar adornment. Second, no Big Man can increase his status by furtively adding a few extra pieces of *pit-pit* cane to this adornment—everybody knows every detail of his life's history and if he were caught cheating he would lose all credibility. Third, the *omak* itself has no intrinsic value, being made from commonly available materials. Fourth, although it indicates a man's worth to the community and his social standing, the *omak* does not indicate in any way his current wealth, only that which he has previously given away during the rituals of his adult life. And it is the giving away, rather than the having, that is of importance here. The next point is a little more nebulous, as it involves understanding why the mature male in the New Guinea Highlands is considered to be more beautiful in an aesthetic sense than the female, and it was while living with the Huli people that I began to see what this actually meant, and to understand the reason why this was so, or more correctly, why it is not also so in the industrialized world.

Nearly all the tribal peoples I have lived with were, until very recent times, warlike, with the young men being initiated into the warrior class on reaching sexual maturity and being responsible for protecting the community and its property. They stayed warriors until their age group relinquished that position to a new group of warriors, possibly five, ten, or even fifteen years later. During this period, they were not normally allowed to marry; marriage was reserved for the village elders who had served their warrior time and had thus earned the right to take a wife. They were, however, allowed liaisons with younger women, married or not, and invariably it was the woman's choice as to who gained her favors. Therefore, it was to the advantage of the warrior to be noticed and to be enticing. This acceptance of female choice is also why the males of many nomad peoples like the Wodaabe make themselves irresistible during their annual *Geerewol* celebration so that they will stand a better

chance of being chosen as a husband or lover. And even where marriage is permitted for young warriors, as it is with the Wodaabe, those who are considered beautiful are more likely to be chosen as a husband and to sire more children from additional clandestine affairs with additional "wives," in addition to affairs arranged by less attractive husbands, in the hope that they will sire beautiful children on their behalf.

The social rules regarding male beauty in the western world were, however, changed from what one might call "the reign of the peacock" during the period of industrialization and revolution of the late eighteenth century—the time that Flügel and others refer to as "The great renunciation of masculine beauty." Henceforth the male's aim was to be useful and productive—the breadwinner and provider—what is often referred to as "the offer of a safe and well-provided nest." They were expected to be correctly attired rather than beautiful, elegant, or modish. And it has remained that way until very recent times.

With the Huli, as with other New Guinea highland tribes I visited, I found that no social position was hereditary—every person must earn their place in society, and this is one reason why they so willingly give up so much for their *omak* or its equivalent. They are respected for who they are and what they have done and certainly not for any family connections or for any sort of ancient lineage. As they each proclaimed, "We all have an ancient lineage and it's one that stretches back to the very dawn of time." And of course they are quite right, we all also have such an ancient lineage. How could it be otherwise?

In our western urban societies, however, although attitudes are beginning to change about family lineage, masculine beauty, feminine attractiveness, and so forth, cheating in what we say about ourselves and our place in society by use of purchasable attributes is an accepted part of the game of life. Through our varying styles of adornment and beautification we create fictional characters, characters approximating those people we would like to be at that moment. In fact, so closely do some people identify with the characters they play that, with the aid of the necessary props, they actually become, in their minds at least, a successful stockbroker, a business tycoon, Prince, Cher, or Cindy Crawford, but rarely themselves.

The trend to fantasize and to adorn our psyche with our dreams has led to an increasing demand for special occasion and performance forms of attire and beautification: lovers' dressing-up gear, to see what fun can be had by reversing the roles or play-acting unfamiliar ones; bondage and sado-masochism sessions; or going to a disco to compete against all those lovely bodies. The accent has in reality become one of dressing the psyche and the imagination, not the body. This has begun to be reflected in the styles being designed in the fashion centers of the world, with Paris seasonal shows in particular now becoming "ten days of madness—of dreams, phantoms and magic. Hollywood-sur-Seine. An extravaganza of color, hysteria, special effects and over-stimulation. The ultimate theatrical production." Many of the famous couture houses even regularly change their designers in order to keep up with the changing times.

This theatricality, aimed at adorning our dreams and our psyche, is further accentuated by music video hype, the unrestrained profligacies of television commercials, the extraordinary styles of makeup and performance clothes worn by many rock and pop artists, and by the outrageous wardrobing or, in some cases, the almost complete lack of wardrobing except for some stick-on sequins, leather straps, metal chains, or the like, in films aimed at the teenage market. The mass media are transforming our notions of dress, ornament, and beauty from the real to a magical coded system of desire, aspiration, and titillation. It is a journey from the actual to a hallucinatory mirage. It totally embellishes our psyche and our inner selves, isolating us from the realities of the real world.

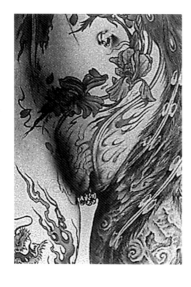

The other side of this development is "reactionary chic," a unique British-inspired tribal development for going forward into the past, or backward into the future. It is a reaction against all other tribal groups—rock, sex, and drugs, lesbians and all that equality nonsense. It's a sort of *Brideshead Revisited*: the traditional country look of tweed coordinates in muted colors, of peaches-and-cream complexions without a hint of makeup, of lisle stockings, and sensible shoes. It evokes Daddy's estate in the country and the old Rolls Royce, Bentley, or Alvis to meet one's friends at the station. It means being adorned absolutely correctly, according to an unwritten set of rules, for each specific social occasion, and it means that looking right according to tradition is far more important than looking attractive or fashionable.

But even in rural England, as in Japan, the highlands of New Guinea, the former Soviet Union, their various satellites and other former communist countries, the tribal lands of the Maasai and the Samburu, or with the nomads of the Niger, the Mexican Indians, the Nuba of the Sudan, and the Xingu of the Brazilian jungle, life is changing. Daddy has died. The estate has been sold, and the heirlooms have been distributed. Other tribes are poaching most of the younger recruits from the followers of reactionary chic, in much the same way that many of the younger members of the Akha, Xingu, Maasai, and so on, are turning away from their traditional ways, forming new alliances. And in some of the more affluent areas of the industrial world, where many younger groups have become totally disenchanted with the over commercialization of life, a new form of urban tribalism is emerging, which, when linked with New Age philosophy, has once again begun to break down the traditions and ways of the older generation in order to create a better, or at least a different lifestyle, and they are marking themselves accordingly, and in the process are creating their own body aesthetics.

I first noticed this change in the late 1980s while living in California, a totally different way of life to that which I had become used to on a small Melanesian island in the South Pacific. Everything on the West Coast seemed to have to be done in such a hurry, and although the people with whom I worked all seemed to be affluent, they were always unhappy and arguing— seldom a smile or a kind word, and they were seldom content with their everyday life. This was a complete contrast from the idyllic tropical island where, although poor, the local people always seemed content with their frugal lifestyle, and the children were always happy and always playing.

While living in California, and a little later in New York and London, I noted what appeared to be a pivotal change in our ever increasingly industrialized world—the wholesale deindividualizing of many members of the population and in some cases of whole indigenous

societies—as if their very souls had been stolen and they were left as empty shells, alive only for the benefit of commercial interests as workers or consumers. When I first started to travel, New York, London, Paris, San Francisco, and Tokyo were all very different from one another. But with the inundation of mass-produced objects and especially of the millions of mass-produced images with which the media assaults our every minute, everything had begun to look the same. It became harder to distinguish between real places and real experiences and those I had experienced while watching television or a film. It was as if my brain had been sabotaged by some sort of virus and my real experiences were being replaced with the collective experiences of the mass media, thus removing me, and presumably everyone else, from our individuality. And for a time, I scarcely knew what to think, especially within the realms of our current topic, human adornment and beautification, because everything else seemed to have been much more important, but was beyond anything that I could actually do to change it, try as I might.

Undoubtedly we were, and for that matter still are, in a collective state of confusion. The structures—political, spiritual, sexual, and personal— that served our parents and grandparents are no longer appropriate. Collective confusion prevails as we seek meaning and harmony in our lives, while knowing instinctively that nothing new can be born without a period of chaos and darkness—which nevertheless we are all trying to avoid. And in trying to find an answer to this conundrum, I reread a number of books on tribal societies, particularly those of the South Pacific where I had lived for a time and where, by and large, the people seemed to be happy enough without all the sophisticated trimmings with which we clutter our lives.

In Stanley Diamond's *In Search of the Primitive* (1954), I came across a clue to the problem: "In machine based societies," he wrote, "the machine has incorporated the demands of the civil power and of the market, and the whole life of society, of all classes and grades must adjust to its rhythms." This is what has happened to us, we have been forced to adjust to the working rhythm of machines and mass production but in a greater degree than Stanley Diamond could have imagined. Our whole lives have become mechanized through the use of computers, conveyor belts, motor cars, time-saving gadgets like electric kettles, vacuum cleaners, television, electric shavers, dishwashers, and the like. And because of this, as he says, time has become lineal, secularized, precious, in the sense that "it is reduced to an extension in space that must be filled up so as not to waste any of it," and thus our non-sacred time, which used to be reserved for ourselves and in which we were able to contemplate and meditate has disappeared— we have become addicted to and ruled by the machines and gadgets with which we surround ourselves and which we mistakenly thought would free us from industrial servitude.

I soon noted the same feeling of powerlessness among many young people, and they told me, in the mixed group therapy sessions that I gave, that regardless of what they thought or did, there was very little they could do to change the world in the way they wished. They had become disenchanted with what they saw as an over-commercialized second-hand life that had removed them from all reality and individuality—even sex seemed to be a second-hand experience. From early childhood, they had experienced, via television and mass impersonal education, everything the world had to offer, from deep sea diving in the Coral Seas, photo safaris in Zimbabwe, fashion shows in Paris, archeological digs, grand feasts, even mixed racial orgies involving men, women, animals, and androgynous beings. Their minds had become a memory bank of second-hand experiences and nothing seemed to have any meaning for them. Everything they did had become inextricably inter-twined with [   ] od of pre-stored images and implanted formula making [   ] oid than human. They wished to reclaim their human [   ] ome were doing this by marking their bodies in various [   ] piercing, branding, scarring, and the like, all of which [   ] ount of physical pain. It seemed only through pain [   ] ack in touch with their bodies. Pain was real and couldn't be experienced via their collective memory bank—it was loaded with a tangible shock that really did say "this is happening to me," and it is this realization that was of importance to them, plus the fact that they were reclaiming their bodies as free individuals, and demonstrating that they had the right to mark them as they chose and nobody had the right to stop them.

I had been lucky it seems, having grown up in a time before television and the media hype and had experienced

life first hand, having been born and raised in London's East End during the depression years and World War II, which in real terms meant that during my formative years I had had very little in the way of home comforts, no money to spend on amusements, very little formal schooling, but a lot of hands-on experience and learning how to make do. Since those early years, I have also been lucky enough to live and work in many other diverse places—in Beverly Hills, on a tropical Melanesian island, with the Huli in the Highlands of New Guinea, the Maasai in Kenya, the Padaung people on the Burmese/Thailand border, the aboriginal wilds of central Australia, and the center of the fashion world in Paris, where my experience of acceptance has been of great advantage.

I have experienced great opulence and thoughtless waste; the glitz of the art and fashion world and the darker reality of greed and bigotry. I have seen people killed by bombs, city centers destroyed by riots, and countries devastated by famine. I have worked with many of the world's most beautiful and talented people and a diverse range of projects with tribal groups. I have slept on beds made from cow dung and been chased by warring tribes. I've had spears thrown at me, been "married" to three tribal "wives" and enjoyed three other long-term de-facto relationships with young women from different cultures of the world, in addition to having been married for fifteen years to an Anglo-Eurasian. I have three children and numerous grandchildren, all of which has reflected on the way I think and what I do. And I was able to call on this experience during the therapy sessions. But after living in L.A. for just over a year, I too found the need to be marked, or rather pierced and tattooed, in order to get back in touch with my primal self. I had become numbed and jaded from the Los Angeles lifestyle. It was then that I met Fakir Musafar (Roland Loomis), the man many regard as the guru of the modern primitives, publisher of *Body Play & Modern Primates Quarterly (BP & MPQ)* and previously a regular contributor to *Piercing Fans International Quarterly (PFIQ)* which has a worldwide distribution network—both publications, along with *Body Art, Secret Magazine, Skin*

Two, *Ritual Magazine*, *Bizarre*, *Marquis* and «*O*» reflect the cutting-edge of today's body aesthetic movement.

I had known of Fakir for some time, having seen his participation in the North American Indian *Sun Dance* where he was featured along with Jim Ward, the founder of *PFIQ* and the underground photographer Charles Gatewood in the cult movie *Dances Sacred & Profane* (1986). As he explained to me when I visited his unique *School of Body Piercing* in California, "The major problem facing many young people today is that they have no real rites of passage. There are no real initiation cere-monies into adulthood left in the western world. Such initiations have to involve some form of physical hardship, pain, or a trial of strength and endurance," It is as if the need to be initiated through a ring of fire is etched into our genes and without it we feel lost and incomplete, lacking an essential part of our human adulthood. Fakir then went on to explain that "if a rite of passage is not provided then the young people will invent one—they will form gangs/tribes/groups...create social problems...seek solace in drugs...even cut initials into their flesh with a pen-knife—or com-mit murder." It seems that to deny our need for rituals that mark the progress from one age group to another is much more hazardous than accepting that it needs to be done, because without a healthy traditional outlet for this essential primal energy, people can do very weird and destructive things. Our primal energy is there whether we want it or not. It is part of our being, so it is better that we mark our bodies with piercings, branding, tattoos, or in some other meaningful way that helps to put us back in touch with our inner being and the essence of our individuality; thus echoing in essence the beliefs of Joseph Campbell mentioned earlier. This I believe is fundamental to an understanding of why so many young people in the industrialized world are marking their bodies and adorning themselves in the off-beat styles they now choose; in so doing they are attempting to form themselves into some sort of tribe with their own dis-tinctive marks of identification.

It was Joseph Campbell who also brought my attention to the work of A. R. Radcliffe-Brown who theorized about the way tribal needs, or sentiments as he called them, worked—as he wrote in *The Andaman Islanders* (1933):

A society depends for its existence, on the presence in the mind of its members of a certain system of sentiment by which the conduct of the individual is regulated in conformity with the needs of the society. Every feature of the social system itself and every event or object that in any way affects the well being or the cohesion of the society becomes an object of this system of sentiment. In human society, the sentiments in question are not innate (as they are in most other creatures with whom we share this planet) but are developed in the individual by the action of society upon him. The ceremonial customs of a society are a means by which the sentiments in question are given collective expression on appropriate occasions. The ceremonial expression of any sentiment serves both to maintain it at the requisite degree of intensity in the mind of an individual and to transmit it from one generation to another. Without such expression the sentiments involved could not exist.

It follows that if the essential cultural sentiments fail to be transmitted from one generation to the next, for whatever reason, then that society will change, and by changing may fail to exist as it merges with others who have similarly lost their cultural anchor. This appears to be what is happening throughout the industrialized world, due, I believe, to the failure of the education system, which in philosophical, psychological, and mechanical terms has failed to grasp the true significance of the responsibility given to them—a responsibility for which they are totally unsuited and unqualified to deal with.

In order to understand why we do what we do to our bodies and why we behave as we do to our and other people's styles of embellishment and body art, we have to understand that it is unnatural for us to live in an industrialized urban environment. When we are forced to do so by economic/commercial necessity, we suffer, and this manifests itself in our outward style of body packaging and our mode of behavior. The fact is, our biology has not had time to adjust itself from our traditional hunter-gatherer way of life, and some young people are beginning to show this in the ways they are marking their bodies with tribal insignia. In evolutionary terms, 10,000 years is a mere drop in the ocean of time and yet our

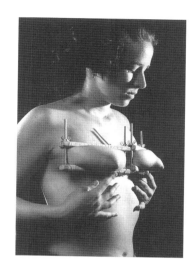

industrialized urban way of life has developed in far less time than 1,000 years. And although we obviously enjoy the fruits of recent industrial progress—cars, television, telephones, fast food, and so on, deep down within ourselves we are missing our natural inheritance.

For countless millennium, our progenitors had lived in small tribal groups and this way of life has, it seems, become part of our biology, part of our very being, which when denied can give rise to grave psychological and physiological problems, in the same way as experienced by our animal cousins when they are crowded together in a concrete zoo. We know what happens to monkeys, the great apes, lions, and the like—they may be well fed and have regular medical help, but they and we know that living in a concrete jungle is a living hell even if we call it civilized and progressive, and this way of unnatural life is being made even worse for us by the ever-increasing demands of commercial interests. There is now little joy left in the workplace—at one time the workplace was a vehicle for a fuller life as well as public good, but now its purpose is motivated solely for private greed. It is against this changing background that we should view the manifestation of the modern primitives, the work of Fakir Musafar, books like *In the Gutter, Strong & Sexy, Decorated Man: The Human Body as Art, Africa Adorned, Massai, The Last Indians, Carnival: Myth & Cult, Hidden Exposures, the magazines BP&MPQ, PFIQ, Les Girls, Transvestites Guide, Skin Two,* and the like. In my formative years many of the books and magazines I now read were forbidden, although I always found the logic for such censorship very difficult to understand. Thankfully such protective prudery is something of the past and if we wish we can now buy books and magazines on bondage, transvestism, body shavers, beautiful bottoms, even African hairstyling and new ways of tattooing and body piercing etc., which are full of many interesting and informative articles. In one issue of *BP&MPQ* for instance Fakir Musafar went into great detail about the pleasures, pain, and art of tight lacing—for many years he made traditional lace-up corsets, which men and women, old and young, used to sculpt their waists down to a mere 12 to 14 inches, and which many of his

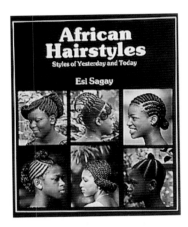

young devotees are now using. Interestingly, after making the film Barry Lyndon (1975), which is set in the mid-eighteenth century, the actress Marissa Berenson told me, when I met her at the opening of the *Fabulous Fashion Exhibition 1907–67* in Sydney, Australia, in which we were both involved, how wonderfully exhilarated she felt after being tightly laced in a whalebone corset for a day, and how marvelous her figure looked.

BP&MPQ has also dealt with the off-beat subject of breast clamping to mold and shape both male and female breasts, and nipple binding and massage to encourage nipple projection—the creating of "natural" nipples and breasts which due to the wearing of a bra have had their growth impeded. "Constant bra wearing during breast development tends to round the breasts and minimize nipples or pronounced areola", and drew my attention to the fact that some cultures encourage the development of nipple and areola "buds" of young pubescent girls, achieving this by a system of alternately binding the nipple itself around the base so that it projects and then massaging it and the surrounding skin with special oils. Tribal peoples see such projecting nipples as a most attractive allurement. *BP&MPQ* went into great detail on many other similar subjects in an attempt to broaden the readers' appreciation of the possibilities of body adaptation and ways of embellishing the psyche.

Other Americans who are also trying to change our attitudes toward the body, sexuality and the human psyche, and recommend that we use its natural source of energy as a natural beautifying therapy as well as an elixir for a happy and more fulfilled life include Fakin Musafar's partner Cléo Dubois, a professional Dominatrix/Dungeon Master who runs an *Academy of SM Arts* and who lectures extensively on bondage, discipline, and consensual sadomasochism; Deborah Anupol, author of *Love Without Limits* (1990) and Ryam Nearing, author of *Loving More: The Polyfidelity* (1991), both of whom are involved in

the *Pali Path, Honolulu Polyamony Network* who believe that sustainable multi-partner relationships are an essential part of the human psyche; the photographers Joel-Peter Witkin and Todd Friedman, who specialize in what many regard as unusual modes of human beauty; Miss Vera, who runs a finishing school in Manhatten for "boys who want to be girls;" the performing artist of female sexuality, Annie Sprinkle, who I met during the British Contemporary Arts Council *Body Arts* tour of Europe in 1995; and Betty Dodson, artist, author, and therapist, whose drawings of women's most intimate allurement struck horror into New York's establishment when first displayed in the mid 1970s. She told me when I interviewed her while researching material for this book, that some years prior to that exhibition, she had fought an even bigger battle against herself and the culturally inherited shame instilled in her by a bigoted form of moralistic education. "As a creative person," she writes in *Sex for One: The Joy of Self Loving*, "I consistently struggled against social restrictions and censorship. However, the worst repression was the kind of censorship I'd been taught to apply to myself." It's a form of censorship that keeps us even from knowing our own bodies, let alone the delights we may be missing out on. The bottom line, of course, is our inability to touch or look at our own private parts, to think of them in aesthetic terms, or to fully enjoy the pleasure nature offers.

Dodson has attempted to open the debate about the aesthetics of all of these body parts and in particular what she sees as being positive about the look of ones own genitals, i.e., liking them—after all, they are the only ones we are ever likely to have. At one time, she held portrait therapy sessions where women came to display and note the different configurations of their genital area and different styles and colorings of pubic hair and inner petals. "Some women had dark, thick bushes and others

OZBEK

fine, wispy hair. One woman had shaved off her pubic hair...the form of her genitals were stark and beautifully two-colored" and she went on to explain that the "colors ranged from pale pink to darkish brown" and some in fact are "like beautiful exotic flowers with shading from pale pink centers to deeply colored outer-lips"—undoubtedly the last remnants of our progenitors' normal mating display. And at a photo session she noted that our much beloved heart symbol "was the shape of a woman's genitals when she held her outer vaginal lips open." Suddenly the St. Valentine's Day heart-shaped card had a clearer meaning, as did Georgia O'Keefe's and other artists' flower paintings, and the flower prints that adorn so many dresses also took on clearer, symbolical significance—or more correctly, the reason for their aesthetic appeal became more apparent. But then we are a culture that, due to our social repression, is hooked on such forms of symbolism, which we see as the essence of beauty without ever quite understanding such beauty's true nature.

I also interviewed a young female photographer who lived near Muscle Beach in Los Angeles and had been working for three years taking photographs of male erections, a subject that is even more taboo than female genitalia. Interestingly, she told me of the problems many male body builders have in regard to penis size. Apparently all the hormones, steroids, and other chemicals they ingest inhibit the growth of this important appendage and many, including the most famous, are having to resort to injections and cosmetic surgery to both thicken and lengthen this feature, and they are having to pad out their scrotum with silicon implants so that they can display a full jockstrap when competing in body building events such as Mr. Universe—removable "artificial" padding being prohibited. A similar nonsense regulation also forces many young women who compete in the numerous beauty pageants and competitions to have breast implants, as their obsessive dieting inhibits the natural growth of these feminine attributes.

I realize the subject I have just mentioned may offend some readers, but no well-adjusted wart hog or mandrill finds anything unpleasant or pornographic in the appearance or behavior of other wart hogs or the physical attributes of their mate. It would be unnatural if they did, and the same should go for homo sapiens. If they do then there really must be something wrong with their way of thinking.

The subject of she-males—transsexuals as well as transvestites—are also of fashionable interest and therefore warrant a mention in this book, as do males who have, with the aid of hormone treatment and gender reassignment surgery, crossed the dividing line and become female, among the first being April Ashley in the early 1960s, who had started life twenty-five years earlier as George Jamieson, and who I knew when she was in her late teens and who as George first brought to my attention the psyche in such matters, being convinced that his own psyche was feminine. This was a subject I also discussed with Quintin

Crisp who, though very feminine, did not wish to become female. But he did live precariously on the borderline between male and female. These trends, together with a general androgynous predisposition, and that of strident and aggressive feminism, which has become increasingly notice-able since the mid-1960s, has resulted in essential changes to our percep-tion of what is, or is not, beautiful about the human body, the human mind, the human psyche, and human ways, particularly within our Western culture. True feminism, as distinct from the 1970s/80s aggres-sive variety, is also beginning to come to the fore, and natural female characteristics, such as a certain voluptuousness of figure, are now also widely admired, although those who control the mass media would have us think otherwise. Nevertheless, the work of the Colombian artist Fernando Botero and the erotic imagery of the Czech photographer Jan Saudek and others are beginning to create wider interest, although I am doubtful if many western people would readily admit to admiring the softly curved voluptuousness as was admired on one Melanesian island in the Bismarck Sea, which I visited some years ago, where one woman, who was around 5'4" tall and weighed just under 300 lbs, was their Queen of Beauty.

Magazine articles on liposculpture, breast implants, penile enlargements, body piercing, tattooing, decorative dental bridges (which are now often encrusted with gold and precious stones) follow the new commercial dictum that money can buy anything. Today, for around $3,000, the body can be permanently freed from all unwanted hair by laser or electrolysis; for $2,000, a nose can be changed; for $2,500, a chin can be reshaped, or for a price, hands can be made thinner…calf muscles added…*derrière* lifted…the inner lips of the vulva can be trimmed…permanent makeup applied by tattoo…one can be made taller or shorter…have colored contact lenses fitted to change the color of one's eyes…and of course having one's hair dyed, restyled, new longer nails fitted, and buy and wear a whole range of ever changing habiliments…. In fact, it would seem that with the new commercial "beauty religion," which is used to dress and adorn the psyche rather than the body, money can buy everything—even a makeover into being a Barbie replica or Schwarzenegger look-alike. And yet those with money who undertake such changes are not among the happiest or the most beautiful people one knows. Beauty, real beauty, is a much more elusive quality. But nevertheless, the beauty we seem to seek, and that which gets promoted by the media does reflect the values and ways of our industrialized society, and therefore can be seen as the true icon of our culture.

In *Marks of Civilization: Artistic Transformations of the Human Body,* the result of *The Art of the Body* symposium held at UCLA in 1983, and published by the Museum of Cultural History at UCLA in 1988; the art historian Arnold Rubin noted how, until then, most anthropologists, scientists, and academics had ignored this essential human art—one of the few forms of popular human expression that is left in this commercialized world, and one that still has an ingredient of magic involved. Speakers told how the various indigenous groups of peoples they have studied all invest their body art with profound cultural, religious, aesthetic, and social meaning. Rubin also noted how, up until that symposium, all of his colleagues in the art and academic world had not thought very much of his research into the world of body marking and manipulation—tattooing, body piercing, scarring, and the like—and, in fact, thought his studies kinky and weird.

Then, in August 1995, an International Conference was held in Seoul entitled *In Pursuit of Beauty* organized by the

IRIAN JAYA

Julie Campbell

International Conference on the Unity of Sciences, with the organization chairman, Professor Frederick Turner of the University of Texas at Dallas proposing that beauty, including human beauty, "had a recognizable biological foundation," thus bringing such human beauty and all of our various forms of body art used to enhance the human form into the realm of academic acceptability. As Turner pointed out, the traditional view of art and beauty was that since they belonged within the sphere of *Geisteswissenschaft* they could not be legitimately studied within the realm of *Natwissenschaft*, with most academics and scientists maintaining that such subjects "were but a trivial fantasy, useful only for passing leisure time." However, in recent years, this picture had undergone a profound change, a change which I have been personally seeking since my postgraduate days.

As Turner observed in his introduction to this symposium:

In a wide range of disciplines—neuroscience, psychophysics, psychology, cultural and physical anthropology, literary theory and criticism, oral tradition studies, visual perception studies, mythology, infant and child development studies, and the evolutionary study of ritual among others—a new approach to aesthetics is being explored. Chaos and complexity theory have demonstrated that most of the characteristics attributed by nineteenth century philosophy of science to the physical universe participates in complex nonlinear dynamical systems in which every part depends upon the behavior of the whole, the whole can be sensitively dependent on the behavior of the parts, and new and unpredictable forms of organization can emerge through spontaneous symmetry-breaking. These nonlinear features are especially characteristic of biological systems, and are so par excellence of the complex feedback processes of the nervous systems of higher social animals such as ourselves.

This new scientific paradigm provides a justification for renewing the great classical and renaissance project of the scientific study of aesthetics. A daring new group of interdisciplinary researches in several fields have begun to ask some fundamental questions: why do human beings across the whole range of human cultures find certain objects, sounds, move-

ments, stories beautiful? Why are the basic genres and forms of the arts culturally universal? What structures and functions of the human brain and sensorium underlie aesthetic experience and competence? Why do scientists report a strong aesthetic element in their research? Do more primitive forms of aesthetic experience and competence exist in nature? What technology, ecological, social or ritual developments might there be, that could provide the adaptive pressure by which our remarkable human aesthetic abilities evolved?

This is a long overdue inquiry, which one hopes may eventually change our understandings about aesthetics and its biological and physiological links in general and human beauty in particular, and I wait with interest to see how such discoveries are going to affect the way we view human beauty in the future. With the biological origins of human beauty now once again under active investigation/discussion, the correlation between sexuality and such beauty is gaining many more supporters and may well prove to be encoded in our DNA. The notion that what we call beauty is not an unmixed idea and that it is intimately united with ideas of carnal pleasure and the drive for procreation is now widely accepted, for it is now realized that sex, rather than being a deadly sin, is simply the process used by Nature to remix the gene pool of human and all other species so that they stay healthy and infection free. I should be noted that the continual remixing of genes helps to overcome various forms of biological attack, with a number of researchers pointing out the important link between many forms of animal "beauty" and their effectiveness as an aid to breeding and survival. This may well be the case in human survival with differing beauty ideals aiding changes in the gene mix and guarantying that the mix is forever changing, thus aiding our chances of survival.

Turner adds further to this belief, explaining in *Beauty: The Value of Values* that breeding success is the main reason why what he refers to as "ritual difference" becomes more pronounced and important: "An individual with better ritual pigmentation, better plumage, bet-

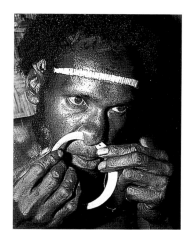

ter-looking reproductive organs, better songs and dance, or better antlers with which to stage the gladiatorial games of sexual rivalry, will end up with more progeny: and so the genes of these qualities can rapidly pervade the gene pool of the species, crowding out the others." The natural world is full of examples of these ritual markings, or beauty differences (as I prefer to call them), that are needed for sexual success, and by admiring such ritual markings and differences, we can earn ourselves a chemical reward, which is almost akin to a pure narcotic pumped directly from the brain into our bloodstream, a chemical "drug" reward that doesn't have the side effects of drugs we ingest. We can also earn this reward if we also partake in certain forms of ritualized sexual activity such as Kundalini and Tantra—techniques that are explained in *Sacred Sexuality* (1995) by A. T. Mann and Jane Lyle, and which are known to improve the health and perceived beauty of regular practitioners as well as aiding the remix of the gene pool.

As Mann and Lyle observed in their introduction, "Many traditions understood and utilised the sacred nature of sexuality, creating personal patterns, collective rituals and magical techniques. These honoured and celebrated sexuality as a powerful tool for spiritual enlightenment, personal growth and ecstatic vision." It seems that such ideas and practices were expunged from our Western culture after the acceptance in the fourth century A.D. by Emperor Constantine of Christianity as the official religion of the Roman Empire. The old belief of pre-Christian times that sensual pleasure and human beauty were divine gifts of the gods was inextricably linked with Devil worship, and were ruthlessly suppressed—hence our neurosis and trouble dichotomy—problems that can only be remedied by rethinking our origins, religion, and the way we perceive the world and our place within it, sentiments that concur with those of the Anglo-Sri Lankan mystic Babagee Attman.

Babagee Attman, who is an expert in Kundalini and Tantra and who studied the *Akashic Chronicle* and how to gain access to the healing qualities of the cosmos in India and Sri Lanka for nearly twenty years, says, "In our conceit and wonderment we are constantly told and believe that we represent the apex of human development and evolution, but

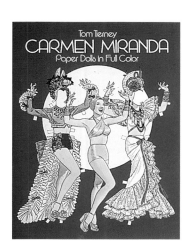

our sexuality—the engine and energy source of life and health—is misunderstood, trivialised and negated. *Sex-Sensual* energy, which is at the very core of the true life force, and which we can readily manufacture on a continual daily basis, is our cosmic connection to personal fulfillment, happiness, health, spiritual involvement and achievement in all aspects of living, and should be celebrated and used to the full instead of being hoarded and confined." Unfortunately, the problem of our attitudes toward sex and sex-sensual energy is quite deeply rooted in our psyche, as is the thought of using Tantra and Kundalini practices. Yet for those, like myself, whose job it is to study contemporary society and our aesthetic and sexual mores, it is becoming harder and harder to accept that the civilization we see around us as highly evolved and desirable, as we seem to be missing out on the very essence of life. Sex and sensuality

within our modern technological world may be big business, and can be used to sell almost anything, but seen from that viewpoint at its most basic level, it is vicious, demeaning, and demanding—the all important sacred consciousness has been lost, warped, distorted. We must learn to rectify this situation if we are going to survive. Whether we like to admit it or not, sex and beauty are at the very core of our existence and should be glorified and celebrated. Interestingly a link has been noted between the human female's beauty and her biorhythms—researchers observe that, for many women, the middle of the monthly cycle,

when they are most likely to conceive, is when they look and feel their most attractive, vibrant, and sexually appealing. Dr. Helen Fisher adds that many of our applied beauty signals also deliberately mimic such natural signals, also noting that we have a storehouse of such inherent natural signals that seem to be etched into our ancient primordial memory, like the "rosy red Revlon mouth mimicking the swollen vulva of our early primate progenitors."

Other researchers have investigated the connection between increased sexual activity and creativity, especially in the realms of Eastern art, and have noted that some cultures go to extraordinary lengths to increase this creative power through increased sexuality using the ancient science of Taoist, Kundalini, and Tantric practices made popular in the West in recent

years by the movies *Sacred Sex* and *Sacred Sex II*—techniques that were originally used for spiritual growth and to achieve perfect cultural harmony and have little to do with the sexual practices of marriage, which unfortunately have more to do with control than enlightenment. In ancient times one of the highest forms of such practices was ritual group sex, the aim being to break through the conditioning of hoarding sex for only one person as happens within marriage—an important step in learning to live harmoniously with other people and to open the pathway to true spiritual, mental, and creative growth—and, of course, to the enjoyment of beauty in all of its forms. I have found in my own life and work that it is essential to free the spirit from all forms of sexual guilt, so that one's inventive and aesthetic nature can flourish unhindered by repressive cultural attitudes, and this is something most people in the West have yet to learn and accept.

As you may now be aware, the sexual element in human creativity, especially in the realm of human beauty, is much more complex and intertwined than most readers would have thought, but the story of the influence and power of sex and sexual activity upon our present condition, and our attitudes and perceptions of human beauty doesn't end there. Some geneticists, for instance, believe that in addition to the sexual force sculpting our bodies, our facial features, influencing our creativity, and controlling our most basic perceptions of human beauty, that the female choice of sexual partners tens of thousands of years ago actually encouraged the development of human intelligence, sculpting our psyche, and shaping all of our behavior and thinking patterns—thus influencing our very lifestyles. Sex is obviously a much more potent force than most people realize; as far as this book is concerned, suffice it to say that such influences do exist and that they are very powerful forces indeed.

There are, of course, a whole array of other attractive, alluring, and beautiful features about the human animal that deserve to be mentioned in a book such as this—i.e., body scent, taste, skin texture, cleanliness, diligence, tidiness, a sense of fun, the way we talk, a quick wit, an agile mind, a pleasant smile, the way one moves, the projection of body language, and so forth. All of these are, or can be, an aid to biological reproduction, if that were still the main aim of our lives. But, as with the more mainstream mani-

MASTERLY DESIGNED HAIRSTYE

festation of beauty, this does not necessarily dictate that this is how an individual will wish to use them. They may simply wish to use such qualities to improve their job prospects, to be one-up on their friends, to enjoy the glances of admiration from potential partners, etc., without a thought of any form of consummation or even liaison—they simply enjoy being beautiful, attractive, alluring, and desirable. For many, that is reward enough.

One only has to check out recent editions of popular fashion and beauty magazines to realize life is changing. A new breed of showbiz royalty is adding to our range of enviable beauty icons. New forms of body decorations are regularly being featured, such as new forms of tattooing using new cutting techniques, new styles of branding, body manipulation, tight-lacing, bondage, S&M, and other styles, have all joined the fray, as have different approaches to hairdressing, nail aesthetics, with female "gladiators" (of various television series) and muscle-ripping female body builders and androgynous men flavoring the mass media imagery. These and many other changes are fortunately being dutifully recorded by such documentary filmmakers and photographers as Charles Gatewood in *Primitives: Tribal Body Art and the Left Hand Path* (1992).

When Gatewood began recording such changes, particularly those being adopted by the underground tribal movement of the mid-1960s in and around San Francisco and the West Coast, he was considered by many Americans to be the *bête noire* of American society—an obsessed and deviant eccentric whose concerns were extremely marginal, and one whom most Americans would have preferred not to have existed. Today, however, as acceptance of public nudity, exhibitionism, body tattooing, various forms of consensual sadomasochistic excess, and the like, have at last entered mainstream culture, his work and images can be seen as uncannily prophetic, as indeed was the remarkable ReSearch publication by V. Vale and Andrea Juno, *Modern Primitives: An Investigation of Contemporary Adornment & Ritual*, which stated in its introduction, "All sensual experience functions to free us from 'normal' social restraints, to awaken our deadened bodies to life. All such activities point towards a goal, the creation of the 'complete' or 'integrated' man and woman.... Our most inestimable resource, the unfettered imagination, continues to be grounded in the only truly precious possession we can ever have and know, and which is ours to do with what we will:

the human body."

Like Gatewood, Fakir, Bill Ward of *PFIQ*, V. Vale of *ReSearch*, and all the others who are involved in the documenting of this wonderful changing world of body art, I am beginning to join in the dance—no longer as an observer but as an active participant. Trying out the new and the unusual, seeking the mystery of the unknown; I'm no longer seeking just the words and the images. I want to be astonished, surprised, and elated as never before. I want to leave the world of rational thought and reason to explore the deeper, more intuitive world in that twilight zone that joins the physical to the psychic—to get in touch with that more ancient source of our being where the mind, body, and spirit are together as one so that I can at last enjoy the pleasures of the now.

But, although all the changes that are now taking place will be dutifully recorded and published, they will nevertheless take some time to be assimilated into our culture as a whole, and only when this assimilation is complete will individuals be able to truly apportion their own involvement and perceptions of beauty upon

them. But change will not end here—out of even more forms of experimentation will come many new styles of human decoration and adornment, and new forms of human beauty that will be used to embellish our psyche, to attract members of the opposite sex, to create envy in the minds of peers, to display the wealth, social position, and aspirations of the wearer, to appease the Gods, and to add variety and excitement to our lives. The new styles will, as always, be a reflection of the social changes taking place in society, and will, hopefully, embrace all of the aims, ambitions, expectations, and dreams of each new generation.

It is my belief that we have now reached that point where we are at last able to come to accept our millions of years of mutually inherited development, so that we can acknowledge and enjoy the diverse magnificence of all the varying ways and styles of human beauty from all areas of this planet, free at last from all forms of preconceptions and outdated

Fat Removal and Transfer
LIPOSCULPTURE

YOUR FIGURE • • YOUR FORTUNE
Cosmetic Artistry with a Touch of Beauty

figurama
UNIVERSAL HEALTH STUDIOS LTD

prejudices. The magical quality of this beauty will hopefully be such that it will burn our blood like powdered glass, while at the same time elating our souls and making our bodies tremble with desire, that moment when we are more alive than at any other time in our lives. After all, such moments are the best device yet invented to ensure that our genes pass on into the next millennium and the millennium after that.

The illustrations I have chosen to convey this diversity, as well as to highlight our inventive spirit and the never ending quest for our own perceptions of perfection, have been culled from a wide range of historic and cultural sources. They are, I believe, truly representative of this particular human talent, as well as being a worthy selection with which to celebrate our newly acquired right to openly display that which in the past has so often been censurable. Such illustrations will also help us expand our notions of the possible, as well as clearly demonstrating to those in authority that there are certain matters beyond their control, and that it is our new belief that there is now no part of the male or female body that is not worthy of embellishment, admiration and display. In fact, such adventurous styles are just as important to our individual and cultural identity as are those areas of our body that traditionally we parade with pride. They are also as vital to our artistic development as new styles of painting, music, poetry, literature, dance, and all other forms of creative expression.

It is my fervent hope that such styles, together with the myriad of others from all other cultural groups from around the world, will continue to be allowed to evolve and flourish. And regardless of any personal idiosyncrasies or cultural foibles—or possibly for this very reason—such styles will continue to be celebrated as legitimate forms of human expression, worthy of a place alongside all other artistic manifestations, as a true reflection of our creativity, sensibility, diversity, and inventive genius. Long may this continue to be so, so that our lives and the lives of our offspring will continue to be enlivened by the new and the different in this never ending quest for our own differing ideals, styles, and forms of human beauty.

EPILOGUE AND ACKNOWLEDGMENTS

As detailed previously, change and difference have always been an essential part of our humanness, and our various styles of self-adornment and beautification are simply one of the ways in which this manifests itself. The human species has never really been static as the documentation of our history testifies. We must accept that change is an intrinsic part of our humanness and appears to have been programmed into our genes to help us survive and thrive. It also appears that regardless of what has happened to our species in the past, many more unexpected things will happen as time progresses, for we undoubtedly live in a changing world. And, for myself, having been born human and raised in one of the largest cities in the world, I wouldn't have it otherwise. But during my years of designing for various manufacturers, working within colleges and universities, running my own fashion business, researching and writing many books on design aesthetics and various forms of body packaging and fashion, traveling the world, and meeting many famous and wonderful people, as well as many ordinary people including those who live in remoter regions, I have come to the conclusion that although change seems to be an essential part of our lives, it doesn't mean that we are happier or more fulfilled because of it.

I have also come to realize that we must not confuse change with progress, or that progress is an inevitable outcome of change. In most cases it simply means "different" and, by its nature, such differences are transitory—an interlude before even more differences come along. And if in our restlessness we begin to actively seek change for its own sake, we should be mindful of not enforcing such a wish for change upon others. The changes we seek or experience are our own—limited, localized, and an outcome of our own ways and needs and are not necessarily compatible with the ways and need of others. And yet today, throughout the remoter regions of the world, various governments, religious organizations, and multinational companies are imposing change upon previously isolated peoples in the name of progress and improvement. But what is being offered is not always progress, nor is it an improvement. More often it is simply social rape and cultural genocide for the sole benefit of the perpetrators. The victims seldom recover.

But, unfortunately, to enforce change upon others also seems to be part of our humanness and it is certainly part of our culture. Our historical records are full of accounts of genocide, just as they are full of the detailed records of the extinction of numerous animal and plant species with whom we once shared this planet, from the dodo to the Tasmanian tiger. And today we are also changing many other aspects of this planet. Our jungles and rainforests are fast disappearing. Our waterways are being polluted. The air we breath is becoming full of harmful chemicals, as is our food. The ozone layer, which protects us from the harshness of the sun's rays and which aided our evolution, is under attack from the misuse of the world's resources. And the rich differences in our human ways and traditions are being eroded.

The speed of this change is accelerating daily. When I first started to travel in the mid-1950s, London, Paris, New York, Tokyo, and Manila were all very different one from another. But now, with the spread of the influence of mass media and multinational companies it's hard to tell one urban area from another. And while I celebrate our growing freedom to explore our personal likes and wishes, I must protest at what I see as imposed change upon others who for one reason or another are powerless to resist the growth of what has become known as the Global Village.

As privileged as I have been during my years of travel, educating myself in tribal ways and researching various aspects of cultural markings, body art, habits of dress, adornment, and beautification, and the benefits I have seen from many of the changes taking place in the world, I cannot hide my deep sorrow and sadness every time I return to a country or village of which I have fond memories, to see for myself the waning traditions. And how the unique modes of body art, tribal markings and styles of adornment, which I had previously admired, and which contain much of the traditions and essence of their ancestors, had diminished, even during their more important festive times.

Only among small out of the way communities and some nomadic peoples who are remote from the normal flow of commercial life and free from such influences as television and tourism, have I noted a real reluctance to change, they prefer instead to utilize a few selected outside influences rather than being swamped by them as so many other cultures have been. But, unfortunately, even here their numbers are beginning to diminish under various government pressures to settle their communities so that their traditional tribal lands can be divided and subdivided and utilized in other more commercial ways.

Thus it is that many of the more unusual traditional techniques and ways of cultural marking and beautification no longer exist, or are becoming increasingly rare, which in effect means that they can no longer be admired, documented, or even photographed. Only existing photographs, many of which are in an advanced state of decay, are a reliable record of their ever having existed. A unique heritage of human aesthetic inventiveness is disappearing and few people are even aware that such a catastrophe is taking place.

The changes taking place in the world undoubtedly mean that our range of visual differences is shrinking, as indeed is the biodiversity of the human species itself along with the biodiversity of many other living things. Remote communities of indigenous peoples who lead unmechanized or nomadic ways of life just don't have the profitable dollar-sign stamp of approval. They don't make a commercial profit so in commercial terms they just aren't worth preserving.

In our hearts we all know that making a commercial profit is not the real essence of life. There are some things in this world that we just can't put a profit value sign on. Fortunately in recent years a number of groups have organized themselves to save such anomalies as the great whales, the giant panda, elephants, rhinos, tigers, and the like. Human diversity is also priceless, yet it is being allowed to slip away. Some of the most unique peoples of the world are now facing extinction through lack of understanding or lack of interest. And in some countries governments have actually introduced policies of genocide neatly couched in sugarcoated words, but I have seen for myself how the Nuba of the southeast Kordofan Province of Sudan are being systematically hunted down by government troops and killed, as indeed happened with the Tutsi Rwandans. Minority peoples in former countries like Yugoslavia are also facing extinction, as are those who live in mineral rich islands like Bougainville in the South Pacific, The Kurds, the Timor islanders, the Dani, Asmat and Jalé of Irian Jaya, and others are also being forced to follow in the footsteps of so many North American Indian peoples and Australian Aboriginals.

The beautiful Jivaro Indians who used to live freely in the border areas between Ecuador and Peru were hunted to the brink of extinction earlier this century by European explorers, who were paid $60 a scalp. The Amazonean Indian and many others are today being killed off by those seeking gold or who wish to "log" their part of the jungle. The Aztecs were slaughtered by the Spaniards as a result of the greed for gold and so on, and the killing still proceeds today in the name of progress. Tribal groups once lived freely in the jungles of southeast Asia, the Congo, and the Amazon while other indigenous peoples inhabited mountainous areas and the vast deserts. For thousands, or maybe tens of thousands of years, tribal peoples have lived in all sorts of environments, but with maps and colonial conquest came the arbitrary division of traditional habitats, and whether willfully or not, international laws have been enacted that gave others rights of ownership over these traditional habitats—hence a reason for systematic genocide.

At the present time there are approximately six thousand distinct cultural groups existing on this planet. The loss of much of their habitat is proceeding so rapidly that on average one distinct group of people, together with its language, its culture, its philosophy, and its knowledge is becoming extinct every week. Fifty-two a year. That's a tragic loss. Others are becoming mortally wounded, often in unexpected ways, such as being made to appear frivolous in circus-like surroundings at holiday resorts, or when their distinctive visual aesthetics are plundered by graphic designers and mass-marketing experts to sell teabags or toilet paper. And ancient cities, which once proudly displayed the art of the indigenous culture, are now being made over into virtual theme parks for the benefit of tour companies, not the residents.

It's as if our differences are being stolen by commercial interests and replaced or homogenized by *Coka-Cola culture* in which we are supposed to eat "Mac-Food," watch "Ted-TV," read "Rupert News," and adorn ourselves in the current industrialized mode according to the dictates of the mass-media moguls, and entertainment conglomerates whose aim seems to be ever increasing profitability. Gone it seems, is the human integrity that once allowed individuality and fidelity to truth to be upper-most in our minds, and that glorified the symbols of independence that each cultural group featured with pride to mark their humanness, yet difference, from others. Being different is now becoming a symbol of not belonging, and being different from us now marks others out as not belonging to our commercial religion and thus is seen as a threat to our progress and profits. Money is now the ruling God of the aimed for homogenized global village, and if these people of difference contribute nothing to the new religion then they, like the heathen of earlier times, do not deserve to survive. Or so it would seem from our current actions.

But their differences, and their right to be different, is at the very core of our humanness and is one of the key reasons why the human species has been so successful and has survived for so long. So if we wish to survive as a species, it is in all our interests to keep our differences and keep our biodiversity. I also believe these differences should be well documented for posterity as should our visual modes of expression, for whether we like it or not the world is going to change quite dramatically in the next few decades and our children and grandchildren have the right to know how their ancestors expressed their art of being human.

It is difficult to draw a sharp line between what should be recorded and what will continue on into the future. For example, how shall we record the changes now taking place within China, which in spite of recent unparalleled industrialization has retained many of its traditions and customs? Japan is also an example that shows no society is truly static or that development and change is in anyway pre-dictable. The well-documented historical processes of our own culture also clearly illustrate this. So with this in mind I am appealing for help and advice from individual readers and organizations who have knowledge, or access to as-yet unresearched photographic material showing the techniques, ways, and traditions of peoples whose culture no longer exists or who are now in the process of dramatic change. Unless these treasures are saved from the ravages of time and climate, they may well become lost forever. Offers of help to save such collections are also most welcome. As I have found with those items in my own archives, it does take a great deal of time and money to restore and preserve fragile images and artifacts, and fortunately this can now be done without putting the original material at risk.

Many such "saved" images have been used in this book. With the aid of a sympathetic editor and the miracle of modern printing technology and computer enhancement, plus a crash course in under-standing the contemporary jargon of Pixel, Megabyte, JPEG, GIF, Gaussian blur, SCSI device, edge enhancement and the like, we have been able to put together a unique survey of what, until now, people from around the world have done to their bodies to change, improve, or beautify themselves.

In addition, in order to show as balanced and informative view of the subject matter as possible, I have taken the liberty of using a number of uncredited images, which by one means or another have come into my possession during my travels, and I would appreciate any information regarding their origins, or that of the current copyright holders, so that I can legitimize their use. Through a variety of clues and the help of various outside agencies and organizations I have been able to attribute most of them; still there are a number I have been unable to trace, but that I felt were too important not to use. I am therefore apologizing in advance to those whose interests I have failed to determine and credit. Information brought to my attention or to that of the publisher will be included in all future editions.

While researching and writing this book, I have also had need to use a great many literary sources, and received a great deal of help from individuals and organizations, both large and small, as well as museums, art galleries, eclectic collectors like myself, photographers, second-hand book dealers and numerous fellow researchers. The total number prevents me from making a detailed acknowledgment of them all, and if by mentioning those to whom I feel I owe most, I omit any that should have been included, let me assure those benefactors with apologies that the omission is inadvertent and if notified, I will remember them in all future editions of this book and its sequel *A Celebration of Human Differences*, which I hope will be published before the end of the millennium as an accompaniment to a planned International Exhibition on the subject.

As we approach the end of this millennium of great change I hope that the people who understand the pressing need will finally band together to aid the survival of the endangered human species. With this in mind, in addition to the dedication featured at the beginning of this book, I now wish to expand that dedication to include all the children of those cultural groups whose traditions and cultural ways, are under threat of extinction, in the hope that in someway or other it will help them save their ways of marking, modifying, and beautifying themselves for future generations to admire and enjoy, thus making life much more enjoyable for us all.

Further information about the above-mentioned projects, offers of help, funding, and advice, or information regarding other matters raised should be addressed to me via the publisher W. W. Norton & Company, Inc., 500 Fifth Avenue, New York, NY, 10110, USA. I thank you in advance for your interest, and wish you all a fulfilled, happy, and visually exciting life.

CAPTIONS

Front Cover: Traditional Japanese *irezumi* tattoo. Photo © Sandi Fellman 1984. Tatoo by Bob Roberts. Model: Adrienne Tolan.

Rear Cover: Unmarried Medlpa woman of the High Plateau region, Southern Highlands, Papua New Guinea partaking in the bi-annual *Mount Hagen Show.* This photograph was taken during my first visit to the *Mount Hagen Show* in 1985. It was during this visit that the concept of this book took on its final form, with the wide range of styles of human adornment and beauty displayed there being the inspiration for my further research—research which subsequently took me five times around the world to visit numerous tribal communities, remote villages, vast urban areas, museums, art galleries, archeological digs, and to meet many photographers, multi-talented individuals, other researchers, authors, artists and the like. This, together with my experience as a child actor, fashion designer, lecturer, illustrator, journalist, author and photographer formed the essence of this book. Photo © Julian Robinson Archives 1985.

Inside Rear Flap: The author. Photo © 1994, James L. Mairs.

6A. Line illustration from the *de-luxe* French magazine *La Gazette du bon ton* 1914. Photo © Julian Robinson Archives.

7A. Line illustration from a 1912 French Art Deco fashion magazine. Photo © Julian Robinson Archives.

7B. Jewelry of a Sumerian lady of rank during the great days of Ur, photographed during a 1920s archeological expedition—the jewelry dating from 2600 B.C. Photo from *Our Wonderful World* (1929). © Julian Robinson Archives.

8A. Contemporary tattooing and piercing. From *Tattoo* (1985). Photo © Stefan Richter.

8B. A young Trobriand bride dressed in her finery and surrounded by her family, ready to receive her first hus-

band. He will move into her village and remain for as long as she decides that he is welcome. When the marriage is over, he simply moves back to his own village. Author's photo taken in 1985. © Julian Robinson Archives.

8C. The author in mix-&-match costume and adornments from around the world, photographed by Roman Cerney in 1992 © Julian Robinson Archives/Roman Cerney.

9A. At a time of change, when it was socially permissible for women to show their ankles. Dresses by the French couturier Drecoll, photo by Talbot from *Les Modes* (1913). © Julian Robinson Archives.

9B. Samo warrior, Western Province, Papua New Guinea. *From Man as Art: New Guinea* (1981). Photo © Malcolm Kirk.

10A. Line illustration by Charles Martin from a 1913 French Art Deco publication. © Julian Robinson Archives.

10B. Line illustration by John Austin from a 1928 publication. © Julian Robinson Archives.

10C. Munchi woman with tribal body scarring. From *Peoples of All Nations* (1922). Late-19th-century photo. © Julian Robinson Archives.

11A. The "Naked" fashion of 1800. Author's photo from an original hand-colored engraving. © Julian Robinson Archives.

11B. Wasp-waisted Melanesian warrior, Bismarck Archipelago. Late-19th-century photo by Dr. C. G. Seligmann. From *Peoples of the World* (1922). JR Archives.

11C. On the set of *The Wild One.* Columbia Pictures publicity photo, 1954. JR Archives.

12A. Ritual costume, upper Sepik region, Papua New Guinea. Author's photo. © Julian Robinson Archives.

12B. Cover of a 1950s chocolate box featuring a painting by Paul Gauguin. Author's photo. JR Archives.

12C. Downbeat casual look of the early-1980s, a reactionary trend against all the high technology clothing styles that were beginning to flood the fashion market. From an Italian magazine 1982. JR Archives.

12D. Engraving of French court fashions by Abraham Bosse, c. 1635. From an early-20th-century publication. © Julian Robinson Archives.

13A. Charles Bronson publicity photo from the mid-1950s. JR Archives.

13B. *Caché-sexe* worn by an unmarried Yetsang woman, Southern Cameroon. Photo by Jaspar von Oetzeu, from *Der dunkle Erdteil: Afrika* (1930). JR Archives.

13C. Hamar tribesman, Southern Ethiopia, having his distinctive clay hair *boro* applied in readiness for a ritual celebration. From *African Ark* (1990), a truly beautiful book from two very talented photographers, who for the past ten years or so have lived with various tribal groups in central and northern Africa. Photo © Carol Beckwith/Angela Fisher (1990).

13D. Farawa warrior, Northern Nigeria, with tribal facial scarring and branding. Photo by W. Hessel, from *Der dunkle Erdteil: Afrika* (1930). JR Archives.

14A. A young Slovakian bride from the village of Hluk near Uherskÿ, Moravian—Slovak border, 1990, soon after the fall of Soviet Communism. Author's photo. © Julian Robinson Archives.

14B. Title page, *Habiti Antichi, et Moderni de tutto il Mondo* (1590). Author's photo from the original publication. © Julian Robinson Archives.

14C. Cover of a 1950s biscuit box featuring Frans Hals' *Laughing Cavalier.* Author's photo. JR Archives.

15A. Wrapper of *Die Galerien Europas* featuring Giovanni Battista Moroni's painting of Antonio Navagero. Author's photo. JR Archives.

15B. The curves of the Far East. From a French theory of art and fashion featured in *L'Amour de l'Art: Le Costume et les Modes* (1952). JR Archives.

15C. Naked but not unadorned. Young unmarried Amazonian Indian women from the Xingu Indigenous Park in Central Brazil. Copyright details not known.

16A. Cover of a 1960s corset box. Author's photo. JR Archives.

16B. Woodcut illustrations from John Bulwer's epic *Anthropometamorphosis* (1650). JR Archives.

16C. Early-20th-century ads. Author's photo. © Julian Robinson Archives.

16D. Title page, *Venus: die apotheoses des Weibes* (1910), featuring the Greek sculpture *Aphrodite of Melos (Venus de Milo)*. Author's photo. © Julian Robinson Archives.

17A. Early-20th-century fashion illustration. Photo by the author from an original 1913 publication. © Julian Robinson Archives.

17B. Hand-colored fashion engraving of a muslin dress for seaside visits, c. 1809. From *La Belle Assemblée*. Author's photo. © Julian Robinson Archives.

17C. Italian shoe ad from an early-1980s Italian fashion magazine. Author's photo. JR Archives.

17D. *Capturing Venus* (1538) from an engraving by Albrecht Dürer. Photo by the author from an early-20th-century art book. JR Archives.

18A. Zulu tribal chief in full regalia. From *Sons of Zulu* (1978). Photo © Aubrey Elliott.

19A. Berber woman of the Ait Hadiddu tribe with traditional facial tattoo. From *Africa Adorned* (1984). Photo © Angela Fisher.

19B. Although poor, British cockneys always made the most of their sparse resources when dressing-up at festive times. Early-20th-century photo of the *Pearly King* and family. From *Costumes of the World* (1922/23). © Julian Robinson Archives.

20A. Contemporary tattooing. From *Tattoo* (1985). Photo © Stefan Richter.

20B. *Beauty Spots*. Ad from a 1960s magazine. JR Archives.

21A. Line illustration by George Barbier from a 1914 French Art Deco publication. © Julian Robinson Archives.

21B. Eyelash ad from a late-1960s fashion magazine. JR Archives.

21C. Unmarried Maasai woman preparing herself for a night of romance. From *Maasai* (1980). Photo © Carol Beckwith.

22A. Lovers' ribbons proudly displayed on the headdress of a Czechoslovakian bride. Early-20th-century photo, from *Women of All Lands* (1925). JR Archives.

22B. Early-1920s shoe ad. Author's photo. © Julian Robinson Archives.

22C. *Body Charms* ad from a 1970s fashion magazine. JR Archives.

23A. *The Eyes of Cairo*. Early-20th-century photo by E. N. W. Slarles, from *People of All Nations* (1922). © Julian Robinson Archives.

23B. Padded bra ad from an early-1950s magazine. JR Archives.

23C. Portrait of a lady wearing a fine *guipure point* lace ruff. From *A History of Hand-Made Lace* (1900). Author's photo. © Julian Robinson Archives.

23D. Late-16th-century engraving of a Venetian courtesan wearing the fashionable 12" *chopines* and "condemned" underpants. Author's photo. © Julian Robinson Archives.

24A. Kara warrior proudly wearing an ostrich-feather head adornment—a symbol of status and bravery. From *African Ark* (1990). Photo © Carol Beckwith/Angela Fisher.

24B. King Bope Mabiinc, Kuba tribe, Kasai, Zaire, in full regalia. Late-1920s photo. JR Archives.

25A. Samantha Fox adorning the cover of *The Best of Mayfair* (1986). © Mayfair/Paul Raymond Publications.

25B. Tribal facial scarring and filed teeth of young Bopoto warrior, Northern Congo. Late-19th-century photo by Sir H. H. Johnston, from *Die Sitten der Völker* (1920). JR Archives.

25C. Young warrior of Kau, Southeast Nuba, Sudan, preparing for the annual *Dance of Love*. From *The People of Kau* (1976). Photo © Leni Riefenstahl.

26A. It takes many hands and much patience to get every feather in the right place and to complete such handsome tribal decorations. Author's photo taken at the bi-annual 1987 Goroka *Eastern Highland Tribal Show*. © Julian Robinson Archives.

26B. Village elder preparing for an important tribal celebration, Southern Highland Province, Papua New Guinea. Photo by the author (1985). © Julian Robinson Archives.

26C. Young Xinguanos warrior of the Amazon jungle, adorned for a tribal celebration. From *Xingu: Tribal Territory* (1979). Photo © Maureen Bisilliat.

26D. Early-19th-century engraving of a Maori chief with traditional *moko* facial tattoo denoting his rank. Photo by the author from an 1880s travel book. © Julian Robinson Archives.

27A. Unmarried Xinguanos Indian during a tribal celebration. From *Xingu: Tribal Territory* (1979). Photo © Maureen Bisilliat.

27B. A beaded gift from a young unmarried Maasai woman admirer, worn to draw attention to the firm buttocks of her *Moran* lover. From *Maasai* (1980). Photo © Carol Beckwith.

28A. Cover of *The National Police Gazette* (Nov., 1879) showing the then-link between tattooing and prostitution. JR Archives.

28B. *Pochoir* fashion illustration with beaded genital symbolism by Bonnotte. From *La Guirlande d'art et de la litterature* (1920). Photo © Julian Robinson Archives.

28C. Adorning what many young American women regard as their most alluring feature, their long and shapely legs. Mid-1920s stocking ad from a weekly women's magazine. Photo © Julian Robinson Archives.

29A. Unmarried Zulu woman of the Mabaso clan, north of Tugela Ferry, South African Republic. From *Sons of Zulu* (1978). Photo © Aubrey Elliott.

29B. Early-19th-century woodcut of Japanese hairstyle published in a 1912 fashion book. Author photo. © Julian Robinson Archives.

29C. Fashion illustration with genital symbolism (1935). JR Archives.

30A. Herman Powers, *Greek Slave*, 1843. This nude sculpture of a slave girl broke the social rules and became famous and much-admired.

30B. Traditional Madrid mantilla from an early-19th-century engraving. Photo by the author, from *A History of Hand-Made Lace* (1900). © Julian Robinson Archives.

30C. A young bride. Engraved illustration from *Le Journal des dames et des modes* (1913). Photo by the author. © Julian Robinson Archives.

30D. *A Lady of the Queens Palace*. Engraving by P. A. Martini, c. 1777, of a woman wearing an extravagant panier-skirted dress. © Julian Robinson Archives.

31A. The allure and symbolism of lace and frills. Late-19th-century photograph. JR Archives.

31B. Illustration by Aubrey Beardsley for *Aristophanes' Lysistrata* (1896). Photo by the author from a 1927 edition. JR Archives.

31C. As 31B.

32A. *Silenus*, Greek sculpture, 2nd half 6th century B.C. Early-20th-century photo. JR Archives.

32B. The ancient Japanese art of adorning the penis during sex play. Mid-19th-century woodcut from the author's collection of erotica. © Julian Robinson Archives.

32C. An erotic religious sculpture from the *Kandariya Mahadev* temple, Khajuraho, dedicated to the Hindu god Shiva. Author's photo, 1996. © Julian Robinson Archives.

33A. *Min*, the ancient Egyptian god of fertility. XVIIIth Dynasty. Photo courtesy of the Library of the Egyptian National Museum, Cairo.

33B. *Kalacha* phallic head adornments worn by Boran elders, Southern Ethiopia. Author's drawings after an illustration by Carol Beckwith.

33C. Indian lovers practicing the erotic art of *Tantra*. Mid-18th-century carved ivory. Photo believed to be early 1920s. JR Archives.

33D. *The Congregation*, admiring a young female. Mid-19th-century lithograph of a Thomas Rowlandson engraving. Author's photo from a 1910 book of erotic art. JR Archives.

34A. *Surprise Surprise*. Line drawing from *The Transsexual Phenomenon: A Trend for the 80s*. © American Art Enterprises, 1980.

34B. Suppressing the male crotch bulge. Corset ad of the mid-1930s. Photo by the author from a 1935 men's fashion magazine. JR Archives.

34C. Admiring a dainty foot. 1880s engraving published in an early-20th-century German book of fetishism. JR Archives.

35A. Fashionable women's shoes of the 1880s. Published in various editions of *Harper's Bazar*, selected from *Victorian Fashions and Costumes* (1974).

35B. As for 35A.

35C. Silhouette illustration of fashionable dress of the 1890s. From the German book on fashion, *Die Mode in der Karikatir* (1928). JR Archives.

35D. *Geisha Painting Her Eyebrows*. Early-19th-century *ukujo-e* print, published in a 1920s French art journal. JR Archives.

36A. *Backstage at the Paris Opera House* (1889) by Jean Béraud. Photo courtesy Musée Carnavalet, Paris.

36B. *La Belle O'Murphy* (1732) by François Boucher. From a French art publication of the 1920's. JR Archives.

36C. A Huli tribesman, Southern Highland Province, Papua New Guinea. Photo by the author (1986). © Julian Robinson Archives.

36D. Engravings of men's fashions, c. 1550. From an early-20th-century German book on fashion by Edward Fuchs. JR Archives.

37A. *Kicks Iron of the Dakota Sioux*. Photo c. 1905 by F. B. Fiske. © Azusa (Historic Photographs) Pub. Inc. 1994.

37B. Mid-19th-century engraving from an 1880 book of tribal peoples. JR Archives.

37C. *Portrait of Henry VIII*, School of Holbein, c. 1537. Early-1920s color photo from an art journal of 1923. Photo by the author. JR Archives.

37D. Unmarried Mendi woman, Sierra Leone, awaiting her rite-of-passage into adulthood. Early-20th-century photo by C. H. Firmin, from *Die Sitten der Völker* (1920). JR Archives.

38A. *Don't Be Flat*. A Frederick's of Hollywood ad for enhancement girdles. Photo by the author from a 1957 film magazine. JR Archives.

38B. *A Calibrated Beauty*. An artist at work, calibrating the measurements of his model. From *Women of All Lands* (1935). © Julian Robinson Archives.

38C. Leather and string skirts worn by engaged young Zulu women of the Tembu clan to advertise their status. From *Sons of Zulu* (1978). Photo © Aubrey Elliott.

39A. The fashionable bustle, c. 1860. © Julian Robinson Archives.

39B. A Harrison Fisher magazine illustration of 1908. Photo © Julian Robinson Archives.

39C. Beauty calibrator invented by Max Factor in 1932 and used to measure young Hollywood actresses for star quality. © Max Factor Cosmetic Co., Inc., 1996.

39D. Leatherwear by Orion of Germany. Photo from *Lack, Leder, Gummi* (1990). © Orion Versand Gmbh & Co. KG., Flensberg.

39E. *Bottom cleavage or décolletage?* Photo from an American Art Enterprise publication.

40A. Samburu Moran warriors braiding each others' hair. From *Samburu* (1990). Photo © Nigel Pavitt.

40B. *Perfect Health Corset* for both mother and child, c. 1890. Photo by the author from a 1891 fashion journal. © Julian Robinson Archives.

40C. Somaliland hairstyling. Early-20th-century photo by R. E. Drake-Brockman. From *Peoples of All Nations* (1922). © Julian Robinson Archives.

40D. Mary Quant's "Pop Art" cosmetic ad, mid-1980s.

41A. Details from 1920s/30s cosmetic and perfume ads. JR Archives.

41B. High-heeled boot featured in the *Custom Shoe Co.* catalog (1984). © Centurion/Spartacus Publications, Inc., Ca.

41C. Bra ad, *Sabrina, the passionate effect* by Perele, c. 1980.

41D. Traditional Balanese teeth filing. Early-20th-century photo. JR Archives.

41E. Exotic platform shoes, © details for 41B.

42A. Italian hairstyling in the late-1960s. From *Italia Mia* (1972). Photo © Gina Lollobrigida.

42B. An ad from a company in Cincinnati, Ohio, selling hair restorer. From a mail order catalogue of 1881. © Julian Robinson Archives.

42C. Ritual painting inspired by the jaguar in preparation for the *Dance of the Urúa Flutes*. Cuyapané tribesman of the Upper Xingu, Mato Grosso, Brazil. From *Xingu: Tribal Territory* (1979). Photo © Maureen Bisilliat.

42D. An early-19th-century dandy from an original engraving, c. 1830. Author's photo. © Julian Robinson Archives.

43A. Details from a perfume ad, mid-1930s. JR Archives.

43B. Biba men's wear and cosmetic ads, early 1970s. JR Archives.

43C. Biba jewelry ad, early 1970s. JR Archives.

43D. Mangbettu woman of the Congo with elongated head and traditional braided hairstyle. Photo courtesy Musée de l'Homme.

43E. As for 43B.

44A. Greek funeral pottery decoration glorifying male sexuality. Detail from an early-1930s art magazine. JR Archives.

44B. A late-19th-century fetish illustration. Photo from a German book of erotica, c. 1925. © Julian Robinson Archives.

44C. Bronze statue of Poseidon (or Zeus) from Histiaea, c. 470 B.C. Photo from a 1920s German art publication. JR Archives.

45A. Body painting of an Amazonian Indian preparing for a religious ceremony. From Xingu: Tribal Territory (1979). Photo © Maureen Bisilliat.

45B. A mid-19th-century dandy from an original engraving, c. 1860. Author's photo. © Julian Robinson Archives.

46A. Detail of Surma body painting, Southwest Ethiopia, in preparation for their traditional donga stick fight: the patterns are used to emphasize their physical beauty. From African Ark (1990). Photo © Carol Beckwith/Angela Fisher.

46B. Traditional penis wrapping of New Hebrides Islanders. Early-20th-century photo courtesy Musée de l'Homme.

46C. As for 46A.

47A. As for 45A.

47B. Members of The Dandy Club, c. 1818. Author's photo from a German book of European fashion. © Julian Robinson Archives.

47C. An array of men's fashions of the 15th/16th century. Illustrations from a 1920s German book of European fashion. JR Archives.

48A. Late-19th-century engraving of traditional West African jewelry from an 1880s travel book. JR Archives.

48B. North American Sioux chieftain and squaw. Early-20th-century colored photo by Hadel & Herbert. Author's photo from Peoples of All Nations (1922). © Julian Robinson Archives.

48C. The allure and beauty of military uniforms is beautifully illustrated by this hand-colored engraving of early-19th-century Prussian officers, c. 1815. Reproduced from a late-19th-century book, European Army Uniforms (1884). © Julian Robinson Archives.

49A. Pre-French Revolution fashionable hats. From Le Cabinet des modes ou les modes nouvelles. Author's photo. © Julian Robinson Archives.

49B. Early-20th-century fashion illustration. Photo by the author from an original 1913 publication. © Julian Robinson Archives.

50A. Mid-1930s American men's fashion ad. From Apparel Arts (1936). Author's photo. © Julian Robinson Archives.

50B. Detail from a late-19th-century article on corsets and the new fashion of "bloomers" (underpants). Author's photo from an original 1895 publication. © Julian Robinson Archives.

51A. Detail from a mid-1980s men's cosmetic ad from a Hong Kong men's fashion magazine.

51B. Page from a mail-order company for fashionable American-made men's wear, c. 1890. © Julian Robinson Archives.

51C. Hand-colored engraving of fashionable men's wear from Le Lion (1850). Author's photo © Julian Robinson Archives.

51D. Les Suppléans. Engraving, c. 1800. Author's photo from an early-20th-century German book of European fashions. © Julian Robinson Archives.

52A. Nell Gwynne by Sir Peter Lely (Pieter Van der Faes), mid-17th-century. Author's photo from an early-20th-century art journal. © Julian Robinson Archives.

52B. The future Lady Hamilton (and mistress to Lord Nelson) working as an artist's model. Engraving, c. 1800. Author's photo from an early-20th-century art publication. © Julian Robinson Archives.

53A. Preparing for a décolletage display, with rouged nipples and push-up corset, c. 1775. Author's photo from an early-20th-century German book of European fashions. © Julian Robinson Archives.

53B. The great fashion accessory of the 1930s, the hat, beautifully displayed on a wax model. Wax models were often used in fashion photography in the 1920s and 1930s as they could be stylized to perfection and this stylization of course affected how people wished to look. Photo from Excelsior Modes, 1934. © Julian Robinson Archives.

53C. Early-20th-century fashion illustration. Photo by the author from an original 1913 publication. © Julian Robinson Archives.

53D. Fashionable Paris hairstyles of the mid-1840s. Hand-colored engraving from Le Bon Ton (1843). © Julian Robinson Archives.

54A. The lipstick craze. Early-1920s illustration by Georges Lepape from La Gazette du bon ton (1920). Author's photo. © Julian Robinson Archives.

54B. The author dressed in Chinese opera garb from Peking (now Beijing). Photographed in 1992 by the anglo-Czech photographer Roman Cerney. © Julian Robinson Archives/Roman Cerney.

54C/D. Shopping for lingerie, a popular fashion in the early 1920s. Author's photo from an original fashion publication of 1922. © Julian Robinson Archives.

55A. Great Frenchy Look. A naughty but nice bra ad of the early 1960s. JR Archives.

55B. Glamorous Tender Tips. A Hollywood-approved breast and nipple enhancer, c. 1960. Photo by the author from a 1960 film magazine. JR Archives.

55C. Edwardian lingerie brought up to date for the American market in the early 1930s by a Paris manufacturer. Photo from an early-1930s Boué Soeurs of New York catalogue. © Julian Robinson Archives.

55D. As for 48C except these are French officers at the time of the Bourbon Restoration, c. 1835.

56A. A Japanese-style illustration. From Jak se Zeny Stroji by Dr. C. H. Stratz, Prague, 1899. © Julian Robinson Archives.

57A. Young Wadaabe woman with traditional kolo facial tattoos. From Nomads of Niger (1984). Photo © Carol Beckwith.

58A. Human-bone nose ornament worn by an Asmat headhunter as a special trophy and symbol of his power. From *Vanishing Tribes: Primitive Man on Earth* (1987). Photo © Alain Chenevière.

58B. Woodcut illustration of a traditional Japanese coiffure, c. 1850. Author's photo from a 1920s Japanese art publication. © Julian Robinson Archives.

58C. Nineteenth-century engraving from an 1880s travel book on Siam (Thailand). Author's photo. © Julian Robinson Archives.

58D. Late-19th-century West African hairstyle, probably from the Bandiagara Plateau, Mali. Author's photo from a 1910 postcard. © Julian Robinson Archives.

59A. Hand-colored engraving by Claude-Louis Desrais. From *Costumes civils actuels des tous les peuples connus* (1787/88). Author's photo from the original engraving. © Julian Robinson Archives.

59B. Hand-colored engraving of a traditional French provincial costume, by Gatine after Lanté. From *Costumes des Femmes du Pays de Caux* (1827). Author's photo from the original engraving. © Julian Robinson Archives.

59C. *Venus of Willendorf* with possible bracelet adornment and braided hair. 25,000–30,000 B.C. Early-20th-century photo. Courtesy Musée de l'Homme.

59D. *Venus of Lespugue* showing a rear-fringed apron worn low across the hips. 25,000–30,000 B.C. Early-20th-century photo courtesy Musée de l'Homme.

59E. As 59A.

60A. Late-19th-century engraving of a North American Indian's headdress. Author's photo from an 1880s travel book. © Julian Robinson Archives.

60B. Young unmarried Ojibwa woman of Algonquian stock, North America. Early-20th-century colored photo. From *People of All Nations* (1922). © Julian Robinson Archives.

60C. Tattooed village cheiften of the Marquesus Islands. From *The Natural History of Man* (1874). Author's photo from the original book. © Julian Robinson Archives.

60D. Tattooed native chieftain of Nulcahiva. Early-19th-century hand-colored engraving from *Voyage Around the World* (1813). Author's photo from the original illustration. © Julian Robinson Archives.

61A. *The Turkish Bath* by Jean-Auguste Dominique Ingres, 1859/62. Early-1920s photo from German book of European Paintings (1922). JR Archives.

61B. Traditional Hungarian costume. Late-19th-century photo by A. W. Cutler, from *Peoples of the World* (1922). JR Archives.

61C. Woodcut by Cesare Vecellio. From *Habiti Antichi et Moderni di tutto il Mondo* (1590). Photo by the author from an original print. © Julian Robinson Archives.

62A. Early-1900s colored photograph by Reutlinger of an evening dress by Doeuillet. From *Les Modes* (1901). Author's photo © Julian Robinson Archives.

62B. Young married Mondi women, Southern Highland Province, Papua New Guinea, participating in a sing-sing celebration. Note traditional cowarie shells worn as fertility symbols. Author's photo (1985). © Julian Robinson Archives.

63A. Line illustration from Fashion & Anti-Fashion (1978) by Ted Polhemus/Lynn Procter, courtesy of Ted Polhemus.

63B. Tattooed hands of a Marquesas chief. Late-19th-century woodcut illustrations from an 1880s travel book of the South Pacific. © Julian Robinson Archives.

63C. Nuba warrior decorated in ochre and oil. From *People of Kau* (1976). Photo © Leni Riefenstahl.

64A. Unmarried daughter of a Samoan Chief. Early-20th-century photo by Muir & Moodie. From *Die Sitten der Völker* (1920). JR Archives.

64B. African Shillules warrior with traditional cow-dung impregrated hairstyle and beadlike *keloid* forehead markings. Early-1920s photo by Hugo Adolf Bernatizik, from *Der dunkle Erdteil: Afrika* (1930). JR Archives.

64C. Xinguano Amazonian Indian warriors preparing their traditional hairstyle for an important religious celebration. From *Xingu: Tribal Territory* (1979). © Maureen Bisilliat.

65A. The pleasures of flagellation, or just the thought of it. 1970s photo courtesy Centurian/Sparticus Pub., Inc., Ca.

65B. Traditional Japanese geisha coiffure. Mid-1920s photo from a travel book of 1929. © JR Archives.

65C. The transvestite phenomna of the early-1980s. From Transvestite Catalog (1982). © Centurian/Sparticus Pub., Inc., Ca.

65D. *I Love You. I Love You. I Really, Really Do.* Illustration by, c. Hérouard, from *La Vie Parisienne* (1919). Photo by the author from the original publication. © Julian Robinson Archives.

66A. Unmarried Surma woman, Southwest Ethiopia, with wood lip-plate labret during the arduous process of lip stretching—a traditional form of cultural beautification, and a sign of her pending marriage. From *African Ark* (1990). Photo © Carol Beckwith/Angela Fisher.

66B. As for 66A.

66C. Publicity poster for the Federico Fellini film *La Dolce Vita* (1960), starring Anita Ekberg. JR Archives.

67A. Traditional Hungarian male dress, village of Mezökövesd. Early-20th-century photo by Cutler, from *Lands and Peoples* (1927). JR Archives.

67B. Line drawing of early-1920s fashionable dress. Photo by the author from an original 1920 French fashion publication. © Julian Robinson Archives.

67C. Mid-18th-century engraving of French court dress. From a 1910 German fashion book. © Julian Robinson Archives.

68A. Unmarried Dinka women displaying their eligibility for marriage—the beads' colors and patterns indicate their families' wealth and thus the expected bride price. From *Africa Adorned* (1984). Photo © Angela Fisher.

68B. Line illustration of an Egyptian circumcision rite, from an ancient burial chamber. Photo by the author from a 1910 German art publication. © Julian Robinson Archives.

68C. Carved painted wood head of Queen Nefertiti. Egyptian, XVIII Dynasty, 1370/1360 B.C. Photo courtesy the Library, Egyptian Museum, Cairo.

68D. Bronze head of an Akkadian King, Nineveh, Iraq, with finely curled beard—a symbol of authority. 2300/2200 B.C. Early-1930s photo. JR Archives.

69A. Faience Snake Goddess, Knossos, 1600 B.C. Photo by the author from an early-1930s art publication. JR Archives.

69B. Mid-19th-century engraving of ancient Greek costume. Photo by the author from an 1870s book of perfume. © Julian Robinson Archives.

69C. Gold funerary mask of Tutankhamen. Egyptian, XVIII Dynasty, 1350 B.C. Note three-eighth inch ear piercing. Photo courtesy the Library, Egyptian Museum, Cairo.

70A. Gold earrings and necklace of Queen Twosre, Egyptian, XIX Dynasty, 1220 B.C. Photo courtesy the Library, Egyptian Museum, Cairo.

70B. Relief carving of the face of the wife of Rameses brother. Egyptian, XIX Dynasty, 1300 B.C. Photo courtesy the Library, Egyptian Museum, Cairo.

70C. Roman statue of a conquering hero with prestigious genital display. Author's photo from a 1912 German art publication. JR Archives.

71A. Late-19th-century woodcut illustrations of fashionable men's wear, c. 1880. © Julian Robinson Archives.

71B. Mid-19th-century engraved illustration of an Assyrian king. JR Archives.

71C. *Pochoir* illustration by Carlos Bady. From the Art Deco folder *La Journée de Mado*, c. 1932. © Julian Robinson Archives.

72A. Early-20th-century photo of a professional Chinese footbinder at work shaping the foot of an 8-year-old daughter of a wealthy merchant. Author's photo from a 1910 German art publication. © Julian Robinson Archives.

72B. Early-20th-century x-ray photo of a Chinese lotus (bound) foot. Author's photo from a 1920s German art publication. © Julian Robinson Archives.

72C. Mid-19th-century engraved illustration of a much admired Chinese lotus foot. Author's photo from an 1880s book; *Oriental Travels* (1887). © Julian Robinson Archives.

72D. Detail from a bondage shoe ad of the late 1970s. © Centurian/Spartacus Pub., Inc., Ca.

73A. *Sexy High Heels* ad. Custom Shoe Co., catalog (1983). © Centurian/Spartacus Pub., Inc., Ca.

73B. Geisha in traditional kimona and *chopines*. Author's photo from an early-1920s Japanese art publication. © Julian Robinson Archives.

73C. Putting on the prestigious marriage anklet, Yafouba Tribe, West Africa. Late-19th-century photo. From *Die Sitten der Völker* (1920). © Julian Robinson Archives.

74A. Mid-19th-century engraving of tribal head-shaping. From *The Natural History of Man* (1874). Author's photo from the original publication. © Julian Robinson Archives.

74B. Traditional neck coil worn by a Padaung woman, Burma-Thailand border. Late-19th-century photo by Sir George Scott. From *Die Sitten der Völker* (1920). © Julian Robinson Archives.

74C. Papua New Guinea Highland tribesmen are very proud of their broad noses, which are made broader and larger by constant manipulation during childhood. Adults use all sorts of fanciful designs to accentuate this distinctive feature—in this case it is decorated with cassowary featherless quills, small *nassarious* shells and scarab beetle horns. From *Ich Komme aus der Steinzect* (1963). Photo © Heinrich Harrer.

74D. Oriental head-shaping. From *The Unfashionable Human Body* (1972). Julian Robinson Library Collection/JR Archives.

74E. Mid-19th-century engraved illustration of a deformed ancient skull, the result of childhood head-binding. Author's photo from an 1880s German anthropological study. © Julian Robinson Archives.

75A. The pleasures of being tightly laced. Original stereoscopic photograph c. 1895. © Julian Robinson Archives.

75B. Sara woman with double labret. Early-1920s photo by Mare Allégret. From *Der dunkle Erdteil: Afrika* (1930). JR Archives.

75C. An 1860s American spoon fronted corset illustration and a 1935 *Roussel* corset ad. JR Archives.

75D. The effects of tight lacing. 1880s illustration. JR Archives.

76A. "Reduce Your Double Chin" ad, mid-1920s. JR Archives.

76B. "Braided Wire Bustle" ad, mid-1870s. JR Archives.

76C. Mid- to late-19th-century crinoline and bustle illustrations from original publications. JR Archives.

76D. A Kaitish woman, Central Australia, having a tooth knocked out during her preparation for marriage. Late-19th-century photo. From *Die Sitten der Völker* (1920). © Julian Robinson Archives.

76E. Beautifying ads, late-1920s. JR Archives.

77A. Melanesian warriors of the Bismark Archipelago with unique nose adornments. Late-19th-century photo. From *Die Sitten der Völker* (1920). © Julian Robinson Archives.

77B/C. Neck rings and beadwork of the Ndebele, 1996. From *The Ndebele: Art and Culture* (1989). Photo © Aubrey Elliott.

77D. Indian religious ascetic with natural untrimmed nails. Early-20th-century photo by Wiele & Klein. From *Die Sitten der Völker* (1920). © Julian Robinson Archives.

78A. Dangaleat, called the Hajjeray, of Chad, West Africa, dancing the *margay jinn*. Note labret and tribal scar patterning. From *Dances d'Afrique* (1978). Photo © Michel Huet.

78B. Traditional Maori chin tattoo beautifying a young Maori woman of noble birth. Early-20th-century photo. From *Peoples of All Nations* (1922). © Julian Robinson Archives.

78C. Young Maasai Moran initiates awaiting circumcision and entry into adulthood. Late-19th-century photo by Underwood & Underwood. From *Die Sitten der Völker* (1920). © Julian Robinson Archives.

79A. Traditional Melanesian tattoo designs of the cheiftain's wife of Nukahiva. From *Voyages Around the World* (1813). Author's photo from the original publication. © Julian Robinson Archives.

79B. Body painting and tattooing of the ancient Picts. From an original engraving by J. Wilkes (1804). © Julian Robinson Archives.

79C. A Samoan tattooing ceremony. A mid-19th-century wood engraving, from *The Natural History of Man* (1874). © Julian Robinson Archives.

80A. The renowned Japanese *irezumi* tattooist Horikin (Mitsuaki Ohwada) with his wife. From *Japanese Tattoo* (1986). Photo © Sandi Fellman.

80B. Mid-19th-century engraving of traditional Japanese *irezumi* tattoo from the Dover Archive publication *Men, a Pictorial Archive from Nineteenth-Century Sources* (1980).

81A. Contemporary blackwork tattoo by Nalla on Blake. Also note stretched earlobes. Photo by Fakir Musafar. © Body Play/Insight Books, Ca.

81B. Line illustrations of traditional Borneo tribal tattoos. Credit & publication as 81C.

81C. Line illustrations of South Pacific Islanders traditional hand and arm tattoos. From *Modern Primitives: An Investigation of Contemporary Adornment and Ritual* (1989). Courtesy Re-Search Publications, Ca.

82A. Traditional back scarification on a young Nuba woman, denoting her marriage and the successful bearing of her first child. Photo © O. Luz/Zefa Picture Agency.

82B. Compilation of various late-19th/early-20th-century tribal tattoo illustrations from various sources. © Julian Robinson Archives

83A. Nuer warrior with traditional forehead scarring and keloid patterning on his shoulders and chest. Early-1920s photo by Hugo Adolf Bernatzik. From *Der dunkle Erdteil: Afrika* (1930). © Julian Robinson Archives.

83B. The art of raised keloid scarring as practiced by the Nuba, Sudan. From *People of Kau* (1976). Photo © Leni Riefenstahl.

84A. Young Shilluk woman of Western Africa, with traditional beadlike *keloid* forehead scarring. Early-1920s photo by Hugo Adolf Bernatzik. From *Der dunkle Erdteil: Afrika* (1930). © Julian Robinson Archives.

84B. Lower lip labret of a young Kirdis woman, Mandara Mountian region, Northern Nigeria. Date and copyright details not known. JR Archives.

84C. The beginning of the 1920s "primitives" influence on beauty and fashion. *Pochoir* illustration by A. E. Marty from *Modes et manières d'aujourd'hui* (1921). © Julian Robinson Archives.

85A. Young Sara woman with random *abaji* facial scarring made to enhance her beauty. Same credits as 84A.

85B. Rendilli Moran warrior with traditional ivory earring, (denoting bravery), splayed front teeth, and traditional hairstyle. From *Rendilli* (1976). Photo © Sicinio Trinci.

85C. Young marriageable Turkana girl with traditional splayed front teeth proudly wearing the bead necklaces of her many lovers which adds considerably to her perceived beauty. From *Turkana* (1975). Photo © Sicinio Trinci.

86A. A young married Toposa woman with traditional facial scars and splayed teeth enhancing her tribal beauty. She is also wearing a lower lip labret and coiled neck torque, gifts from her husband prior to their marriage. From *Africa Adorned* (1984). Photo © Angela Fisher.

86B. Young Dayak mother from an inland Kenyah village, Kalinantum (Indonesian Borneo), with traditional elongated earlobes. From *Pagan Innocence* (1960). Photo © K. F. Wong.

87A. A Kikuyu candidate for the circumcision rite-of-passage to full warrior status and adulthood, a status eagerly looked forward to as it allows him to take a lover. From *Kikuyu* (1975). Photo © S. Trinci.

87B. *Medicine Crow*. Late-19th-century photo from the AZUSA Historical Collection of North American Indian photographs. © AZUSA Pub., Inc., 1994.

87C. Traditional shell septum-pierced nose decoration of an Asmat head-hunter, Southern Irian Jaya. From *Ich Komme aus der Steinzeit* (1963). Photo © Heimrich Harrer.

88A. Ex-Sergent-Major RSM Crozier sporting his famous beard and wearing all the symbols of the British realm, frozen in time on his uniform of a Yeoman Warder (Beefeater) of the Tower of London. Photo courtesy of Yeoman Warder Crozier.

88B. At the *Eunoto* ceremony, Maasai *Moran* warriors painting themselves with white clay prior to their becoming village elders. Note split foreskin circumcision. From *Africa Adorned* (1984). Photo © Angela Fisher.

88C. Late-19th-century wood engraving. From a German book of *European Fashions* (1912), compiled by Edward Fuchs. JR Archives.

88D. *Train Your Moustache*. Late-19th-century ad. JR Archives.

89A. Traditional hairstyling with plaited side-wings decorated with an ostrich feather. Early-20th-century photo from *Peoples of All Nations* (1922). © Julian Robinson Archives.

89B. *Edwards Harlene Hair* ad, c. 1890. JR Archives.

89C. Cover of *La Revue des Folies Bergère* 1925. Photo by the author from his collection of Art Deco publications. © Julian Robinson Archives.

90A. Ad for "The Ideal Man" from the Indian edition of *Vanity Fair*, which I purchased in Delhi in 1996 whilst attending the *Miss World* carnival. JR Archives.

90B. Sculptured head of a young Greek athlete from a German art publication, c. 1930. © Julian Robinson Archives.

90C. Line illustrations of Greek costumes. From *Ancient Greek Female Costumes* (1883). © Julian Robinson Archives.

91A. Marble relief showing the birth of Aphrodite. Central panel from the Ludovisi Throne. Greek, 460 B.C. 1920s photo from a German art publication. JR Archives.

91B. A mid-1920s perfume ad featuring a painting of a young woman by Pierre Auguste Renoir. From a deluxe fashion magazine of the period. © Julian Robinson Archives.

91C. "Inspecting her jewels after death." Greek grave stele of Hegeso Dipylon cemetery, 400 B.C. 1920s photo from a German art publication. JR Archives.

91D. An illustration after those by Hanky Panky. Featured in *Modern Primitives: An Investigation of Contemporary Adornment and Ritual* (1989). © V. Vale/ReSearch Publications, Ca.

92A. French ad of the early-1930s. © Julian Robinson Archives.

92B. Ad from a late-19th-century New York mail-order catalogue. Photo © Julian Robinson Archives.

93A. Fashion illustrations from the 1935 French fashion magazine *Chiffon*. © Julian Robinson Archives.

93B. Walter Crane's chromolitho illustration for *Aladdin and His Wonderful Lamp* (1876), which helped to prepare young readers' minds for the later *Art Nouveau* style. Author's photo from an original print. © Julian Robinson Archives.

93C. A Hollywood Cleopatra redesigned in the Art Deco style by Travis Banton under the direction of Cecil B. DeMille, starring the French actress Claudette Colbert. Paramount publicity photo from a 1934 film magazine. JR Archives.

94A. *Masterpiece Makeovers: Three Renaissance Beauties Go Modern*. An Italian ad/editorial promoting the use of cosmetics, early-1980s. JR Archives.

94B. *Who Has the Best Figure in Hollywood?* Cover of *Photoplay*, a film fan's magazine of the early 1930s. © Julian Robinson Archives.

94C/D. As 94A.

94E. Mid-16th-century woodcut illustrating the fashion for face patches. Author's photo from a 1910 German art book. © Julian Robinson Archives.

95A. *A Medieval Court of Love*. Woodcut illustration by Thomas Wright. From *Womankind in Western Europe* (1869). © Julian Robinson Archives.

95B. Chocolate box cover featuring a painting by Paul Auguste Renoir. JR Archives.

95C. Engraved illustration of Medieval English court dress. From the *Girl's Own Paper* (1880). © Julian Robinson Archives.

96A. *Birth of Venus* by Sandro Botticelli (1486). 1920s photo from a French art publication. JR Archives.

96B. *Honouring a Lady*. Medieval book illustration featured in a German art publication of the 1920s. JR Archives.

96C. *A Day's Falconry*. A woodcut illustration by Thomas Wright. From *Womankind in Western Europe* (1869). © Julian Robinson Archives.

96D. *Primavera* by Sandro Botticelli (1478). Photo from a mid-1920s French art publication. JR Archives.

96E. *Les Nois de Janvier*. From a Book of Hours (1416). 1920s photo from a French art publication. JR Archives.

97A. Detail from *The Three Graces* by Hans Baldung Grien, early-16th-century. Photo from a mid-1920s French art publication. JR Archives.

97B. *Archduke Maximilian* by Jalcob Seisenegger, mid-16th-century. Photo from an early-1930s German magazine. JR Archives.

98A. Ladies at the tournament displaying their finery, and drawing attention to their facial beauty. Chromolitho illustration from *Womankind of Western Europe* (1869). Author's photo © Julian Robinson Archives.

98B. The fashionable bum-roll. Late-16th-century engraving included in *Illustrierte Sittengeschichte* (1909). © Julian Robinson Archives.

98C. Clandestine meeting in a *Garden of Love*. Chromolitho illustration from *Womankind in Western Europe* published in 1869. Author's photo © Julian Robinson Archives.

98D. Mid-17th-century engraving of European courtier, c. 1630. From a German book of fashion, compiled by Edward Fuchs (1912). © Julian Robinson Archives.

98E. As for 98D.

98F. As for 98D.

99A. *Venus à la Coquille*. An early 16th century engraving by Benoist after the central figure in Titian's painting *Venera Anadiomene* (1520). Photo from an early 20th century German book of erotica. JR Archives.

99B. *Venus attending to her toilette* (and displaying her very feminine charms for the delight of the observer) by Francesco Bissolo, mid-16th-century. Photo by the author from *Venus die apotheose des Weibes* (1909). © Julian Robinson Archives.

99C. *Virgin and Child* by Carlo Crivelli. Late 15th century. To some extent our perception of the aesthetic merit of such paintings and the beauty of the central figure will depend on our religious beliefs, knowledge of the art of painting, our subliminal response to various forms of symbolism, juxtapositioning of pattern and details, and a whole range of other responses all of which add up to a subjective judgement of its beauty. Photo from a mid-1920s French art journal. © Julian Robinson Archives.

99D. *Blanca Maria Sforza* (wife of Emperor Maximilian I) by Bernhard Strigel. Early-16th-century. Photo from Die Mode (1914). © Julian Robinson Archives.

99E. Decorative engraving from M. Augustin Challamel's *The History of Fashion in France* (1882). © Julian Robinson Archives.

100A. Sixteenth-century *Ceinture de chasteté* or chastity belt from the collection in the Musée de Cluny. Photo from an early-20th-century German book of erotica, which inferred that such belts were worn as a form of titillation—the giving of the key to one's lover being the main aim. JR Archives.

100B. Baroque pearl Renaissance jewelry, c. 1580. Early-20th-century photo from a 1920 French publication. JR Archives.

100C. Sixteenth-century iron corset from the collection housed in the Musée de Cluny. Early-20th-century photo from an early-20th-century German book of erotica. © Julian Robinson Archives.

101A. "Sinful" decorative buttons, c. 1660. From a German fashion book, c. 1910. JR Archives.

101B. *La Schoon Majken*. An early-17th-century engraving of a Belgian "House of Beauties." Photo by the author from an early-20th-century German book of erotica. © Julian Robinson Archives.

101C. *The Voice of God Against the Sin of Pride* (1683). From a German publication of 1912. JR Archives.

101D. Raphael's use of phallic symbolism (detail). Photo from an early-1920s French art publication. JR Archives.

102A. A lady attending to her toilette while Rubens skillfully displays her sensual curves. Early-17th-century painting featured in *Venus: die apotheose des Weibes* (1909). © Julian Robinson Archives.

102B. Mid-16th-century court fashions. From a late-19th-century engraving included in a German book of European fashion (1912). © JR Archives.

102C. French courtier fashion, c. 1690, after an engraving by J.D. de St. Jean. Note the *de rigueur* muff and face patches. Photo from an early-20th-century German publication. JR Archives.

102D. Details as 61C.

103A. Details as 61C.

103B. *John and Bernard Stuart* (men of fashion) by Sir Anthony Van Dyck. Early-17th-century. Photo by the author from a 1922 German art journal. © Julian Robinson Archives.

103C. *A Lady of Fashion* displaying her beautiful guipure lace collar and cap, and at the same time concealing her hair and ears because of their perceived sexual association. Painting by M. Hiert, c. 1642, from a 1926 photo in a French art journal. JR Archives.

103D. *Portrait of a Young Woman* by Piero del Pollaiuolo, c. 1475, with her ears concealed, as was the fashion at the time, because of their perceived erotic symbolism. Author's photo from a 1926 French art publication. © Julian Robinson Archives.

104A. The famous *Directoire* beauty Madame Récamier by François Gérard. Photo courtesy Musée Carnavelet.

104B. French court fashions, c. 1787. Hand-colored engraving by Claude-Louis Desrais, *Magasin des modes nouvelles françaises et anglaises*. Author's photo. © Julian Robinson Archives.

105A. English fashions of the late-18th-century. Hand-colored engraving from Niklaus Wilhelm Innocentius von Heideloff, *Gallery of Fashion* (1796). Author's photo. © Julian Robinson Archives.

105B. An engraved illustration of a fashionable man's wig of the mid-18th-century. © Julian Robinson Archives.

105C. *Preparing the Fashionable Wig*, c. 1785. Engraved illustration from a German book of fashion, c. 1912. Author's photo. © Julian Robinson Archives.

105D. Men's wigs just prior to the French Revolution. Hand-colored engraving by François-Louis-Joseph Watteau, *Le Cabinet des modes ou les modes nouvelles* (1785). Author's photo. © Julian Robinson Archives.

106A. Admiring the delights of a young court beauty—the much discussed Fragonard painting *The Swing* (1769). Photo from a 1927 French art journal. JR Archives.

106B. *A Fashionable Lady of 1800 in Dress and Undress*. Hand-colored engraving, c. 1800. Author's photo. © Julian Robinson Archives.

106C. *A Scene at a London School of Beauty and Deportment*, c. 1800. From an engraving featured in a 1910 German book of fashion compiled by Edward Fuchs. Author's photo. © Julian Robinson Archives.

106D. Ingres' famous and influential painting *La Source* (1856). An early-1920s photo from a French art journal. JR Archives.

107A. Engraved illustration *An Abridgment of M. R. Pope's Essay on Man*, invented, designed, and printed by V. Green, 1769. Author's photo from an original print from his collection of rare fashion illustrations. © Julian Robinson Archives.

107B. *An Essay on Women by Various Authors*, illustrated, engraved, and printed by I. Roberts, 1769. Author's photo from an original print. © Julian Robinson Archives.

107C. A fashionable gathering at a London theatre in the early-19th-century. Hand-colored engraving from *Life in London* (1822). Author's photo from one of his original prints. © Julian Robinson Archives.

107D. Napoleon in his influential riding habit, first adopted as a form of modernist dress by the British aristocracy, and then metamorphosized by changing times into today's business suit. Early-20th-century photo of the 1810 painting. JR Archives.

108A. Early-19th-century wood engraving of the Italian sculptor Antonio Canova's *Three Graces*. © Julian Robinson Archives.

108B. Hand-colored engraved fashion plate of 1806 showing the latest "naked" French fashions. From *La Belle Assemblée* (1806). Author's photo from an original hand-colored print. © Julian Robinson Archives.

108C. Fashionable men's wear, c. 1841. Hand-colored engraving showing the gradual metamorphosing of traditional men's wear designs—styles that are still widely admired today. Author's photo from an original print. © Julian Robinson Archives.

108D. Swiss peasant costume of the 18th-century. From an original painting by D. A. Schmid contained in a 1920s European travel book. Photo © Julian Robinson Archives.

109A. *Tableaux Vivants* or "Poses Plastiques/Living Pictures." Advertising broadsheet, c. 1845—evidence of a mid-19th-century *Playboy* era. Image from an early-20th-century German erotic publication. JR Archives.

109B. Admiring a pretty foot and, unwittingly or not, showing an attractive leg and possibly much more, plus intoxicating the admirer with a little natural body scent. An 1840s print featured in *Die Frau in der Karikatun* (1906). Photo © Julian Robinson Archives.

109C. The beginnings of fashionable sports for women. Author's photo from an original 1840s hand-colored fashion engraving. © Julian Robinson Archives.

109D. Fashionable laced-up form-sculpting corset. Hand-colored engraving from *Le Petit Courrier des dames* (1837). Author's photo of an original print. © Julian Robinson Archives.

110A. *The Pleasures of Cross Dressing*. An 1840s print from an early-20th-century German erotic publication. JR Archives.

110B. Mid-19th-century pleasures of the flesh, before the age of the cinema and of television. An 1850s illustration featured in *Illustrierte Sittengeschichte* (1912). © Julian Robinson Archives.

110C. The fun of fancy dress—a good way of expanding new ideas about women's dress styles and for testing moral attitudes. Author's photo from an original 1840s hand-colored fashion engraving. © Julian Robinson Archives.

110D. A mid-19th-century chromolitho illustration of an earlier Thomas Rowlandson illustration, showing the delights to be gleaned from an uninhibited dancer of the times—it was *de rigueur* for women of all classes not to wear underpants as they were thought to be lust provoking. © Julian Robinson Archives.

111A. Hand-colored fashion engraving. From *Le Petit Courrier des dames* (1854). Author's photo from original print. © Julian Robinson Archives.

111B. Traditional 18th-century Tirolean costume of the Brandenberg District. From a book of illustrations by Hammerstein. *Trachten der Alpenlander* (1930). Author's photo. © Julian Robinson Archives.

111C. Hand-colored engraving of early-19th-century fashionable hats *Costumes Parisiens*. From la Mésangère's *Le Journal des dames et des modes* (1815). Author's photo from an original print. © Julian Robinson Archives.

112A. Chromolitho print from *A New Matrimonial Ladder*, c. 1850. Author's photo from an original print. © Julian Robinson Archives.

112B. Advertisement for the fashionable crinoline, c. 1860. JR Archives.

112C. Hand-colored fashion engraving published during the reign of the bustle. From the English women's magazine *The Queen*, c. 1874. Author's photo from an original print. © Julian Robinson Archives.

112D. Bum-pad fashion accessory, c. 1870. JR Archives.

113A. Exploring remoter regions, but still confined by the fashionable dress of the period. A mid-19th-century engraving from *Modes and Manners of the XIX Century* (1909). © Julian Robinson Archives.

113B. Late-19th-century engraved illustration featured in a French publication of the period. © Julian Robinson Archives.

113C. Chromolitho print from *The Lady's Toilet* (1845). Author's photo from an original print. © Julian Robinson Archives.

114A. A chromolitho illustration from *Undine: A German Legend* by Julius Happner, published in 1885. Such illustrations helped to broaden young readers' minds, thus sowing the seed for future change. Author's photo from an original print. © Julian Robinson Archives.

114B. A new generation of young women, c. 1882, were undoubtedly destined to grow up with notions of physical beauty that were quite different from their non-physically experienced mothers. As the article for which this illustration was made said, "Gymnasiums for young women are a very new idea" and it suggests the young women removed their stays (corsets) before partaking in such "strenuous exercise." Chromolitho illustration designed by R. W. Maddox for *Every Girl's Annual* (1882). © Julian Robinson Archives.

114C. Corset illustration from an 1880s ad. JR Archives.

115A. *The Wheel of Fashion*, an 1840s engraving from a French fashion magazine of the period. © Julian Robinson Archives.

115B. Late 19th century engraving of near nude dancing at a New York burlesque theatre, featured in an early 20th century German book of erotica. JR Archives.

115C. A duel of honor between two women. From a mid-19th-century print illustrated in an early-20th-century German book of erotica. © Julian Robinson Archives.

115D. Corset and bustle ads from the 1870s. © Julian Robinson Archives.

116A. A frontier bride in breeches. Photo of an 1895 wedding published by Lawrence Langner in *The Importance of Wearing Clothes* (1959). JR Archives.

116B. *Odalisque*. A nude photograph published in Paris in 1899. © Julian Robinson Archives.

116C. Line illustration of a scene in a West Coast dance hall in the mid-1880s showing the preference of young women to show their legs—a trend that would soon transform Western fashions. JR Archives.

117A. "The Folly of the Corset." Illustration from an 1880s English magazine. © Julian Robinson Archives.

117B. An 1890s photograph of a wasp-waisted actress wearing a fashionable whalebone corset, laced to 15 inches. Such actresses and *demimondaines* were avidly sought by rich paramours— millionaire bankers, industrial barons and the like—and those who envied their success soon followed their fashion lead. Photo from a 1905 art journal. JR Archives.

117C. Line illustration of fashionable dress c. 1895 (note the veil). JR Archives.

117D. Late-19th-century line engraving from a magazine of the period. © Julian Robinson Archives.

118A. *Little Egypt*. Late-19th-century French photograph from the author's collection. © Julian Robinson Archives.

118B. An American woodcut ad *How to make women beautiful*, c. 1880s. © Julian Robinson Archives.

118C. A leading lady at the *Gaiety Theater* in tights, proudly displaying the then-fashionable hour-glass figure. Author's photo of an original 1889 chromolitho illustration. © Julian Robinson Archives.

119A. Underwear as outerwear—a waist-sculpting corselette in red satin worn over a darker red velvet afternoon dress, c. 1880. Author's photo from an original print. © Julian Robinson Archives.

119B. Early-20th-century fashion illustration. Photo by the author from an original 1913 publication. © Julian Robinson Archives.

119C. An illustration by the prolific artist Gustave Doré whose work is full of sexual symbolism and whose illustrations were later to be a great influence on advertising and films—Cecil B. DeMille was known to be a great admirer of Doré's work and based many of his film sets around his work. © Julian Robinson Archives.

120A. *The Queen's State Robes*. An 1870s woodcut illustration of the British aristocracy's dress of rank (1876) showing their somewhat idiosyncratic figure shapes. © Julian Robinson Archives.

120B. An 1880s dandy, Henry Cyril, Earl of Uxbridge, and soon to be the fifth Marquess of Anglesey. A photograph from *The Album: A Journal of Photographs* (1895) which was printed using the newly introduced "half-tone" screen method of reproduction. © Julian Robinson Archives.

120C. Late-19th-century woodcut illustration of fashionable young men. © Julian Robinson Archives.

121A. *Folies-Bergére* poster featuring the dancer Loie Fuller. Late 19th century. Photo © Julian Robinson Archives.

121B. Poster in the fashionable *Art Nouveau* style designed by the Czech artist Alphonse Mucha. JR Archives.

121C. *Folies-Bergére* bare bottom publicity poster, "*Sans Culottes, Mesdames!*". © Julian Robinson Archives.

122A. Japanese-inspired chromolitho illustration published as the frontispiece to the first *Girl's Own Annual* (1880) which helped to broaden the young reader's mind, thus opening the pathway for future change. © Julian Robinson Archives.

122B. Cosmetic ad for *Japanese complexion powder*. Late-19th-century. JR Archives.

123A. WWII pin-up *The Utility Suit* by David Wright. Published by the English magazine *The Sketch* (1942). Author's photo from his collection of WWII pin-up illustrations. © Julian Robinson Archives.

123B. Cover of *Les Modes*, No. 47, November 1904. Author's photo from an original publication. © Julian Robinson Archives.

123C. As if to greet the new century it became fashionable for women's ankles to be displayed in decorative stockings. At first they were only glimpsed—a tease—but gradually the feminine leg was to transform our western way of dress. Ad, c. 1902, featured in *The Unfashionable Human Body* (1972). JR Archives.

124A. Air travel has greatly influenced our way of life and perception of both beauty and fashion. Photo by Luza-Moral, *Excelsior Modes* (1934). JR Archives.

124B. Cover of *La Femme Chic* (1928), featuring an illustration by P. Jiguet. © Julian Robinson Archives.

124C. The allure of the bathing costume. French postcard, c. 1905. Photo © Julian Robinson Archives.

124D. A fashionable motorist, c. 1908. © Julian Robinson Archives.

124E. Fashion silhouettes, 1400 to 1900. From a 1920s theatrical magazine. JR Archives.

125A. Fashionable nude sunbathing in Germany in 1905. Chromolitho illustration from *Die Frau als Hausärztin*. Author's photo © Julian Robinson Archives.

125B. Corset ad, c. 1910. From a magazine of the period. JR Archives.

125C. Corset ad, c. 1910. © Julian Robinson Archives.

126A. A Gibson Girl-influenced dress featured in *Les Modes* in 1901. Photograph by Reutlinger. © Julian Robinson Archives.

126B. Pochoir print of fashionable Parisian hats. From *La Femme Chic* (1912). © Julian Robinson Archives.

126C. The growing influence on fashion and beauty of the automobile. Ad, c. 1910. Photo © Julian Robinson Archives.

126D. The influential American beauty Miss Camille Clifford, the original Gibson Girl and wife of the illustrator Charles Dana Gibson. Photo from a 1906 fashion magazine. JR Archives.

126E. *At a Paris couturier*, models displaying the latest fashions. From a French fashion magazine of 1905. © Julian Robinson Archives.

126E2. *A Gibson Girl*. An illustration by Charles Dana Gibson, detailing the daringly new swimming costumes of the early 20th century. Published in a 1905 women's magazine. Photo © Julian Robinson Archives.

127A. An American beauty, *After the Dance*, illustrated by Harrison Fisher, 1907. Photo © Julian Robinson Archives.

127B. Detail from a poster advertising the new and influential fashion for the "movies." *Cinématographe Lumière*, c. 1910. Photo © Julian Robinson Archives.

127C. The revolutionary French couturier Paul Poinet with his wife, both dressed in Persian-style costumes for their famous *One Thousand and Second Night* fête held in 1911. © Julian Robinson Archives.

127D. A woman of adventure with her new flying machine, *Femina* (1911). © Julian Robinson Archives.

128A. Perfume ad for *Seduction*, "*Le parfum des Élégantes.*" From a French fashion magazine, c. 1905. © Julian Robinson Archives.

128B. Perfume ad illustrated by Paul Iribe. From *Luxe de Paris* (1913). © Julian Robinson Archives.

128C. Gate-fold from the theatre program of the *Ballets Russes* production of *Schéhérazade* designed by Leon Bakst (1910). © Julian Robinson Archives.

128D. Fashionable line illustrations, c. 1910. © Julian Robinson Archives.

129A. Fashion line illustrations, c. 1912. © Julian Robinson Archives.

129B. The new fashion for garters, designed to draw attention to the wearer's legs. From *Shadowland* (1928). © Julian Robinson Archives.

129C. *Pochoir* fashion illustration of a dress by Martial et Armand. From *Luxe de Paris* (1913). Author's photo © Julian Robinson Archives.

129D. *Pochoir* fashion illustration by George Barbier. From *Le Journal des dames et des modes* (1914). Author's photo © Julian Robinson Archives.

129E. George Barbier's "new woman." *Pochoir* fashion illustration published in *Modes et manières d'aujourd'hui* (1914) from the author's collection of Art Deco pochoir prints. © Julian Robinson Archives.

130A. Colored fashion photograph by Reutlinger. From *Les Modes* (1915). Author's photo © Julian Robinson Archives.

130B. Leon Bakst designs for the *Ballets Russes* production of *Schéhérazade*, 1912. Photo from a book written on Diaghilev and the *Ballets Russes* in 1922. © Julian Robinson Archives.

130C. Mademoiselle Lantêlme. Photo from an early-1900s French fashion magazine. © Julian Robinson Archives.

130D. Detail from an early-1920s ad for hair care products. Photo from a women's magazine of the period. © Julian Robinson Archives.

131A. Line illustration by Ronald Balfour. From *Rubaiyat of Omar Khayyam* (1920). © Julian Robinson Archives.

131B. *Pochoir* fashion illustration by Simon A. Puget of a dress by Paul Poiret. From *La Gazette du bon ton* (1914). © Julian Robinson Archives.

131C. The film actress Theda Bara, the idealized *femme fatale* of the pre-1920s. Publicity photo for *Salomé* (1918). JR Archives.

131D. *Pochoir* book illustration in the fashionable Persian style by Léon Carré. From *Le Jardin des caresses* (1914). Author's photo from an original print. © Julian Robinson Archives.

132A. An early-1920s illustration from *La Vie Parisienne*, "I haven't a thing to wear." © Julian Robinson Archives.

132B. Ad for beautifying the human nose, c. 1910. JR Archives.

132C. Ads for beautifying women's hair, c. 1925. JR Archives.

132D. Line illustrations from *La Vie Parisienne* (1922). JR Archives.

132E. Cosmetic ad, *"Teindelys Parisien,"* c. 1920. JR Archives.

133A. An ad for breast cream and body powders from a mid-1920s copy of *La Vie Parisienne*. JR Archives.

133B. An introduction to topless/see-through fashion. *Pochoir* illustration by Charles Martin from *La Gazette du bon ton* (1920). Author's photo. © Julian Robinson Archives.

133C. *Pochoir* illustration by Jamine Aghion. From *The Essence of the Mode of the Day* (1920). Author's photo. © Julian Robinson Archives.

133D. Publicity photo of Max Sennett's *Bathing Beauties*. From an early-1920s film fan magazine. JR Archives.

134A. Foyer card advertising the 1928 film, *Our Dancing Daughters*, starring Joan Crawford. Photo © Julian Robinson Archives.

134B. The Italian-born Hollywood actor Rudolph Valentino in one of his famous roles as an Arab sheik. Publicity photo for the Allied Artists' film *Son of the Sheik* (1926), from a film fan magazine of the period. © Julian Robinson Archives.

134C. Nazimova, the Russian-born Hollywood actress. Publicity photo for the 1922 film *Salomé*, from a film fan magazine of the period. JR Archives.

134D. "In homage of the female body." Illustration from a mid-1920s copy of *La Vie Parisienne*. © Julian Robinson Archives.

135A. Line drawings by Benito. From *La Gazette du bon ton* (1923). © Julian Robinson Archives.

135B. Publicity photo of the Anglo-Chinese-American actress Anna May Wong. From a mid-1920s film fan magazine. Photo JR Archives.

135C. Detail from a mid-1920s corset ad. JR Archives.

135D. *Pochoir* fashion illustration of the latest men's wear, illustrated by Leon Bonnette. From *La Guirlande d'art et de la littérature* (1920). © Julian Robinson Archives.

135E. Details as 135D above.

135F. *Pochoir* fashion illustration of *"Le Gantier préféré par Aléxandrine"* by Jean Grangier. From *La Gazette du bon ton* (1925). © Julian Robinson Archives.

136A. Warner's corselette ad, c. 1925. JR Archives.

136B. Men's wear ad, c. 1926. © Julian Robinson Archives.

136C. Publicity photo of the Swedish-born Hollywood actress Greta Garbo and her favorite leading man of the late 1920s, John Gilbert. Photo from a Czechoslovakian film magazine (1929). © Julian Robinson Archives.

136D. The African-American dancer Josephine Baker at the *Casino de Paris*. Late 1920s ad. JR Archives.

136E. Detail from a French ad for wrinkle prevention. Late 1920s. JR Archives.

137A. Fashionable line illustration of a young girl about town dressed in an adaptation of a man's evening suit. Mid-1920s. JR Archives.

137B. Illustration from a 1920s French eye make-up ad. JR Archives.

137C. *Pochoir* fashion illustration by George Barbier. From *Falbalas et Fanfreluches* (1925). Author's photo. © Julian Robinson Archives.

137D. French fashion illustration featuring designs by Jean Patou and Drecoll with an American jazz band in the background—American jazz was very fashionable in Paris throughout the 1920s. Author's photo from *Art-Goût-Beauté* (1922). © Julian Robinson Archives.

137E. "The alchemy of industrialized beauty." A 1929 illustration from *Science Wonder Stories* courtesy of Ted Polhemus' *BodyStyles* (1988).

138A. By the late 1920s the influence of the so-called "primitive" style was much in evidence in fashion and advertising, with traditional ways of dress, such as this one from Southern Africa, being widely distributed in such publications as *Our Wonderful World* (1929). © Julian Robinson Archives.

138B. An early-20th-century photo of mid-European peasant costume. From *Customs of the World* (1929). © Julian Robinson Archives.

138C. North Indian *Sikh* with splendid beard. Early-20th-century photo from *Lands and Peoples* (1928). Photo © Julian Robinson Archives.

138D/E. "What's the Difference." Two illustrations from *The Way of the World* (1926), which skillfully compared and documented both tribal and Western customs—the illustration above is of North American Haida Indians partaking in a ritual, while the illustration below is of participants in the annual *Horn Dance*, Abbots Bromley, England. Photo © Julian Robinson Archives.

139A. Traditional dress of Japan. Late-19th-century photo published in *Lands and Peoples* (1928). © Julian Robinson Archives.

139B. An illustration showing the beginnings of the unisex fashion trend. Magazine illustration of the late-1920s. JR Archives.

139C. Princes of an ancient Mongolian tribe in full regalia. Late-19th-century photo published in *Peoples of All Nations* (1922). © Julian Robinson Archives.

139D. Early-20th-century photo of traditional Greek dress. From *Die Sitten der Völker* (1920). © Julian Robinson Archives.

139E. Sara woman with double labret. From the influential German book by Hugo Adolf Bernatzik, *Der dunkle Erteil: Afrika* (1930). JR Archives.

139F. Nuba woman with labret, partaking in a festive celebration. From *Der dunkle Erteil: Afrika* (1930). JR Archives.

140A. *Pochoir* illustration by George Barbier showing the fashionable use of opium in the 1920s. From *Le Bonheur du jour ou les grâces à la mode* (1924). Author's photo © Julian Robinson Archives.

140B. Detail of a jewelry ad, c. 1929. Author's photo © Julian Robinson Archives.

140C. Mid-1920s cover of *La Vie Parisienne* commenting on the fashionable primitive trend *A Pale Imitation*. Author's photo © Julian Robinson Archives.

140D. Cinema foyer card ad for Howard Hughes' *Blonde Bombshell* (1933), starring Jean Harlow. Author's photo © Julian Robinson Archives.

140E. Men's wear ad, c. 1928. Photo © Julian Robinson Archives.

140F. Ad for banishing "unsightly" hair growth, c. 1930. Photo © Julian Robinson Archives.

141A. *Pochoir* illustration by George Barbier of fashionable sunbathing. From *Le Bonheur du jour ou les grâces à la mode* (1924). Author's photo © Julian Robinson Archives.

141B. Detail for a 1920s cosmetic ad. © Julian Robinson Archives.

141C. Detail from a shoe ad, c. 1928. Photo © Julian Robinson Archives.

141D. "Beauty Is in the Eye of the Beholder." *Pochoir* illustration by Nelly et Jean (Jean Dulac) from *Nous Deux* (1929). Author's photo from his extensive collection of Art Deco prints and publications. © Julian Robinson Archives.

141E. As detailed for 141D.

142A. Cover of the English edition of the American magazine *Harper's Bazar* designed by the Russian Art Deco illustrator Erté (1934). Photo courtesy Erté.

142B. Publicity photo of Marlene Dietrich in the German film *The Blue Angel* (1930), which catapulted her to instant stardom and changed forever our cultural view of beauty and femininity. UFA photo featured in a Czechoslovakian film magazine of 1931. JR Archives.

142C. Hollywood costume designers, with the aid of willing stars, helped promote the figure-hugging bias-cut dresses that were designed to be worn without any form of under-clothing so that intimate physical features could be clearly seen. Hollywood publicity photo from a 1934 Czechoslovakian film magazine. JR Archives.

142D. Cosmetic ads such as this helped to break down restrictive social mores. Mavis ad, c. 1932. JR Archives.

142E. *Dress and Beauty,* magazine cover featuring a drawing of the *Venus de Milo* (1936). Author's photo from the original publication. © Julian Robinson Archives.

142F. *No More Freckles* and *Coryse Face Powder* ads, c. 1930. Photo © Julian Robinson Archives.

143A. *Hawaiian Tattoo* lipstick ad, c. 1935. Photo © Julian Robinson Archives.

143B. Cosmetic ad, c. 1928. Photo © Julian Robinson Archives.

143C. *Dreams of the Kama Sutra.* The *Kama Sutra* and *Dreams of the East,* together with other erotic and sex-sensual books, were very fashionable in the early-1930s, with their influence spreading into films, advertising, and all forms of commercial enterprise. Author's photo © Julian Robinson Archives.

143D. Cover *"La Revue de Casino de Paris"* by Zig. His design emphasizing the models' scanty costume and long legs, both growing trends in feminine beauty, which have continued to the present day. Author's photo. © Julian Robinson Archives.

143E. The Busby Berkeley chorus line on the set of *The Kid from Spain.* Publicity photo for the 1932 Samual Goldwyn film. JR Archives.

143F. Publicity photo of the German actor/director Eric von Stroheim from an early-1930s Czechoslovakian movie magazine. JR Archives.

144A. Idealized western beauty as perceived by Emile Aubrey in his painting *La Voix de Pan* (1936). Author's photo © Julian Robinson Archives.

144B. Cover of *Screen Play* featuring Marlene Dietrich (1933). Photo © Julian Robinson Archives.

144C. Cover of *Modern Screen* featuring the English actress Merle Oberon, whose grandfather was Indian (1936). Photo © Julian Robinson Archives.

144D. Publicity photo of Greta Garbo as *Mata Hari* (1931). The head-dress was designed by Gilbert Adrian, MGM's most talented and prolific costume designer. Photo from a mid-1930s Czechoslovakian movie magazine. JR Archives.

144E. Typical *Film Fun* magazine cover of the mid-1930s. JR Archives.

145A. American 1930's ad. JR Archives.

145B. "A New Face—A New Future." Early-1930s ad for face lifting and other forms of cosmetic surgery. Photo © Julian Robinson Archives.

145C. *Beauty Parade, What Men Like* cover design of the mid-1930s. Photo © Julian Robinson Archives.

145D. Clarke Gable and Jean Harlow adorning the cover of the Italian magazine *Zenit* (1933). Author's photo © Julian Robinson Archives.

145E. Fashionable men's wear designs of 1935. From *Apparel Arts.* Author's photo © Julian Robinson Archives.

146A. The fashionable mud-bath, c. 1935. From an English magazine feature on *Beauty and Health.* Photo © Julian Robinson Archives.

146B. Publicity poster for *Moon Over Miami* (1941) starring the ex-Busby Berkeley chorus girl Betty Grable, redrawn and airbrushed to idealized Hollywood perfection by the master of wartime pin-ups, Alberto Vargas. Photo © Julian Robinson Archives.

146C. French fashion illustrations of the mid-1930s. From the magazine *Chiffon* (1936). Photo © Julian Robinson Archives.

146D. Body painting publicity photo of the mid-1930s promoting the use of a new range of Max Factor cosmetic colors. Photo courtesy Max Factor Cosmetics, Inc.

146E. Magazine illustration of the late 1920s, *Now what should I choose?*. © Julian Robinson Archives.

147A. French line illustration, c. 1930. JR Archives

147B. Busby Berkeley's favorite chorus girl, Toby Wing, giving beauty hints. From *Film Fashions* (1934). Photo © Julian Robinson Archives.

147C. The great Renaissance painters were influential in the art of hair-dressing in the mid-1930s under the guiding hand of *Antoine of Paris.* Author's photo © Julian Robinson Archives.

147D. French *Vogue* with a drawing of a topless sun bather, 1934. © Julian Robinson Archives.

147E. Betty Grable, the famous wartime pin-up and Hollywood movie star. Cover of *Movie Story* (1942). JR Archives.

148A. Ad for a 1944 wartime pin-up calendar designed by the popular Alberto Vargas. JR Archives.

148B. A Varga wartime pin-up from *Esquire* magazine. Photo from an original print. JR Archives.

148C. An English wartime pin-up by David Wright, published by *The Sketch* (1942). Author's photo from the original pin-up calender. © Julian Robinson Archives.

149A. Detail from a French wartime stocking ad. JR Archives.

149B. As detailed in 148B.

149C. An illustration by Pierre Louchel of French wartime fashions. From *La Femme Chic*, October 1943. © Julian Robinson Archives.

149D. Lastex publicity ad extolling the beauty of stretchable and flexible corsets. From *Film Fashionland* (1936). Photo © Julian Robinson Archives.

149E. "I Want to Be Beautiful," and according to the subheading most women would endure torture if necessary. Gate-fold article on the new modes of beautification in the late-1930s published in a popular English weekly. Photo © Julian Robinson Archives.

150A. As 148C.

150B. Wartime cover of *La Femme Chic* (1943), featuring a drawing of the latest Paris couture fashions by J. C. Horamboure. Photo © Julian Robinson Archives.

151A. A John Austen line illustration, c. 1930. Photo © Julian Robinson Archives.

151B. Kauil tribesman, Laiagam, Western Highland Province, Papua New Guinea. From *Man as Art: New Guinea* (1981). Photo © Malcolm Kirk.

151C. *The Wild One*, originally released as *Hot Blood*, 1953. Note that Marlon Brando was given a stubble and ruffled hair—a symbol of the changing times—for the second release. Columbia Pictures publicity posters.

152A. Max Factor cosmetic ad featuring the Hollywood actress Jane Russell and her use of *Pan-Cake* foundation and powder, courtesy Max Factor Cosmetics/JR Archives.

152B. The influence of Marilyn Monroe, star of *Gentlemen Prefer Blondes*, *Some Like It Hot*, and many others, still lingers on in the cosmetics industry. This ad is from the mid-1980s, courtesy of Max Factor Cosmetics.

152C. Detail from a late-1940s corset ad. JR Archives.

153A. *Gentlemen Prefer Blondes*. Film ad (European edition) 1953/4.

153B. The reintroduction of television in Europe after the end of WWII was much publicized, although the actual audience was very small. Only in the U.S. was the commercial potential fully realized, and it was American television's profitability that has allowed its influence to reach every corner of the globe. BBC TV publicity photo 1946.

153C. Elvis Presley and his 1957 film *Jailhouse Rock* added an essential new, young, rebellious quality to how men should look, supplementing the groundwork change already achieved by Marlon Brando and his contemporary James Dean. Publicity poster courtesy MGM.

154A. Tom Kelley pin-up of Marilyn has continued to be an inspiration to many illustrators and artists. This one, by Wolfgang Hülk was used as a gate-fold in the first issue of the fetish, fashion fantasy magazine «O» in 1989. © Wolfgang Hülk.

154B. The release in 1958 of *Cat on a Hot Tin Roof* starring Elizabeth Taylor added an additional change in attitudes to the changing times. This MGM publicity poster was used for its European release.

154C. The delights of tight corsetting to achieve a narrow waist and to emphasize the female bust and derriere was reborn after the end of WWII. Inspired by Christian Dior's *New Look*, dress manufacturers began to focus on women's curves, aided by a new range of corsets. This one, called *The Merry Widow*, is by Warner, c. 1951. JR Archives.

155A. The original Marilyn Monroe *Golden Dreams* calendar, published in 1951 by John Baumgarth Co., Ill., catapulted her to instant fame. The photographer was Tom Kelley, who supplied the flip-side of a similar photo to *Playboy* for use in its first edition, published in 1953. JR Archives.

155B. Publicity photo of a leather-clad Brigitte Bardot—the young French beauty icon of the early 1960s. Photo from the JR Archives.

155C. James Dean in *Rebel Without a Cause* (1955) added to the changing ideals of the young. The film's wide international distribution helped to unify the voices advocating change. Warner Bros. publicity poster for its European release, from the JR Archives.

156A. By the mid-1960s the plastic doll *Barbie* was beginning to have an influence on the thinking and ideals of the young and that influence was to grow as her devotees became wage-earners and could afford to imitate her dress style and stylized "beauty." An early *Barbie* catalogue cover, c. 1960, from the JR Archives.

156B. Publicity poster for Carnaby Street—symbol of the *Swinging London* era and home to many of my design students. Publicity poster, JR Archives.

156C. An ad featuring the young English model Jean Shrimpton for the international cosmetic firm Revlon, from the 1960s. JR Archives.

157A. An English ad for *Beatle Boots*, c. 1965. Courtesy Ted Polhemus.

157B. With the coming of the miniskirt, a previously neglected erogenous zone was displayed beautifully and is captured in this photo by the Italian actress Gina Lollobrigida. © Gina Lollobrigida, *Italia Mia* (1972).

157C. By the mid-1960s social mores among the young had irrevocably begun to change and this was reflected in their styles of clothing, perceptions of beauty, and modes of behavior. This photo says it all. It was taken at a London rock concert, part of the *Chelsea Students' Carnival* (1967). © Frank Habicht; *Young London: Permissive Paradise* (1969).

157D. Cover of a 1966 edition of *Millie the Model*, whose effect on the dress styles and ideas of feminine beauty of its young readers was profound. Heroines such as Millie were able to disregard all the normal stultifying and outdated social rules about acceptable behavior, dress codes, and modes of beauty, the effects of which are still very much in evidence today. Photo from the JR Archives.

158A. The German model Veruschka wearing one of my designs made for a Park Lane boutique, photographed by Helmut Newton and published by English *Vogue* in 1965. Publicity window card courtesy Helmut Newton and Julian Robinson & Associates Pty. Ltd. (The author is the model sitting in the front—gee, how he has changed).

158B. "The Dress You Dream About." A popular magazine article of the mid-1950s which promoted the aging journalist's ideal. But this was soon to change once the younger readers began to demand a voice in how they should dress. Magazine from the JR Archives.

158C. In 1966 the West Coast based designer Rudi Gernreich launched his range of topless bathing suits and evening dresses upon an unsuspecting world. This photo is from an article I wrote for a London newspaper at that time, courtesy Erich Locker.

158D. One of the author's designs from the early-1960s that caught the eye of *Vogue*'s fashion editor. Shop window card © Julian Robinson & Associates/JR Archives.

158E. Frederick's of Hollywood *Pad It* bra, mid-1950s. JR Archives.

158F. The Carnaby Street style at the time of *Swinging London*, c. 1967. At that time it was the aim of the new group of young designers to make even ordinary looking young women seem irresistibly attractive by virtue of the symbolism of their clothing styles. Photo courtesy Clive of London.

159A. An ad needing little comment, except to say that prior to 1960 a young woman's navel was considered obscene by most censors and its exposure was condemned as a form of sexual licentiousness. JR Archives.

159B. *The Language of Legs* and other mid-1960s ads. JR Archives.

159C. Working with Jean Shrimpton and photographer David Bailey. Jean is wearing one of my designs made for Sylvia Mills, U.K., while I assist David as photo stylist. The result was published by English *Vogue* (1963). Photo courtesy Sylvia Mills, U.K./Julian Robinson & Associates Pty. Ltd.

159D. In the early-1970s I wrote an article on the first of the Japanese designers to set up a fashion business in Paris. His name was Issey Miyake, the rest is legend. This is one of his mix-and-match designs. Photo courtesy Issey Miyake which was used in that article.

160A. Twiggy as photographed by Richard Avedon. Photo courtesy Twiggy (Leslie Hornby) and Richard Avedon.

160B. The fashion for *hot pants* finally hit Paris couture in 1972. Photo courtesy The International Wool Secretariate, Publicity Division.

160C. Publicity sales poster for *Life Australia* featuring the newest styles of *derrière décolletage* swimwear from American West Coast designers. Poster, c. 1967, from the JR Archives.

161A. The Wodaabe nomads during the *Geerwol* celebrations. The unmarried men make themselves as attractive as possible in the hope of being chosen as a husband or lover. This concept of female choice may seem to be at odds with our own cultural ways, but as Carol Beckwith explained at one of our meetings, female choice is also at the root of our own pair-bonding system, it's just that our cultural ways seem to prefer to disguise this most basic fact. From *Nomads of Niger* (1984). Photo © Carol Beckwith.

161B. Massai *Moran* in their prestigious lion-mane headdresses, which denote courage and skill during the killing of a lion. From *Africa Adorned* (1984). Photo © Angela Fisher.

162A. Psychedelic fashions, the outcome of hallucinatory drug use and television. This design is by the New York designer Oscar de la Renta. Photo by Horn/Griner 1967 © Telegraph Group Ltd., London.

162B. The early 1970s *Art Deco Revival* was much featured in the popular press. This costume design for the *Folies-Bergère* by the Russian born Erté (Romain de Tirtoff) from his 1929 New York exhibition catalogue was one of the illustrations I used for a television program I did on the subject which featured Erté and his work. Photo © Julian Robinson Archives.

162C. Drawing by Steffi Schirrmacher. From a photograph in the British Museum publication, *Ethnic Jewellery* (1990). © Julian Robinson Archives.

162D. Author's drawings of Nagas jewelry. The Nagas inhabit the mountainous areas of Northeast India which I trekked through in 1988—the jewelry being from my own collection. © Julian Robinson Archives.

163A. Woodcut illustration of a Marquesan chief with distinctive shell ear adornments. From *The Natural History of Man* (1874). © Julian Robinson Archives.

163B. Fine examples of traditional purdah, worn throughout the Muslim areas of the Middle East. Anyone who has travelled through the extensive desert regions would quickly understand how such veils originated—it is extremely hot and dusty, and after a few days I, too, adopted a form of head-covering and veiling. However, the exact location, tribe, date, photographer, and publication from which this image came is not known. Information please. JR Archives.

163C. A Guna woman of the Comarca de San Blas archipelago south of Panama wearing a traditional gold nose ring. From *The Last Indians: South America's Cultural Heritage* (1981). Photo © Fritz Trupp.

163D. Plumes of a *okcadedié* headdress adorning a Quená tribesman, a descendant of the awesome Kaiapó nation, who now live in harmony with other Amazonian Indian peoples in central Brazil's Xinge Indigenous Park. From *Xingu: Tribal Territory* (1979). Photo © Maureen Bisilliat.

163E. Henna and bejewelled hands of what appears to be an Indian bride, although the exact location, date, photographer, and publication from which this image came is not known. JR Archives.

163F. Contemporary packaging of traditional Indian henna, purchased in Bombay in 1986. Photo ©. JR Archives.

164A. Unmarried Xinguano Indian women of central Brazil parading during one of their religious fertility festivities. *From Xingu: Tribal Territory* (1979). Photo © Maureen Bisilliat.

164B. Mangbetu women, Nanga region of Zaire, photographed in 1955 during a marriage ritual. They are each wearing a *negbe*, a sort of buttock decoration made of beaten bark and decorated with individual geometric patterns of their own design. Both men and women have elongated skulls, shaped during childhood by cloth bindings, with the women braiding their hair over wickerwork frames into tall funnel-like cylinders From *Danses d'Afrique* (1994). Photo © Michel Huet/Hoa-Qui Photo Agency.

164C. Traditional North Indian tribal jewelry, which is still worn in many country areas. Early-20th-century photo from *Die Sitten der Völker* (1920). © Julian Robinson Archives.

165A. Young Kayan woman, Sarawak, Borneo, with highly decorated and inlaid teeth. From *Decorated Man: The Human Body as Art* (1979). Photo © Charles and Josette Lenars.

165B. Highland warriors of the southern border area between Irian Jaya and Papua New Guinea, who still proudly wear their curved penis gourds. While there in 1985 and again in 1992, I was able to collect a few fine specimens, purchased from the wearers, and I can assure the reader that without their gourds, these warriors are still very impressive. The exact date, photographer, location, and publication from which this image came is not known. Any information would be appreciated. JR Archives.

165C. Elongated earlobes of a Kayan of Sarawak, Borneo. From *Pagan Innocence* (1960). Photo © K. F. Wong.

165D. Hair jewelry of the Bororo, a nomadic people living between Senegal and Chad, south of the Sahara desert. From *The Last Africans* (1977). Photo © Gert Chesi.

166A. A Zulu chief. The photographer Aubrey Elliott explains, "When I met him during my visit to the Zulu and Ndebele peoples of South Africa in 1996, [he] was a truly handsome man—one of the finest examples of masculine physique for which the Zulu are justifiably proud." From *Sons of Zulu* (1978). Photo © Aubrey Elliott.

166B. A village elder of the Pokot who, as a sign of respect for his having survived the rigor of their normal spartan lifestyle, is allowed the privilege of special forms of decorative and symbolic jewelry, which include a septum-piercing leaf shaped adornment made of what is referred to as German silver (aluminum). From *The Pokot* (1975). Photo © S. Trinci.

166C. A young woman from the Mendi area, Southern Highland Province, Papua New Guinea, preparing to partake in annual Mount Hagen Show—a three-day event involving some twenty-five or more tribal groups in dancing, chanting, and display. Author's photo, 1986. © Julian Robinson Archives.

167A. A late-19th-century engraving of an Indian silver necklace, but exact details, area of origin, age, etc. are not known. © Julian Robinson Archives.

167B. Ritual dance costume photographed by Michel Huet during his mid-1950s expedition into the remoter regions of West Africa, and which, as he told me shortly before his death in 1996 is unfortunately rarely seen nowadays. Photo © Michel Huet/Hoa-Qui Photo Agency.

167C. As 162D.

167D. An 1880s engraving of an Amazonian Indian with unique lip labrets that appear to have been made from jaguar claws. © Julian Robinson Archives.

168A. *Adam & the Ants*. Pop-star publicity poster (1981). JR Archives.

168B. *Kiss* album cover for their *Destroyer* LP (1976), by the talented designers Woloch & Kelly. JR Archives.

168C. *Vanishing Tribes* by Alain Chenevière (1987)—a truly wonderful book, which acted as an inspiration to me during my research and fueled my resolve to try to organize an end-of-millennium photographic exhibition celebrating our wonderful human differences. From *Vanishing Tribes: Primitive Man on Earth* (1987). Photo © Alain Chenevière.

169A. *The Dallas Cowboys Cheerleaders*, a truly American tradition and one that expresses the American ideal of young womanhood, a sentiment expressed in an English magazine of the mid-1970s that accompanied this photo. JR Archives.

169B. *Cicciolina: The Rise of the Roman Empress* (1985). An X-rated movie starring Cicciolina, an ex-anglo-Italian stripper turned politician who I met during a visit to Prague in 1991, and Tracy Adams with whom I worked while living in LA. JR Archives.

169C. Bra and lingerie ad. Compiled by the author from a *Fredericks of Hollywood* catalogue, 1991. Photo from the JR Archives.

169D. Filmmakers, especially those working in the growing X-rated movie market were, by the mid-1970s becoming tired of just displaying naked female bodies and acts of fornication, and loved to find new ways to dress their actresses which drew attention to the then-neglected alternative erogenous zones. The director of *Wild Gals of the Naked West* must have loved these designs to ring-the-changes, so to speak. Photo from the JR Archives.

170A/B. Mid-1970s photos aimed at reviving the 16th- to 18th-century courtly art of pubic hair decoration published in *Club International* (1976). Photos © Club International/Paul Raymond Publications.

170C. Heart-shaped pubic hair styling. Photo © Club International/Paul Raymond Publications (1976).

170D. As 170C.

171A. A "Big Man" from the Medlpa people of the Papua New Guinea central highlands—believed to be descended from a Negro population that invaded Melenesia some ten thousand years ago—preparing for an important sing-sing. Author's photo, 1986. © Julian Robinson Archives.

171B. The fascinating *Mud Men* of Makehuku village, Asaro area, Eastern Highland Province, Papua New Guinea, photographed by the author on his third visit to PNG in 1988. © Julian Robinson Archives.

171C. Participation in sing-sing celebrations for most female members of the indigenous people of Papua New Guinea is limited. Not so for the Medlpa whose womenfolk actively organize and participate and are adorned to the hilt, as can be seen from this photograph, taken by the author in 1986. © Julian Robinson Archives.

172A. Publicity images used to promote Claude Montana men's wear. Author's composite of Antonio Lopez illustrations. JR Archives.

172B. *Women's Bodybuilding Fashions*. Composite picture by the author (1990). JR Archives.

173A. *The New Biba* ad, early-1970s. JR Archives.

173B. The Pretty Boys of Thailand take center stage at the *Alcazar*, in Pattaya, South of Bangkok. In beauty, they certainly rival the Thai females, with both being, in aesthetic terms, among the luckiest cultural groups on earth. © Alcazar (1985).

173C. *Stolen Sweets* magazine cover, 1933. It was magazines such as this that many of the young *Swinging London* designers of the early 1960s grew up with, and it was this influence, together with that of Busby Berkeley style musicals and so forth which created such a revolution in young modes of beauty and dress. © Julian Robinson Archives.

173D. Advertising poster for the Paramount release of *Barbarella* (1967), starring an often sparsely clad Jane Fonda. Photo courtesy John Phillip Law (the blind angel seen in the top right hand corner of the poster whom I met recently whilst visiting LA).

174A. *Body Painting* from an article published in the British *Mayfair* magazine (1988) suggesting that such styles may one day replace party wear. For the adventurous, who live in the warmer west coast climate, this might be possible, but for the majority it is only a pleasant thought. Photo © Mayfair/Paul Raymond Publications.

174B. Cover of the *Star Video* catalogue, late-1980s. JR Archives.

174C. An example of the changing dress and beauty rules of the 1980s. Author's composite and colorization. JR Archives.

174D. Leather corset, black stockings, high-heeled boot, a whip, and studs—a fetish delight and one that Richard von Krafft-Ebing would have delighted analyzing. Photo © Centurian/Spartacus Publications, Inc., Ca., 1980.

175A. *New Wave Hooker*, starring a very young Traci Lords, with whom I was lucky enough to work while living in L.A. Photo from the JR Archives.

175B. *Zou Zou*, a now defunct glossy magazine featuring Haysi Fantayzee on the cover. Photo © JR Archives.

175C. The sexually ambiguous Boy George and his *Culture Club*. European tour publicity poster, mid-1980s. JR Archives.

176A. *Sex Cat* and *Fantasy Fun* lingerie ads, late-1970s. JR Archives.

176B. *Take Me Home.* Advertising/publicity poster featuring Cher. Photo JR Archives.

176C. The delights of bondage, which was given a boost in popularity around the world by such films as *Batman II*. Photo © Centurian/Spartacus Pub., Inc., Ca., 1980.

177A. The ancient art of nipple-painting, revived in the early-1970s by *Club International* (1974). Author's photo from his collection of erotica © Club International/Paul Raymond Publishing.

177B. *The Red Devil* in red plastic. From «*O*»: *Fetish:Fashion:Fantasy* (1989). Photo © Peter W. Czernich.

177C. *Transvestite* sales catalogue of 1982 with over 100 pages of things to buy if you were a male and wished to take on the symbols of femininity. © Centurian/Spartacus Publications, Inc., Ca.

177D. *Les Girls: Boys Will Be Girls*: A glossy publication extolling the delights and beauty of being a she-male. Issue No.1, 1980. JR Archives.

178A. Thailand ad for *Batman Returns* (1992), which features Michelle Pfeiffer in a bondage-inspired leather catsuit. JR Archives.

178B. High-heeled bondage boots from the author's collection of contemporary bondage wear. JR Archives.

178C. Bondage wear illustration from a 1983 sales catalogue. © Centurian/Spartacus Pub., Inc., Ca.

179A. Black leather lace-up corset from the *Dark Garden (San Francisco)* catalogue, modeled by JoAnna. Photo by Egon Du Bois. © Dark Garden, Ca., 1993.

179B. *Far-Out Fashion.* An authors montage of Spartacus bondage illustrations, 1997. © Julian Robinson/Spartacus Pub. Inc., Ca.

179C. Designs and illustrations of cuffs and bondage wear from The *Bondage* and *Slave Trainer* catalogues published by Centurian/Spartacus (1985) and collaged by the author. © Julian Robinson Archives/Spartacus Inc. Ca.

180A. I could write a book about the symbolism of frills and their use in women's dress. This wonderful example is by the Paris couturier Pierre Balmain, for whom I worked as a freelance designer in the mid-1960s. Like so many other fashion designers, he was gay and loved pretty dresses with lots of frills and lace. His motivation seems to have been subliminal—a longing to symbolically create that very feminine feature that the frills symbolized but which he, being male, did not possess. Fashion ad (1980). JR Archives.

180B. Thierry Mugler fashion ad of the late-1980s. JR Archives.

180C. The author dressed in 1920s Chinese Opera costume—part of his collection of theatrical costumes, during a 1992 photo session with the anglo-Czech photographer Roman Cerney. Photo © Julian Robinson Archives/Roman Cerney.

181A. An aristocratic couple of quality and fashion, engraved by Giacomo Franco, c. 1550. From *Die Mode* (1914). © Julian Robinson Archives.

181B. Participants in the annual *Basel Fasnacht Carnival*, Switzerland, whose costuming and makeup is quite different from the norm and challenges the observer's sense of aesthetic rightness. From *Carnival: Myth and Cult* (1980). Photo © Alexander Orloff.

181C. Unmarried Nuba woman preparing for the *Dance of Love* at which she may chose any male, or several males to fulfill her erotic expectations. From *People of Kau* (1976). Photo © Leni Riefenstahl.

182A. A. young Maasai *Moran* wearing a handsome feather ruff. From *The Last of the Maasai* (1987). © Mohamed Amin.

182B. Samburu splendor and vanity. From *Africa Adorned* (1984). Another truly wonderful book, which documents numerous dying traditions in loving detail. Photo © Angela Fisher.

182C. Unmarried woman from the Mubi Valley area, Southern Highlands, Papua New Guinea, with her body glistening with oil from the tigaso tree. Author's photo, 1985. © Julian Robinson Archives.

182D. Late-19th-century wood engraving of a Melanessian warrior. JR Archives.

182E. Line illustration, c. 1930. Photo © Julian Robinson Archives.

183A. Camera stylization of the young Jean Harlow who, under the guiding hand of Howard Hawks, became the archetypical platinum blonde. Early publicity photo, probably for *Hell's Angels* (1930). Photo from a Czechoslovakian film magazine of 1933. © Julian Robinson Archives.

183B. Line drawing of aristocratic splendor of the mid-15th century. JR Archives.

183C. Ad for the *Mystere* range of cosmetics manufactured by Rochas. Mid-1980s. JR Archives.

183D. Line illustrations of women in trousers, c. 1880 and 1930. © Julian Robinson Archives.

184A. Gatefold of *Moulded Body Tops* (modern day corsets). From the Australian fashion magazine *Mode*, 1980. © Mode/ACP Publishing Pty.

184B. Cesar Romero, a leading romantic Hollywood actor of the 1950s was one of the super studs, who fired women with desire. It is little known, however, that such stars required many hours of make-up and styling before they appeared before the publicity camera, and that expert lighting was a vital tool in creating the allure of beauty or handsomeness that their fans craved, as indeed was the studio lighting during the making of the films themselves. Many Hollywood stars not only had their own make-up team, but their own lighting technicians, camera crew, wardrobe staff and so on in order to achieve the final look for which they were famous. Photo courtesy Max Factor Cosmetics, Inc.

184C. Veruschka (Vera Lehndorff) being painted by the artist Holger Trulzsch. From *Veruschka: Transfigurations* (1986). Photo © Vera Lehndorff/Holger Trulzsch.

184D. An English ad for men's evening dress, showing the latest mid-1920s style for "tails," in midnight blue with two rows of braiding down the side of the trousers—a style which today is usually only worn by head waiters in traditional restaurants. Photo © Julian Robinson Archives.

185A. *Portrait of a Gentleman* by Giuseppe Ghislandi. Early-18th-century picture from a 1927 Czechoslovakian art magazine. Photo © Julian Robinson Archives.

185B. Punks window shopping in central London, 1985. Photo © Real London.

185C. "We Can't All Be Perfect." Jack Lemmon and Joe E. Brown in a United Artists publicity photo for *Some Like it Hot* (1959). JR Archives.

185D. "Boys Can Be Girls." Another United Artists publicity photo for the 1959 film *Some Like it Hot*, in which Tony Curtis and Jack Lemmon play the parts of female musicians. JR Archives.

185E. Clint Eastwood. Publicity photo probably for the 1969 United Artists film *Two Mules for Sister Sara*. Photo JR Archives.

186A. *Razzle Dazzle* Burlesque featuring the trend-setting British dance group *Hot Gossip* (1980). Photo JR Archives.

186B. Traditional Japanese *Irezumi* tattoo photographed by Sandi Fellman, advertising her highly successful exhibition at the Williams College Museum of Art. Photo © Sandi Fellman, 1984.

186C. Cover of Val Hennessy's landmark book, *In the Gutter* (1978). JR Archives.

186D. Line illustrations of fashionable men's wear, c. 1912 and 1860. © Julian Robinson Archives.

186E. Line illustration, c. 1920. Photo © Julian Robinson Archives.

187A. Hand-colored fashion illustration of fashionable men's wear, c. 1829. From *The Gentleman's Magazine* published in London by John Bell. Author's photo © Julian Robinson Archives.

187B. *Wearing My Y-Fronts*. Detail from a unisex coordinates ad for *Bo-Bo Kammsky Separates*. Photo by the author from a mid-1980s Australian fashion magazine ad. JR Archives.

187C. Portrait of Antonio Navagero by Giovanni Battista Moroni, 1565, from a 1927 Czechoslovakian art magazine. Photo © Julian Robinson Archives.

188A. *Corsets for Men*, (as well as women). From a unisex catalogue of crossdressing published in the early 1980s. © Centurian/Spartacus Publications, Inc., Ca.

188B. Detail from a *Frederick's of Hollywood Bum-Pad* ad, mid-1960s. JR Archives.

188C. Today's acceptable display, which symbolizes that of our primordial ancestors—see photo and caption below. Photo © Steve Fee.

188D. A male chanona baboon admiring the pink blossom of a young female—a symbol of her fertile state, remnants of which still live on in our own collective memory of a time when we, as a species, admired such symbols. Photo © C. Haagner/Adrea Photo Agency.

189A. An American *Braided Wire Bustle* exported to England to improve the allure of women's dresses in the 1880s. Photo © Julian Robinson Archives.

189B. Line drawing from an early-20th-century German book of 19th-century European fashions: *Fashionable Padding c. 1869*, after an illustration by Hadd. © Julian Robinson Archives.

189C. The allure of contemporary tight lacing. Photo © Trevor Watson, 1990.

189D. A much-admired female derrière featured in the popular English magazine, *Men Only* (1976). Photo © Men Only/Paul Raymond Publications.

189E. Ad for *Lee Jeans* (1980). Photo JR Archives.

190A. Cover of *Strong & Sexy: The New Body Beautiful* (1983). JR Archives.

190B. *Folies Bergére* publicity poster, 1980. Photo JR Archives.

190C. Cover of *Body Play & MPQ* featuring a tattoo photo by Elyse Reghr. © Body Play/Insight Books, Ca.

190D. Arnold Schwarzenegger in competitive form. From *Arnold Schwarzenegger: A Portrait* (1990). Photo © George Butler.

190E. *Mr. Atlas* ad about why a young man should become a muscleman. Author's photo from a 1949 American magazine. JR Archives.

191A. Elaine's muscles. Photo © Rennie Ellis, 1985.

191B. Frances, the first female champion. Photo © George Butler.

191C. The world's best muscle men in competition in 1980 for the *Mr. Olympia* title, and for the seventh time the winner was Arnold Schwarzenegger. Photo © George Butler.

191D. The world's best muscle women in competition in the early-1980s. *From Pumping Iron II: The Unprecedented Woman* (1984). Photo © George Butler.

192A. The contemporary art of branding, or the "Kiss of Fire" as the West Coast practitioner and teacher Fakir Musafar prefers to call it. Photo © Body Play/Insight Books, 1994.

192B. Contemporary body piercing. Photo © Cheyenne Morrison/The Piercing Temple (1997).

192C. A bondage scene from a 1983 illustration by Tealdo (Jim Tealdo of South California). © Centurian/Spartacus Pub., Inc., Ca.

192D. Contemporary tattooing and piercing. From *Tattoo* (1985). Photo © Stefan Richter.

193A. *Another Love*. A 1925 George Barbier illustration from the collection of the author. © Julian Robinson Archives.

193B. Contemporary ear piercing with gold stretcher. © Cheyenne Morrison/The Piercing Temple (1997).

193C. Cheyenne's tongue. © Cheyenne Morrison/The Piercing Temple (1997).

193D. "Body Piercing," a chart by Doug Malloy from V. Vale and Andrea Juno's landmark book *Modern Primitives: an Investigation of Contemporary Adornment and Ritual,* © ReSearch Publications, San Francisco, Ca.

194A. The art of cut-tattooing demonstrated by Raelyn Gallina. Photo by Fakir Musafar. © Body Play/Insight Books, Ca., 1990.

194B. Contemporary nipple jewelry, 1985. Photo © Centurian/Spartacus Publications, Inc., Ca.

194C. Rose tattoo featured in *Sex Watching* (1988). Photo © Prof. Mitton Diamond.

195A. Preparation for *The Shavers Convention*, 1985. © Club International/Paul Raymond Publications.

195B. Eyebrow tattooing and piercing, featured in *PFIQ No. 39* (1992). Photo © Todd Friedman/Piercing Fans International Quarterly.

195C. Jen's tattoo and piercing, featured in *PFIQ No. 39* (1992). Photo © Todd Friedman/Piercing Fans International Quarterly.

195D. Paula, pierced by Mr. Sebastion. Photo © Christine Alicino, courtesy Modern Primitives/Research Publications, Ca.

196A. "Body Art" ad 1992. Photo courtesy Ted Polhemus.

196B. Line drawing by the author of an Allen Jones "table." © Julian Robinson Archives.

196C. An Allen Jones mixed-media sculpture, late 1960s. Photo © Allen Jones.

196D. The delight of stockings and a suspender belt. © as for 195A.

197A. A she-male in all his/her glory. From *Les Girls: Boys Will Be Girls* (1980). © Holly Publications.

197B. A Fernando Botero fashion drawing from French *Vogue*, 1982. © French Vogue/Condé Nast Publications, Inc.

197C. A Fernando Botero sculpture photographed by the author. © Julian Robinson Archives 1993.

198A. Cover of André Virel's wonderful book *Decorated Man—The Human Body as Art* (1979), featuring many fine photographic images by C & J Lenars. Photo © C. & J. Lenars/Draeger et Cie.

198B. Cover of *Eternal India* by Indira Gandhi (1980). © Jean-Louis Nou/Edita SA.

198C. A young male star at the *Alcazar,* a transvestite revue, Pattaya, Southern Thailand. Photo JR Archives.

199A. *The Rolling Stones.* A promotional poster for their 1984 European tour. Photo JR Archives.

199B. Young female from the Mendi area, Southern Highland Province of Papua New Guinea, participating in the Goroka biannual *Eastern Highland Tribal Show* along with twenty-five other tribal groups, 1988. Author's photo. © Julian Robinson Archives.

199C. Kauil tribesmen from Laiagam Village, Western Highland Province, Papua New Guinea, resplendent in their birds-of-paradise feathered headdress, cassowary-bone hair spatulaés, large bailer-shell chest adornment, and stylistic face painting, parading for an *ink pomba* ceremony, part of the annual *mok ink* ritual. Author's photo, 1989. © Julian Robinson Archives.

200A. A young Samburu woman wearing a fine *Mporro* necklace indicating her married status. From *Samburu* (1990). Photo © Nigel Pavitt.

200B. Padaung brass long-neck beautifying coil, which, once the neck has reached the predetermined height, is never removed. It is not tight to the neck, however, and the wearer is freely able to move her neck within the coil without difficulty. Author's photo 1993. © Julian Robinson Archives.

200C. Jivaro tribesman from the upper reaches of the Amazon on the border of Peru. From *The Last Indians: South America's Cultural Heritage* (1981). Photo © Fritz Trupp.

201A. Maasai girls putting on their tribal jewelry in the hope of attracting a young *Moran* lover. From *Maasai* (1980). Photo © Carol Beckwith.

201B. Samburu elegance—the ivory ear ornament and stylish hair indicate his membership in the elite *Moran* (warrior class) and that he has shown considerable bravery in the killing of a lion. From *Samburu* (1990). Photo © Nigel Pavitt.

201C. A truly beautiful Peul woman from Djenné, Niger, fully adorned in local jewelry. From *The Last Africans* (1978). Photo © Gert Chesi.

201D. A Samburu bridegroom elaborately painted for his wedding—his betrothal is symbolized by his wearing his mother's copper earring. From *Samburu* (1990). Photo © Nigel Pavitt.

202A. *Central Europe's Most Beautiful Knees.* From the collection of erotic images by the Czech artist Jan Sandek, featured in *Jubilation and Obsessions* (1995). © Jan Sandek/Art Unlimited.

202B. Sharon's corseted body sculpting. Photographed by Fakir Musafar and featured in *Body Play & MPQ* (1994). © Insight Books, Ca.

203A. Fakir Musafar, *Self Portrait,* 1975. Photo © Body Play/Insight Books, Ca.

203B. A young female participant with magnificent keloid scarification participating in the annual mating dance of the Sara people, Maro, Chad. From *Danses d'Afrique* (1994). Photo © Michel Huet/Hoa-Qui.

204A. Japanese sword and serpent's tail *irezume* tattoo by Horiyoshi III. From *Japanese Tattoo* (1986). Photo © Sandi Fellman.

204B. Jen's labia piercing and tattoo, featured on the cover of a 1992 edition of Piercing Fans International Quarterly. Photo © PFIQ/Todd Friedman, 1992.

205A. Male leather chastity belt. Ad from *Bondage & Slave Training* catalogue, 1980. © Centurian/Spartacus Publications, Inc., Ca.

205B. Debra, 1990. Photo © Todd Friedman.

205C. Boned, lace-up leather corset by *Dark Garden (San Francisco)*, modeled by Indra. Photographed by Peter DaSilva. © Dark Garden, 1994.

205D. Detail from a bondage ad featured in *Sweet Gwen's Bondage Catalog*, 1984. © Centurian/Spartacus Pub., Inc., Ca.

206A. *Hair Sensations for Men* who wish to be, for a time, dressed like a woman. From *Transformation*, a mail order sales catalogue for transvestite and transsexual products. © Transformations, UK, Inc./JR Archives.

206B. *Female Human Face Mask* (other details as 206A).

206C. *Rubber Female Torso Suit* with specialized anatomical features. A page from Centurian's *Whole Catalog of the Exotic and Bizarre* (1982). © Centurian/Spartacus Pub., Inc., Ca.

207A. The Japanese art of erotic ribbon work. Mid-19th-century woodcut. JR Archives.

207B. Earl Van Aken, pierced by Gauntlet. From *Primitives: Tribal Body Art* (1992). Photo © Charles Gatewood.

207C. Cover of *PFIQ No. 17* (1983) featuring a photo by Fakir Musafar. © Piercing Fans International Quarterly/Gauntlet Inc., Ca.

207D. Blake's stretched earlobes. From *Body Play & MPQ* (1993). Photo © Fakir Musafar/Insight Books, Ca.

208A. Kirk, tattooed by Leo Zulueta. From *Primitives: Tribal Body Art* (1992). Photo © Charles Gatewood.

208B. A Todd Friedman photo featured in *The Secret Fetish Photo Anthology* (1995). © Todd Friedman/Secrets Magazine.

208C. Ron Athey's throat and chin tattoo. © as for 207B.

209A. The Bororo Fulani, Dakoro area, Niger, during their annual *Dance of Love*. From *African Dance* (1995). Photo © Michel Huet/Hoa-Qui Photo Agency.

209B. A fine *Gue Ba* headdress indicating that the wearer is a member of the Akha tribe who live in the hills of the Golden Triangle, Northern Thailand. Author's photo, 1985. © Julian Robinson Archives.

209C. Ndebele neck and body adornments photographed in the South African republic by the author at a coming-out party after weeks of fattening combined with an image by Aubrey Elliott. © Julian Robinson Archives/Aubrey Elliott.

209D. An Achuar girl from Ipiak, upper Amazon. From *The Last Indians: South America's Cultural Heritage* (1981). Photo © Fritz Trupp.

209E. A beautifully scarred unmarried Dangaleat woman, also called the Hajjeray, Korbo village, Chad, during the annual *margay jinn*, at which love or lust matches are consummated. From *African Dance* (1995). Photo © Michel Huet/Hoa-Qui Photo Agency.

210A. An engaged young Zulu woman of the Ntombela clan displaying her new status in her elaborate and colorful adornments. From *Sons of Zulu* (1978). Photo © Aubrey Elliott.

210B. A fun black leather party skirt. From «O»: *Fetish:Fashion:Fantasy* magazine, early 1990s. Photo © Peter W. Czernich.

210C. Indian tribal piercing from the Orusa area of the mideast coast of India, Saora tribe. From a mid-1930s French magazine. JR Archives.

211A. Black front-laced corset by *Tantalizing Fashions*, UK. Featured in «O»: *Fetish:Fashion:Fantasy* magazine, 1989. © Peter W. Czernich.

211B. Breast clamping. Photo by Fakir Musafar for *Body Play & MPQ*. © Insight Books Ca., 1995.

211C. Adorned to perfection in a coat of scars and natural oils during the annual Nuba Dance of Love, awaiting her turn to chose a lover. From *People of Kau* (1976). Photo © Leni Riefenstahl.

211D. Detail of a late-19th-century corset ad. From a catalogue of *Corset and Bondage Fantasies* (1981). © Centurian/Spartacus Pub. Inc. Ca.

212A. Cover of *African Hairstyles* by Esi Sagay (1983). © Esi Sagay.

212B. A page from *African Hairstyles* showing contemporary modes of cornrowing. © Esi Sagay (1983).

212C. Credits as 90C.

212D. *Dress Your Eyes*. Ad for Yves Saint Laurent eye makeup, mid-1980s. JR Archives.

212E. Detail from an eyelash ad, late 1960s. JR Archives.

213A. A wonderfully elaborate tribal coiffure made with the aid of ground ochre, cow dung, and urine. Early-20th-century photo of a Shilluk warrior. From *Die Sitten der Völker* (1920). © Julian Robinson Archives.

213B. *Make an Impression*. An ad for impressed hair patterning. Mid-1980s. JR Archives.

213C. Ad for *Sloane Ranger/Brideshead Revisited* style of English country clothing, c. 1990. Photo © Swaine & Adeney.

213D. A wonderful velvet cocktail dress worn with a plumed hat—stylish English dressing of the early-1980s. From a Mayfair boutique ad. JR Archives.

214A. Naomi Campbell modeling an Ozbek dress from his autumn 1991 collection—headdress by Phillip Treacy. Photo © Rifat Ozbek, London.

214B. A young Tiwa Indian from New Mexico. From *Decorated Man: The Human Body as Art* (1979).© Charles and Josette Lenars.

215A. Details as 215B.

215B. *An Urban Girl*. Photo © Trevor Watson.

215C. *Gods of Earth and Heaven*. Photo © Joel-Peter Witkin, 1990.

216A. The author in a mix-and-match array of tribal jewelry and body adornments, 1992. Photo by Roman Cerney. © Julian Robinson Archives/Roman Cerney.

216B. A young Mehinaku tribesman of the central regions of the Amazon jungle proudly wearing his father's necklace of jaguar claws. From *Xingu: Tribal Territory* (1979). Photo © Maureen Bisilliat.

216C. Cover of «O»: *Fetish:Fashion: Fantasy* (1990). Photo © Peter W. Czernich.

216D. Amazonian Indian of the Aripaktsa tribe, Juruena river area of Central Brazil, wearing macaw and toucan septum ornament. From *Primitive Peoples Today* (1960). Photo © Edward Weyer, Jr.

217A. Cover of *Irian Jaya: The Timeless Domain* (1990). © Julie Campbell.

217B. A young tribesman of the Huli tribe, Southern Highland Province, Papua New Guinea, with a fine yagama headdress resplendent with iridescent-blue fan-shaped plumage from the breast shield of the superb bird of paradise. © Malcolm Kirk, 1980.

217C. "Is nakedness more appealing?" A well thumbed page from a mid-1970s edition of the English magazine *Men Only* which had traveled halfway round the world before I acquired it in the Highlands of Papua New Guinea in 1985 from a local Huli tribesman. Such photos are highly sought by highland warriors. This one cost me my spare Reeboks. Photo © Men Only/Paul Raymond Publications, 1975.

217D. Dinka warrior from the border area of Kenya and the Sudan in traditional beaded corset. From *Africa Adorned* (1984). Photo © Angela Fisher.

218A. Although they were forcibly removed from much of their traditional tribal land, where for countless generations they had respected and lived in harmony with the wild animal population such as elephant, rhino, lion, gazelle, and the like, the Maasai still retain many of their traditions, with the young *Moran* warriors spending hours adorning and beautifying themselves and partaking in various rites and rituals. Under government pressure however, this is beginning to change. As Carol explained when we last met, such change is inevitable, but she believes we should do all we can to document that which still remains so that there is at least a record of its existence for future generations to see. Currently she and her friend Angela Fisher are filming such last rites and rituals. From *Maasai* (1980). Photo © Carol Beckwith.

218B. The young of the historic Kaiapó people, now living in the Xingu Indigenous Park in the center of the Amazonian jungle in central Brazil, together with the remnants of other indigenous peoples—about 2,000 in all from an estimated 4 million who used to live in the vastness of the jungle before Spanish and Portuguese conquest—still retain some of their traditions as can be seen here—a young unmarried woman dressed in feather finery while partaking in an ancient ritual. From *Xingu: Tribal Territory* (1979). Photo © Maureen Bisilliat.

218C. A new generation of Amazonian Indians—young Yanomami from the border area of Venezuela sporting traditional stick labrets and septum

nose decorations. From *The Last Indians: South America's Cultural Heritage* (1981). Photo © Fritz Trupp.

218D. A young unmarried woman being painted for the Yamaricumá ceremony, which only happens every few years, when the women take over the running of the village and hunting from men—a reminder of ancient times of Amazons when a matriarchs ruled the village and the jungle. Once painted, the women wear the splendid feathers normally reserved for their menfolk. *From Xingu: Tribal Territory* (1979). Photo © Maureen Bisilliat.

219A. Dani warrior from the highland area of Irian Jaya adorning his nose with a traditional boar's tusk. From *Irian Jaya: The Timeless Domain* (1990). Photo © Julie Campbell.

219B. A Thierry Mugler publicity photo from his 1991 collection publicized around the world. © Thierry Mugler/Studio (Australia) 1991.

219C. A Cairo belly dancer of the mid-1980s. JR Archives.

219D. Cover of *Carmen Miranda*: a book of cutouts. JR Archives

220A. Details as for 216A.

220B. An elaborately costumed participant in Trinidad's famous annual *Kings and Queens Carnival*. From *Carnival: Myth and Cult* (1980). Photo © Alexander Orloff.

220C. Mid-1980s *Cooler* ad featuring *Rio Carnival* style influence that was gaining in acceptance at that time. JR Archives.

221A. Early-20th-century line drawing. © Julian Robinson Archives.

221B. A late-19th-century engraving of a Zulu chief of the Goza clan. From *The National History of Man* (1874). © Julian Robinson Archives.

221C. Krall chief, Southern Africa. From *Sons of Zulu* (1978). Photo © Aubrey Elliott.

221D. The author in 1993 on the border of Burma and Thailand with two members of the Padaung people. In the village where I stayed there were 36 children of whom only 6 had opted to continue the long-neck tradition of tribal beautification—a sign of the changing times and one which indicates that within another generation or two such forms of cultural

marking will have disappeared from this planet, to be remembered only by photographs such as this. Photo © Julian Robinson Archives.

222A. A Japanese woman of fashion during the *Edo* period, painting her teeth black. *Ukiyo-e* print by Utamoro II, early 19th century. Photo from an early-1920s German art magazine. © Julian Robinson Archives.

222B. A colored woodcut by François-Louis Schmied, *La Cantique des Cantiques*, 1925. Author's photo from an original print. © Julian Robinson Archives.

222C. Cover of an early 1990s *Hair Dressing* magazine, which I purchased in a village in northern Thailand while living with the Padaung people. JR Archives.

223A. The complete businessman's tattoo, giving him the power of being tatooed without a visible hint. From Tattoo 1985. Photo © Stefan Richter.

223B. Traditional *Fouta Djallon Peul* hairstyle, which is made over a cane and wire framework worn by a young woman from Labe, Guinea, West Africa. Early-20th-century photo from *Die Sitten der Völker* (1920). © Julian Robinson Archives.

224A/D. Young unmarried Trobriand Islanders preparing for a night of lovemaking, an important part of their annual Yam Festival. Author's photo, 1988. © Julian Robinson Archives.

224B. *Liposculpture* ad 1995 which extolls the beauty of fat removal. JR Archives.

225A. Line illustration by the American artist Ray Sullivan. From *Eighth Annual of American Advertising Art* (1929). Photo © Julian Robinson Archives.

INDEX